LANGUAGE LEARNING AND INTERCULTURAL UNDERSTANDING IN THE PRIMARY SCHOOL

Language Learning and Intercultural Understanding in the Primary School shows how to deliver a progressive and holistic embedded language curriculum. It provides guidance on inclusive approaches for students with English as an additional language, including native speakers in the target language as well as language awareness activities that maximise links with learning in English.

Practical and accessible, it contains classroom examples, plans, resources and pedagogical approaches all underpinned by theory, research and practice. Each chapter examines specific themes relating to language, culture, identity and wellbeing, providing rich discussions and a range of perspectives. Case studies 'bring to life' the examples provided, and reflection points offer the reader the opportunity to pause and consider an idea, resource, or challenging concept before moving on.

Presenting a lived narrative of shared voices, the authors invite readers to learn about their own cultural and linguistic identities and how these relate to their practice. This is a must-read for teachers, language specialists and school leaders who wish for a clear rationale for the role of language, culture, identity and wellbeing within and beyond the curriculum.

Wendy Cobb is a passionate advocate of holistic language teaching, developed through her experiences of leading a primary-languages teacher training programme, cross-phase languages initiatives, international partnerships and a research and knowledge exchange project focusing on emotional health in schools.

Virginia Bower has a very strong interest in literacy and language, particularly in relation to pupils learning English as an additional language. She has published books on early literacy, poetry and supporting pupils with EAL, and in 2020 her publication with Routledge, *Debates in Primary Education*, brought together a range of current and key issues relating to teaching and learning in the primary school.

LANGUAGE LEARNING AND INTERCULTURAL UNDERSTANDING IN THE PRIMARY SCHOOL

A Practical and Integrated Approach

Wendy Cobb and Virginia Bower

LONDON AND NEW YORK

First published 2022
by Routledge
2 Park Square, Milton Park, Abingdon, Oxon OX14 4RN

and by Routledge
605 Third Avenue, New York, NY 10158

Routledge is an imprint of the Taylor & Francis Group, an informa business

© 2022 Wendy Cobb and Virginia Bower

The right of Wendy Cobb and Virginia Bower to be identified as authors of this work has been asserted by them in accordance with sections 77 and 78 of the Copyright, Designs and Patents Act 1988.

All rights reserved. No part of this book may be reprinted or reproduced or utilised in any form or by any electronic, mechanical, or other means, now known or hereafter invented, including photocopying and recording, or in any information storage or retrieval system, without permission in writing from the publishers.

Trademark notice: Product or corporate names may be trademarks or registered trademarks, and are used only for identification and explanation without intent to infringe.

British Library Cataloguing-in-Publication Data
A catalogue record for this book is available from the British Library

Library of Congress Cataloging-in-Publication Data
A catalog record for this book has been requested

ISBN: 978-0-367-65498-6 (hbk)
ISBN: 978-0-367-65500-6 (pbk)
ISBN: 978-1-003-12973-8 (ebk)

DOI: 10.4324/9781003129738

Typeset in Interstate
by Apex CoVantage, LLC

To all those advocates for language learning – keep going!

CONTENTS

List of figures viii
List of tables ix
Acknowledgements x
Foreword xi

Introduction 1

1 **Language awareness** 10

2 **Inclusive approaches to language learning** 28

3 **Language, culture and identity** 46

4 **Language and wellbeing** 67

5 **Language and gender** 84

6 **Languages across the curriculum** 99

7 **Progression in language learning** 119

8 **Assessing progress in language learning** 141

9 **Leadership of languages – a whole-school approach to planning and implementing a language-focused curriculum** 158

10 **Concluding thoughts** 180

Index 189

FIGURES

0.1	The AMLA Model (Cobb, 2014)	2
2.1	Monolingual language mat	39
2.2	Language mat template	39
2.3	Bilingual (Portuguese/English) language mat	40
3.1	Interdependence between language, culture and identity	47
3.2	Understanding terminology	48
3.3	A continuum of competence	49
3.4	Seven characteristics of culture	50
3.5	Finding names in the home environment	56
7.1	Extending patterns	131
10.1	Teachers leading the way	182

TABLES

1.1	Language poster	15
1.2	Latin legacy	17
1.3	How others use languages	21
2.1	Early morning routine in a Reception class	34
3.1	Names and naming practices	55
4.1	Polite classroom responses and language of clarification	71
4.2	French and Spanish emotion words	78
5.1	Exceptions to the Spanish *o/a* gender rule	86
5.2	Gendered and gender-neutral nouns	88
6.1	SWOT analysis	105
6.2	4C's Curriculum	107
6.3	AMLA scheme overview	109
6.4	*Jacques a dit* instruction words and actions	109
6.5	French colour words and suggested gestures	113
6.6	Snip lotto sheet	114
6.7	Probability table when rolling two dice	114
7.1	Grammatical forms with examples in the French language	121
7.2	Question-and-answer phrases in the French language	123
7.3	AMLA thematic scheme overview	127
7.4	'Can do' statements for speaking	128
7.5	Language awareness through colours	132
8.1	Prompts for learners, to enable teacher assessment of intercultural understanding	145
8.2	Lexical set – at the seaside	154
8.3	Lexical set – at the seaside – in two languages	155
9.1	Links between the English curriculum and the languages curriculum	163
9.2	Implementing cognitive principles	173
9.3	SWOT analysis	177
9.4	Challenges and responses	178
10.1	Professional development resources	184

ACKNOWLEDGEMENTS

We would like to acknowledge the huge support of family, friends and colleagues during the writing process and to also express particular thanks to David Matthews, without whose initial vision for the AMLA project, this book would never have happened.

FOREWORD

One of the frustrations of working in schools is that the political agenda rarely coincides with a feasible educational agenda. Children can be affected by two or three changes in policy, as governments come and go, during their time at school. Throw in the added complication of academies being able to set their own curriculum, and it is easy to see how an inter-school initiative, however lauded at its inception, can founder.

Those of us involved in the Accelerated Modern Languages Acquisition (AMLA) project were tremendously excited when learning an additional language became compulsory for all primary school children. We knew that British children, far from being fortunate in being native speakers of the new *lingua franca*, were in fact disadvantaged. Start learning a language before you are eight years old, and a rich array of synaptic pathways will be forged, benefitting intellectual development across every discipline. The widespread belief that learning another language was pointless, because everyone spoke English anyway, was damaging. With AMLA, we hoped that we could inspire secondary schools and their feeder primaries to collaborate on a modern language teaching-and-learning scheme, focussing on a common language across the age range. I remain convinced that such a scheme would have seen the majority of children taking a GCSE in a modern language at the end of Key Stage 3, with improved attainment in English and mathematics as a result.

The AMLA project, sadly, could not command sufficient resources to rise above all the other pressures on primary and secondary schools at the time. There was simply too much going on and, for many schools, a modern language initiative which involved cross-phase liaison was too costly an exercise. The result, of course, has been a steady dwindling in the number of pupils taking a modern language beyond GCSE. University courses are under threat and now, post-Brexit and post-Erasmus, there is a real risk that having the skill to converse in a language other than one's natal tongue will bypass many Britons.

But that gloomy prognosis ignores people like the authors of this great book. I am in awe of Wendy's dogged determination in continuing to refine and develop the AMLA teaching and learning materials, fostering old contacts and forging new ones to bring this book to print. At the heart of language learning is the desire to reach out and connect. I have no doubt that this book will do just that. And I look forward to the day when being able to speak and listen in another language is a skill that every child and young adult strives to acquire.

David Matthews
Head Teacher (2004–2015), St. Andrew's Church of England
School and Sixth Form, Croydon

INTRODUCTION

How the book came about

This book was a joy to write, as it afforded us the opportunity to join forces and bring together thoughts and ideas, research and experience, knowledge and skills relating to language that were accumulated over decades of working in different educational settings. One of the key driving forces behind the ideas in this book was a theoretical model initially established by a primary/secondary school languages development project, with which Wendy was involved – Accelerated Modern Languages Acquisition (AMLA). The aim of this project was to provide an accessible and consistent approach to how teachers can deliver a progressive and holistic embedded language curriculum.

The AMLA project was led by David Matthews, Head Teacher of St. Andrew's Church of England School and Sixth Form, Croydon, and the project team comprised of David, Wendy (author and editor of the AMLA materials) and Sue Keeler, linguist and translator of the AMLA resources. Before developing the theoretical rationale underpinning the AMLA approach, which was designed to support teachers in primary feeder schools preparing to deliver languages as a statutory subject at Key Stage 2 and accelerated language learning in the secondary school, the project team spent time researching effective language-learning pedagogy in national and international contexts and visited primary schools in England developing models of bilingual teaching. Participating in a funded project researching practice in schools was a real privilege; it offered us the unique opportunity not only to observe good practice but also to identify opportunities to bridge gaps and unlock possibilities, drawing on what evidence and experience suggest might work best in diverse contexts.

The AMLA project's launch coincided with the publication of Tinsley and Comfort's research report 'Lessons from abroad: International Review of Primary Languages' (2012). The review summarised national and international evidence of the cultural, cognitive and literacy benefits across the curriculum of language learning and emphasised the potential of studying different languages and cultures through broad-based programmes to contribute to what Tinsley and Comfort describe as a 'unique dimension' of a school's curriculum (2012, p. 27). The AMLA team elected to further investigate 'The Use of Language Other Than English' policy (LOTE) (Victoria University, no date) in Victoria State, Australia, and its emphasis on the potential of languages to 'nurture reflective, deep and creative thinking' and

DOI: 10.4324/9781003129738-1

2 Introduction

to cultivate 'culturally distinctive fields of knowledge' (p. 31); the LOTE focus on learner 'self-reflection' was to become a particular influence on the subsequent AMLA theoretical model.

The AMLA team believed that building a language-aware school, where community languages and diverse experiences are celebrated, is an important step in achieving a broad and progressive programme which allows for the development of learning in the primary school and its extension in Key Stage 3 and beyond. The team also promoted the need for schools to design opportunities for 'immersing' children in language in meaningful contexts, including through linking learning with other subjects of the curriculum.

The AMLA approach is underpinned by three key aspects of language:

- Language as communication;
- Language as culture;
- Language as identity.

Language awareness cuts across all three strands, as illustrated in Figure 0.1.

The team used the AMLA model to develop a language awareness programme, a thematic Scheme of Work for Key Stage 2 and cross-phase transition projects. These resources were disseminated to schools through a programme of professional development opportunities and through free access to materials via an online portal, and project outcomes and resources were shared through an Association for Language Learning Conference Presentation (Cobb and Matthews, 2014). The postponement of the planned statutory primary languages provision in England by the coalition government from 2010 to 2014, and the concurrent cessation of funding for primary languages development, meant that the project's initial momentum was stalled in line with many other local authority-funded language initiatives at that time.

Mindful not to waste the project's initial creative impetus, for this book we have drawn on and extended many of the ideas and resources developed through the AMLA project and are grateful for David's support and encouragement to complete this publication.

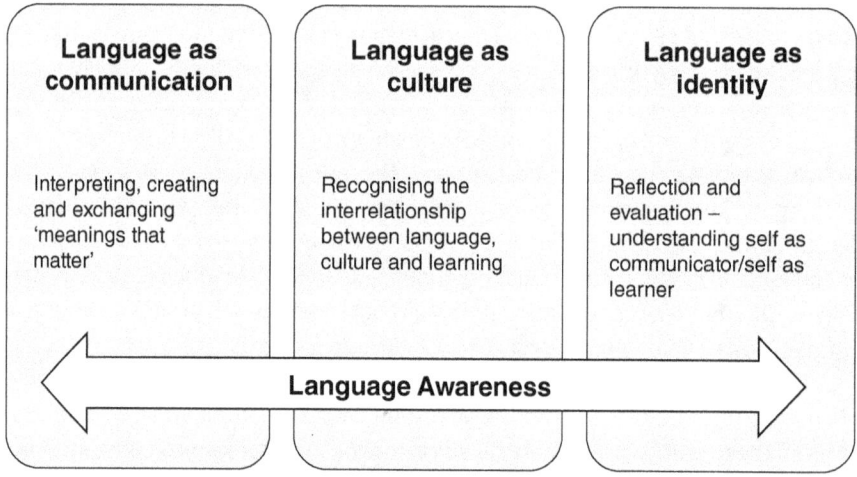

Figure 0.1 The AMLA Model (Cobb, 2014)

Our philosophies

One of the key philosophies that underpins all the chapters in the book is that a holistic approach to language and raising language awareness is likely to benefit both teachers and the taught. We put forward the idea that the ethos and ensuing pedagogy and practices in educational settings would benefit from an integrated language policy. Schools often have a foreign languages policy, an English as an additional language policy and an English policy, and we argue that, in order to raise the status of language and raise awareness about language, these would be better under one umbrella. Usually there would be a lead teacher for each of these, but imagine the power of a combined role (preferably adopted by more than one member of staff) that looked at language across the curriculum and in every aspect of school life. This may be utopian, and we acknowledge this, but at the very least, making the connections between these aspects of teaching and learning has the potential to ensure that children are better able to recognise and respond to the power and responsibility of language and what it can do for us.

Utopian or not, our ideas and suggestions are based on years of experience, research and listening to the views and perspectives of children, student teachers, experienced practitioners and senior leaders. Our aim and indeed our hope, is that you get to know us as you move through the book, in terms of our linguistic and cultural identities, and begin to identify why we believe what we do and how this relates to our practice. In turn, we hope this enables you to reflect on your own linguistic and cultural identity, and the influences thereon, and through this, better understand those you teach. Our intention has been to produce an authentic, lived narrative, with our own and others' voices speaking out from the pages, raising issues, acknowledging challenges and suggesting possibilities. We hope our voices will emerge and, in general, the chapters refer to 'we' as they are all co-authored to a greater or lesser degree. At times however, for the sake of authenticity, we will be specific about the author – either Wendy or Virginia – particularly when the example is very personal to one of us. What follows is a little more about us both and our backgrounds, which will enable you to identify the origins of our interest in this area.

About us

Wendy – Although I had only one experience of foreign travel with my family during my early childhood, I had a vivid imagination, and every night in my dreams I 'travelled' to different worlds and became someone else quite removed from the introverted, shy young girl that everyone else saw. These worlds were inspired by the films that I watched and the books that I read.

I was jealous when my older sister's secondary school arranged 'pen pal' exchanges with French students, as my school did not, so I persuaded my mum to organise for me to join an exchange group and at the age of twelve, I travelled with a group of students, none of whom I knew, to stay with a French family for three weeks during a very hot summer, never having met the family before and knowing just a handful of French phrases. I vividly recall how excited I was by the smells and tastes of family meals and being thoroughly spoiled by my French 'mum' who did everything she could to put some fat on my skinny frame. I returned to the small French town, aged fifteen, to spend Christmas with my new family and remember feasting and dancing into the early hours of Christmas Day morning at a traditional Christmas Eve banquet (*Le Réveillon*).

I studied French, Italian and Latin at secondary school with taster classes in Mandarin and Esperanto (a constructed international auxiliary language intended for use as a universal second language). At university, for my English degree, I opted to major in Old and Middle English from the second year, largely because I found it easier than some of my peers to translate Old English texts because of the grammar parallels with Latin, and also because of my fascination with history. I had planned to head off around the world on my own to teach English after university, but instead came home to marry my husband. When my two boys were little, I taught myself Spanish from a grammar translation book then began to speak the language a little at a Spanish evening class. By this time, my stepbrother had married a Spanish girl who introduced me to new family traditions, such as racing to eat twelve grapes as each clock bell tolls at midnight on New Year's Eve!

Once my children were both at school, I trained to be a primary teacher. Strangely, I did not feel I had the knowledge and skills to teach languages at secondary school; besides, I loved the variety of primary teaching. I was subject coordinator for music and 'gifted and talented', before persuading my head teacher to allow me to take on leadership for languages. I became a leading teacher for creativity and primary languages and was offered a local authority advisory role developing cross-phase languages networks. This was a role I loved, which involved me working on Content and Language Integrated Learning (CLIL) projects with the local university and meeting many inspirational language leaders at annual primary language conferences.

Alongside my local authority work, I was invited to lead a pilot teacher-education course for language specialist primary teachers in London schools. When the three-year pilot ended, I returned briefly to school leadership and then completed my master's degree in leadership resilience alongside a variety of coaching, advisory and teacher educator roles. Language, culture, identity and wellbeing became integral elements of my master's journey as I explored my own and other leaders' autobiographies.

When two language specialist alumni working in feeder primary schools suggested my name to secondary head teacher, David Matthews, I became the educational consultant for the AMLA project, and the spark for this book began. I have been lucky to have worked with many supportive leaders like David and Virginia, who have encouraged my passions for creative projects, such as this co-authored book, which has been a joyous journey and an opportunity to revisit some of the memories of students, teachers and leaders who have shaped my understanding of the power of language and intercultural understanding to change lives and reimagine futures.

Virginia - Language and its power has held a fascination for me since secondary school. I can remember two particular instances that have stayed with me, to the point that I can recall the room and where I was sitting on both occasions. The first was an English lesson, where the teacher introduced Chaucer and said, 'I just want you to sit and listen, with your eyes closed, and don't worry if you do not understand'. We were all a bit surprised by this but obediently did as we were asked. The teacher began reading, and she read for about twenty minutes. We were completely mesmerised by the sound of the new language, despite having very little idea about the content. The power of language indeed – to get thirty teenage girls to sit in a trance-like state! The second example was my first German lesson. I had not enjoyed learning French, as the teacher had very little control, and we were all quite badly behaved (I do not look back and feel proud of this). I did not, therefore, approach my first brush with German with any excitement, particularly as, at my school (a selective girls' establishment), it was those who were considered 'less intelligent' who did German, and the others did Latin (hardly the best for one's self esteem!). However, what a different experience this was; an engaging teacher; a language that seemed to speak to me; pedagogies which supported and inspired. I was hooked! Looking back, these influences were profound in several ways. They instilled a love of language, despite my negative experience with French; an understanding of the importance of powerful pedagogies and strong relationships between pupil and teacher; and a realisation that there was a wide world out there to be explored, in terms of language through the ages, places to go and people to meet.

Since those teenage years, I have had the good fortune to work with children and adults from different cultures who speak different languages, in both primary education and the university setting as well as outside of education spheres. Whilst working as a Year 6 teacher, I embarked on a part-time, three-year master's degree, focusing on literacy and language, which further ignited my fascination with the power of language, linguistic diversity, accent, dialect and finding an oral and written voice and identity. When I moved to work in Initial Teacher Education, I had the opportunity to use and follow up on these interests and experiences, but more specifically focusing on supporting children with English as an additional language. This led me to embark on a six-year, part-time PhD, involving data collection over two years, one day a week, in an early years and primary setting. The study used elements of ethnography, allowing me to immerse myself as a researcher in the setting and to gain the perspectives of the children and adults over an extended period – an absolute privilege. During this time, I also published a book with Open University Press entitled *Supporting Pupils with EAL in the Primary Classroom* (Bower, 2017), which provided me the opportunity to share some of my findings in a more practical publication that I hoped practitioners would find useful.

I now divide my life between England and Portugal, enjoying the challenge of learning another language and being lucky enough to spend a great deal of time immersed in a very different culture. The more I find out about the Portuguese people and their way of life, the more I realise how important it is to spend time getting beneath the surface of a country and its people, and to go beyond the immediate judgements – both positive and negative – we are inclined as humans to make when encountering the new and unfamiliar. Delving beneath the surface, through extended conversations, research, developing relationships, exploring the landscape, the politics, the traditions and everyday way of life has enabled me to further realise how very different we all are, according to our backgrounds and upbringing, but also how those very things that make us human provide the means to negotiate and celebrate these differences. This book – working with Wendy – has provided the opportunity to share many of these thoughts and ideas, and it has been a real pleasure to write.

The structure of the book

Each chapter examines specific themes relating to language, culture and identity, providing rich discussions and a range of perspectives derived from theory, research and practice. As well as these discussions, there are supplementary elements in each chapter: case studies, reflection points and author dialogue. Case studies are used to illustrate particular points and to 'bring to life' the examples provided, with at least two in every chapter. The reflection points model those in the AMLA model and offer the reader the opportunity to pause and to consider an idea, resource or a challenging concept before moving on. They might also be useful for staff meetings, student teacher seminars or to ignite discussion between colleagues. The third element is author dialogue, and these are written conversations between us. These came about because, inevitably when planning and writing this book, we engaged in many conversations, trading viewpoints, perspectives and ideas, alongside deciding on the more pragmatic and technical aspects of book writing such as structure, chapter titles, word length etc. Often, we would end up saying, 'It would be really useful to include this exchange of ideas in Chapter X', and this led to a deliberate inclusion of snippets of conversation bringing forward ideas or questions or differences of experience. We hope these enrich the chapters – they certainly enriched our knowledge and understanding!

Here is a summary of what you can expect in each chapter:

Chapter 1: Language awareness

There are four key sections in this first chapter: Conscious perception: building on early awareness; Knowledge about language; Language use: a shift in focus; and The role of the teacher. Examples are provided of how to promote and build language awareness across the curriculum, and there is a focus on how this awareness is of benefit to native speakers and those with English as an additional language.

Chapter 2: Inclusive approaches to language learning

This chapter focuses on two key themes, both of which are central to the idea of an inclusive approach to language learning. Firstly, we examine why it is important to maximise children's existing language skills and ensure that we build on these. We then put forward the argument that, by taking a bilingual approach to learning and teaching, planning and resourcing, a more inclusive ethos will be achieved, where a celebration of language and multilingualism is embedded in everyday practices, enhancing the lives of all children.

Chapter 3: Language, culture and identity

This chapter examines aspects of the complexity that lies behind ideas relating to language, culture and identity, and we argue that an understanding of this complexity, and of how we can use it in empowering ways, is vital to all educators. One of the key messages we hope to convey is that a school ethos which puts language, culture and identity at the forefront of its considerations for *all* staff, children, their families and the local community, will provide a more safe, supportive, nurturing, creative, inclusive, innovative and forward-thinking environment, where learners thrive and flourish.

Chapter 4: Language and wellbeing

Learning communities that are built on healthy relational cultures are foundational to both student and staff wellbeing. Protective factors for positive mental health include a positive school climate that enhances belonging and connectedness. This chapter focuses on why children's mental health is so important and how our own autobiographical insights can enhance our approach to supporting children's wellbeing. We examine the idea of language development as an indicator for wellbeing and how language play is a potentially powerful aspect of this. The importance of choice of lesson content is presented and how social and emotional learning are closely bound up with the teaching and learning of language, including a focus on limiting language performance anxiety.

Chapter 5: Language and gender

In this chapter, we consider how the pro-social and language-aware classroom can mitigate the potentially damaging impact of gender discrimination, bias and gender stereotyping on a child's developing sense of identity. Ideas relating to grammatical gender, gendered language, gender-inclusive language and social gender will be explored, as well as potential issues including false gender-neutrality and the impact of misgendering. Practical responses and approaches will be discussed and a set of prompts provided to support gender-inclusive teaching.

Chapter 6: Languages across the curriculum

This chapter begins by considering the idea of a positive pedagogue and how positive pedagogy is essential in a classroom that promotes a cross-curricular approach to language learning, and we explore the theory behind Content and Language Integrated Learning (CLIL) to provide a rationale for embedding the target language across the curriculum. The chapter then examines both discrete and embedded language learning before exploring the cognitive and wellbeing impacts of multi-tasking in the bilingual classroom. Ideas are introduced whereby the language teacher can make connections with the wider curriculum, with specific subject examples.

Chapter 7: Progression in language learning

In this chapter we consider expectations for progression in language learning, with a focus on progression in foreign language teaching in the language-aware classroom. We begin the chapter by looking at some general expectations around the core content of language schemes of work in the primary years before providing some specific examples relating to grammatical features, communicative competence and developing a metalanguage. The chapter then moves on to examine planning for progression, drawing on examples from each element of the Accelerated Modern Languages Acquisition (AMLA) project resources with a focus on embedded language learning and Content and Language Integrated Learning (CLIL). There is then a more specific focus on how progression in language learning can be promoted by a curriculum area – in this case creative arts. The final section explores how 'big questions' can be investigated to the advantage of both language progression and a curriculum area.

Chapter 8: Assessing progress in language learning

This chapter is built around three principles taken from the Expert Subject Advisory Group for Modern Languages (2015), focusing on assessment that fosters motivation, enjoyment and progress in language learning. These principles also include ensuring that assessment enables learners to feel confident through building resilience, enthusiasm and persistence. This involves embedding assessment into the language learning process and recognising that the learning of a language includes making mistakes, whilst having high expectations of learners. Throughout the chapter, we suggest ways that we might assess progress, adhering to these principles and looking beyond the more traditional methods of formative and summative assessment.

Chapter 9: Leadership of languages – a whole-school approach to planning and implementing a language-focused curriculum

We believe that all teachers are language teachers and that leadership can take place at all levels. Because of this, as teachers we are always tackling complex issues and facing 'big questions'. We decided therefore, to base this chapter around five 'big questions' designed to provide ideas for designing a whole-school approach to planning and implementing a language-focused curriculum, where leadership is shared and all stakeholders involved. The five questions are:

- What are the aims of the wider school curriculum?
- Where should we position English/L1, ancient/modern languages, language awareness and English as an additional language within school policy?
- Who should lead on language-focused curriculum development, and how can language leadership promote democratic citizenship?
- How can we engage children with 'big questions' through the language curriculum?
- How can we know whether the curriculum is meeting the stated aims?

Chapter 10: Concluding thoughts

The main aim of this final chapter is to provide ideas for moving forward. Whilst acknowledging all that we have written about in the previous chapters, it looks beyond these themes to a more personalised approach to development. We begin by examining the importance of considering our own values and principles for teaching and learning and then move on to link this with the importance of teacher agency. The benefits of professional learning and development are discussed, with reference to resources you may find useful. We provide some examples of mistakes we have made along the way, with the intention of reassuring our readers that, as humans, these mistakes are inevitable, to be embraced and will help us move forward. The chapter, and indeed the book, concludes with a final author dialogue, where we put forward our vision for the future in terms of language-aware classrooms.

Before we finish this introduction, we wanted to share a quote from a child in Virginia's class many years ago, who said, 'I love it when you read to us, miss, as I can hear the voices in my head and picture all the people'. We hope that, through this book, you will hear the voices of many, picture different circumstances and contexts, embrace differences and be inspired to be an advocate for the overt celebration of language and culture and to be an ally to all those you encounter within this challenging yet rewarding entity that is learning and teaching.

References

Bower, V. (2017) *Supporting Pupils with EAL in the Primary Classroom*, London: Open University Press.

Cobb, W. (ed.) (2014) *Language Awareness Programme*, Croydon: Accelerated Modern Language Acquisition.

Cobb, W. & Matthews, D. (2014) 'Language as communication, culture and identity', Association for Language Learning 2014: Language World, Lancaster, 4–5 September.

Expert Subject Advisory Group Modern Foreign Languages (2015) 'Assessment in modern foreign languages in the primary school', Available at www.all-languages.org.uk/wp-content/uploads/2016/01/ESAGMFLGroupAssessmentStatement.pdf (Accessed 19.02.2021).

Tinsley, T. & Comfort, T. (2012) *Lessons from Abroad: International Review of Primary Languages*, CfBT Education Trust, Available at www.educationdevelopmenttrust.com/EducationDevelopmentTrust/files/cc/ccead869-2418-4cad-b04a-d4ae98097448.pdf (Accessed 21.12.2020).

Victoria University (no date) 'The use of languages other than English policy', Available at https://policy.vu.edu.au/document/view.php?id=192&version=1 (Accessed on 03.03.2021).

1 Language awareness

Language: *'The systematic, conventional use of sounds, signs or written symbols in a human society for communication and self-expression'.*

(David Crystal, 1995, p. 454)

Introduction

With a book such as this, where there are notionally so many essential themes and ideas to be discussed, it is difficult to decide on an order of chapters, as there is no single chapter more important than another; and yet, the hierarchy of 1, 2, 3 . . . would seem to suggest this! Such a choice must be made however, and we opted to begin by focusing on the idea of language awareness, to raise the status of this topic from the very start, enabling us then to move in different directions – all closely interwoven but examining key themes from a range of perspectives. Something that determined the choice was the word *awareness*, as we believe that this needs to underpin all our work as educators. Awareness of difference. Awareness of diversity. Awareness of others' perspectives, feelings, beliefs, emotions. And so many of these aspects are influenced by language. A deep, secure knowledge and understanding of language strengthens our ability to empathise, collaborate, develop long-lasting relationships and communicate across social, cultural and linguistic boundaries.

The sections in this chapter have emerged from specific words and phrases in two definitions of language awareness, that we found particularly useful. In the first, Zaidi (2020, p. 270) refers to language awareness as, 'an understanding of the human faculty of language and its role in thinking, learning, and social life.' We appreciated the emphasis on *human* here and the subsequent link to the inherent sociability of the human race, as without an understanding of the importance of language to support the development of relationships, community ties and familial connections, life is a struggle. Zaidi also includes a reference to thinking and learning and how language awareness has a significant role in these aspects of being human, all of which underpin the ideas in this chapter and throughout the book.

Alongside this, we have borrowed from the Association for Language Awareness (ALA) (2020, no page) this definition which, although different, demonstrates parallel ideas: 'explicit knowledge about language, and conscious perception and sensitivity in language learning, language teaching and language use.'

DOI: 10.4324/9781003129738-2

There is much to ponder in this definition, including an emphasis on knowing *about* language but also the ways it can be used. The words *perception* and *sensitivity* are powerful, particularly with an emphasis on the preceding word *conscious*, which elevates the responsibility level for those of us working with young learners, to ensure that this consciousness is raised and maintained.

The themes which have emerged, therefore, and within which ideas will be explored alongside practical suggestions, are as follows:

- Conscious perception: building on early awareness;
- Knowledge about language;
- Language use: a shift in focus;
- The role of the teacher.

Throughout the chapter, we provide practical examples of how to build language awareness across the curriculum and explain how this awareness can also support progress in English and other languages, for both native speakers of English and those learners with English as an additional language.

Conscious perception: building on early awareness

A realisation that language is power generally emerges at a very young age. Babies soon understand that a particular sound they make elicits a specific response and that their carers are in their power! In this way, they learn from the people around them, the contexts and settings which form part of their lives and the degrees of interaction they are exposed to (Bower, 2017). This awareness – arguably both innate and learnt – continues to affect our lives – relationship forming, learning, acquiring goods, achieving goals – as we move through childhood, teenage years and into adulthood. However, the extent to which these abilities are capitalised on in school life is variable, and we would argue that a more systematic, overt and celebratory approach to language awareness – across languages and cultures – would benefit all children and enable them to utilise language for communication and self-expression in a way that enriches their lives and the lives of those to whom they are connected.

Raising awareness about language in schools can start at a very early age; indeed, evidence would suggest the earlier the better in terms of taking a plurilingual approach, which exposes very young learners to different languages and cultures. Nicholas and Lightbown (2008, p. 39, cited in Corcoll, 2013) write that 'the period between 2 and 7 years of age is a time during which children's knowledge about language and about the language(s) they hear around them develops rapidly and, to a very large extent, without instruction or intention'. This would suggest that anything we can do to provide an environment that nurtures this development will be of great value.

Research undertaken by Coelho, Andrade, and Portugal (2018) adopted the Awakening to Languages (AtL) approach with pre-school children in Portugal. With AtL, the focus is on a wide range of languages, underpinned by the idea that a plurilingual approach can lead to better academic performance, specifically in terms of:

- Building more complex sentences and improvement in writing competence;
- Phonological awareness and reading comprehension;

- Improved perception, concentration and selective attention;
- A tendency to learn other languages more easily alongside 'communicative sensitivity' (ibid., p. 201); and
- An ability to adapt speech to suit the needs of the listener.

Interestingly, there is also evidence to suggest plurilinguals have higher-paid careers as they move through life (uoguelph.ca, no date). With all this potential in mind, Coelho, Andrade, and Portugal (2018) wanted to explore the benefits of the AtL approach with pre-school children in terms of their communicative competence. They asked the children which other languages they would like to learn in addition to their native Portuguese, and the children opted for Spanish, Italian, French and English. Activities were carried out in these different languages, including listening to and re-telling stories, watching videos, practising tongue twisters and playing games. Assessment of progress focused on oral production, oral comprehension and oral interaction, and the key findings were that children enjoyed the activities and were very keen to discuss linguistic diversity and offer their opinions. They were also eager to learn about other languages and cultures and to discuss differences, and it was felt that an enriched linguistic environment emerged within the school.

Another study, conducted by Karagiannaki and Stamou (2018) in a Greek school with six- and seven-year-olds, used fairy tales to develop children's critical language awareness. The idea was to use alternative versions of fairy tales to promote an examination of the world through different lenses. Other aims were to support the children with making connections between ideas and working out the authors' intentions by recognising implied messages in the texts. One of the key strategies was role play, as it allowed the children to be active learners, to reconstruct the tales and represent them in their own ways, to 'become' other people. Although not a plurilingual approach, the questions used in Karagiannaki and Stamou's research could easily be applied to activities which involve more than one language:

- What version of the world has been constructed here?
- How are relationships and identities revealed?
- How are the messages conveyed in terms of the language used?

The following case study describes some classroom activities which also used tales, but took a bilingual approach and, after the case study, we will use Karagiannaki and Stamou's questions to explore how the activities might have been extended to raise children's language awareness further.

> At the time, I (Virginia) was working in a class with eight- and nine-year-olds. I wanted to raise their awareness of different languages in a relaxed and fun way, which I could then build on in different areas of the curriculum. I decided to use a popular traditional tale with which I was fairly sure they would be familiar – The Three Little Pigs – as I had in my possession a dual language picture book version of this story in Portuguese and English.

> Firstly, I read the story in English to remind the children of the series of events, the settings and the characters. This took some time, as the children were commenting on their younger days and how they loved fairy tales, who used to read to them before bedtime, reading to younger siblings etc. It was worth taking time with this, allowing the children to make comments, discuss and ask questions, as this raised their interest and motivation for future tasks. I then asked the children to work in groups to come up with a list of key words and phrases from the story that they could remember. Each group then shared their word lists, and these were written on a flipchart which remained highly visible and available for a few weeks and became part of a plurilingual working wall.
>
> I then explained to the children that I was going to read the same story but in Portuguese, showing the pictures so that they could follow along, reassuring them that it did not matter if they were unable to understand any of the words – they could just sit back, listen and absorb. However, I emphasised that they were welcome to interrupt the reading to ask questions, talk about anything that came into their minds or to identify vocabulary that interested them. After the initial reading in Portuguese, time was given to share ideas, note down any words and discuss their thoughts. We then went through the story again, with it projected onto the whiteboard so that the children could identify some key fairy tale language and compare words and phrases in both languages. For example, an obvious phrase is *Once upon a time*, and they were very interested to see whether there are any similarities with how this is written in the two languages. This led to a whole discussion around the phrase *Once upon a time* – what does it signify? What does it actually mean? Where did it originate?
>
> Words and phrases in Portuguese were added to the working wall, and these were used over the next few weeks to create bilingual glossaries, language mats and lexical sets (lists of words focused on a particular topic). With the use of these resources and translation websites, we wrote a whole class sequel (albeit very basic) to The Three Little Pigs, in Portuguese, which we shared with other classes.

So, with this case study in mind, let us return to Karagiannaki and Stamou's questions:

- What version of the world has been constructed here?
- How are relationships and identities revealed?
- How are the messages conveyed in terms of the language used?

These could be adjusted to promote children's thinking in terms of what they have achieved and to raise awareness of language:

- How has our version of the world of fairy tales changed through reading in another language?
- What words are used in each language to reveal relationships and identities?
- What words are used in Portuguese and English to convey key messages?

Later in the chapter, when we examine language awareness in terms of language use, we will look at some more examples of how dual language texts might be utilised. For now, though, we are going to move on to looking at the benefits of learning *about* language.

> Think about why this raising of awareness about language through the use of picture books is so useful. Are there other resources and pedagogies that you have observed or used that are also both powerful and motivating for children?

Knowledge about language

I (Virginia) recently had an amusing conversation with my partner, who said he had been reading a Tweet which talked about somebody who had a doctorate and had written over ten books but had to research what was meant by 'fronted adverbial' so as to be able to support their eight-year-old child with their home schooling. My partner (who was a head teacher and then went on to lead a large university department, as well as being the editor for many years of an international peer-reviewed journal) related this to me, paused and then said, 'What *is* a fronted adverbial anyway?' Now, this came from somebody who I refer to as the 'King of the split infinitive' (see later discussion on this) and, as my chief editor, delights in finding many errors in my writing!

You may feel we have gone a little 'off piste' here, but the aim of this anecdote is to identify how teaching children about language can, if we are not careful, evolve into something that is of very little use and is merely 'mechanistic learning based on prescriptive principles' (Koller, 2018, p. 5). In this instance, children know particular terminology relating to grammatical forms and functions and, within the confines of prescribed activities can insert appropriate words. However, they may lack deeper knowledge of why the positioning of words and phrases can have such fundamental effects on meaning and the evocation of thoughts and feelings and power.

We are certainly not saying that children do not need knowledge about language – quite the opposite. But they need *useful* knowledge about language, which raises their language awareness and empowers them to use language – both oral and written – in the most effective ways. One approach to increasing children's knowledge about language is through a study of morphology (the study of words) and etymology (the history and origins of words and phrases). If children can begin to see 'behind' the words they are using, to discover the origins and connections with other languages, to recognise language patterns and exceptions, then they are opening the portal to a fascinating world of words and deeds, of languages familiar and strange, of cultures and traditions known and new. This does not have to be dry, teacher-transmitted knowledge; instead it can most usefully be implemented through games and investigations.

Games and investigations

The invaluable asset of games and investigations is that they can be used across the curriculum, linking subjects and building on concepts, or they can be used as standalone activities, perhaps at the start or end of the day or for homework. This section provides some examples, which aim to teach children about language and raise their awareness of features of their own and other languages. You can of course adapt these ideas to suit your own classes.

Table 1.1 Language poster

	French	Portuguese	Spanish	German	Dutch	Polish	Others
tree							
root							
leaf							
flower							

The first activity we call 'Getting to the root of the matter' which is in itself a play on words, as the investigation is related to trees. This gives you a powerful starting point for discussion, as you can talk about what is meant by this phrase and how it links with roots in the natural world. Begin by asking children to research what the word for *tree* is in different languages. They can work in groups using technology, or you could set this as a homework activity that they then report back on. You could create a poster for the class, as shown in Table 1.1. As the children make their discoveries, they can fill in the poster and the discussions can begin.

The word for tree in Portuguese is *árvore*, in French is *arbre*, in Italian is *albero* and in Spanish is *árbol* – all descending from the Latin *arbor*. In German it is *baum*; in Dutch it is *boom*. Hopefully, the children will make these discoveries. The next part of the investigation is to think of questions that they want to ask about their findings. They could post these in the class question box.

It is likely that one of the questions might be, 'Why then, do we say in English, 'tree', which sounds and looks very different from words used in other European languages?' They might also wonder why the Portuguese, Spanish, French and Italian words are all very similar, why German and Dutch are similar etc. The etymological roots of *tree* are from the Old English form: *trēow, trēo*. The etymological roots of *baum* are from Middle High German and Old High German. You can see how this investigation could go down layer by layer – let the children run with it.

Then, perhaps, take it in a slightly different direction. In English, there are two words closely connected to the Latin-based vocabulary relating to trees – *arbour* (an area often built for shade, where the roof and sides are made from trees or plants, trained over a framework) and *arboretum* (where many trees, plants, shrubs etc. are planted and used for educational, scientific or leisure purposes). Children could start to group words together according to their origins and investigate why words may have changed over time and in what ways. Let them lead on this – it is an investigation, so there are no boundaries. You could certainly take this a step further by including reference to the findings and the ongoing investigation in other curriculum subjects.

A similar activity using words of Latin origin is 'Latin Legacy', which is an example from the AMLA language awareness programme (Cobb, 2014) (see the introductory chapter for details about the AMLA project). Before we explain what this activity entails, you might find it helpful to have a little background knowledge. We noted earlier that the etymological roots of *tree* are from the Old English form: *trēow, trēo*. 'Old English' is the name given to the earliest recorded stage of the English language, a period lasting about 700 years, beginning around the time of the arrival of the Angles, Saxons and Jutes, Germanic settlers who invaded Britain in the 5th and 6th centuries. Prior to this time, during the Roman invasion of Britain, Latin was the pre-eminent language of the elite. Old English borrowed very few words from Latin; more words began to be borrowed during the Middle English period – a period of significant language shifts, including many French influences following the Norman conquest in 1066 – and this increased significantly from 1500. These increased Latin (and Greek) language borrowings were sparked by the Renaissance, an intellectual and cultural movement which reawakened interest in the classical civilisations of ancient Greece and Rome and which coincided with the new technology of the printed word, enabling wider access to great literature (Smith, 2016).

We have included this background information as a reminder that languages are constantly evolving and that learning about language is a dynamic process. Each word has its own story, and each writer and orator add their own history to an interpretation of the word. English, in particular, is a multicultural language, increasingly used by non-native speakers as societies have become globalised (Yamada, 2010). All languages shift over time, and although there will always be those who may seek to influence language use such as the grammarians who argue that it is incorrect to split an infinitive – despite some notable authors breaking this rule such as Chaucer, More, Keats, Spencer, Twain, Kipling, Conan Doyle and Hardy (Freeman, 2013) – it is young people in particular through their social interactions and cultural expressions who enable languages to grow.

Let us digress a little further here (hang on in there – we will get to our 'Latin Legacy' activity!) using the example of the split infinitive to make a point about the fluidity of language learning. Debates about the origin of the split infinitive rule continue, with some arguing that it should not be split (e.g. 'To go boldly') and some who argue that it can be split to suit the context ('To boldly go'). It is suggested that the rule that infinitives should not be split stemmed from a desire for the English language to be more like Latin, which had one word for the infinitive (for instance *scribere*, Latin for 'to write') (Merriam Webster, 2021), although there is a lack of evidence to support this argument (Owen, 2016). The rule is sometimes argued to be about clarity of meaning, although there are some cases where it may be better to split the infinitive, for instance where so doing might improve clarity or avoid the language sounding overly formal (Evans, 2016). Consider for instance the following sentence where the use of the split infinitive is clearly appropriate: 'The price of eggs is expected to more than triple because of panic buying following a reported chicken blight.'

What we are trying to demonstrate here is that, when we are teaching children about language, focus needs to be on the importance of conceptual understanding and interpretation of language features as opposed to simply learning a set of rules. As we explore further in Chapter 9, grammatical knowledge is just one aspect of communicative competence.

So, with this in mind, on to our next activity. In the maths curriculum, children are introduced to Roman numerals, numbers which were represented by combinations of letters from the Latin alphabet (I, V, X, L, C, D and M). 'Latin Legacy' uses the Latin words for the numbers 1 to 10 for an investigation into English derivatives. We have given some examples in Table 1.2.

This activity is useful on several levels. There are clear links with the Latin words and numbers in other Latinate target languages, such as the Spanish number words *uno, dos, tres, cuatro, cinco, seis, siete, ocho, nueve, diez* and those in Italian: *uno, due, tre, quattro, cinque, sei, sette, otto, nove, dieci*. Knowing the Latin (or Latinate) numbers is also useful for

Table 1.2 Latin legacy

Latin number	English derivatives
1 unus	unicycle
2 duo	duet
3 tres	trio
4 quattuor	quartet
5 quinque	quintuplet
6 sex	sextuplet
7 septem	September
8 octo	octopus
9 novem	November
10 decem	decagon

examining the meanings of and remembering words, including maths terminology. Dabell (2018, no page) suggests that every subject has its own language – maths for example uses specialist vocabulary, grammatical structures and symbols – and that therefore we are all multilingual. Dabell adds that becoming fluent in maths is a communication journey with roadblocks to navigate, just like any other language-learning process, and that we should not underestimate the cognitive load on learners. Activities such as 'Latin Legacy' can support that load and can ensure that children are actively involved with their learning about language.

At the start of this section we emphasised the usefulness of games to support learning about language. An excellent game to practise word roots is 'Vocabulary Tennis'. For this game you will need to organise the students into two teams (or groups if you have a large class). The teams stand on opposite sides of the classroom. Explain that you are taking the role of umpire, and then 'throw' the students a word root – *friend*, for example. One team says a word containing the word root – *friendly* – and the other team has to respond with another word – *friendship*. If a student repeats a word or takes longer than a specified time, the other team wins a point. Play with a new word root for a new point.

As we discuss in Chapters 6 and 8, deliberate practice and motivating, unpressured 'test' situations, like Vocabulary Tennis, are important strategies for mastering language concepts. We suggest that these types of playful word-root challenges will help build key language knowledge that will scaffold learning across the curriculum.

Wendy: One of my former educational roles was an achievement coach which involved me working with teachers to support removing barriers to learning and raising expectations and achievement for vulnerable groups. Many of the barriers focused on communication issues, and these often stemmed from the way key vocabulary was used during the lesson, with an assumption that the children understood the concept because they were 'familiar' with it, in the sense that the word been used recently and had been 'taught' in previous years. Yet many subject specific words can be really confusing for children. Consider maths words that have different meanings in everyday contexts, such as odd, even, mean and right (as in 'right angle'). This vocabulary confusion can be particularly frustrating for children with English as an additional language tackling word problems in a subject where otherwise they might be able to demonstrate their knowledge and understanding well. Virginia, do you have any advice for teachers about how to build language awareness and knowledge about language into their planning and teaching to address these issues?

Virginia: This is such an important point, Wendy, and careful attention to this can make a considerable difference to children's access to curriculum subjects and concepts. Firstly, having two learning objectives for each lesson is really useful: an objective focusing on the content learning of the lesson and a language-focused objective. For example, the 'normal' learning objective might be 'To identify a range of settings for stories' and the language-focused objective would be 'To explore language associated with story settings'. Now, this second objective can be tackled in a number of ways, and I will briefly describe two of these.

Firstly, you could pre-teach the vocabulary which will be needed for this lesson – *forest, woods, pirate ship, castle, desert island, outer space* – and this could be with small groups of children who you have identified would benefit from this intervention – perhaps with the words translated into their first language if they are EAL learners. The pre-teaching session could take place just before the lesson or first thing in the morning when the children are doing settling in work, or the week before and then set as homework. The second way is to include this in the first part of your lesson and include all the children. So, you might ask, 'Who can tell me what a story setting is? Who can name some different settings?' These words would need to be recorded on the flipchart/working wall (and, potentially could be translated by you or the teaching assistant there and then or once the children begin independent work to acknowledge the languages spoken in your class) so that children could use them during that lesson and beyond. I always made the children a small 'book' each – just lined paper stapled together for each topic – and they could create their own dictionaries/glossaries as they progressed through the unit of work.

Language use: a shift in focus

By 'a shift in focus' we mean away from knowledge *about* language towards an understanding that language is for using. That language is 'dynamic and situational' (Radinger, 2018, p. 64) influenced by us as people, our emotional connections and of course the historical and political contexts in which we live our lives.

It is such a joy when you start to see learners moving on from their knowledge about language to seeing how language can work for them in a range of contexts. Often this then comes full circle to knowing more about language because of how it has been used and the results of this. Let us return to our fronted adverbial example. There are several ways of teaching this aspect of grammar and here are three:

1. Introduce the term 'fronted adverbial' and show the children some examples. They then input appropriate fronted adverbials into sentences, perhaps on a worksheet;
2. Find a story or a poem that includes examples of fronted adverbials and read the text, pausing to point out fronted adverbials. The children then look through a range of texts and highlight examples of fronted adverbials;
3. Find a story or poem that includes examples of fronted adverbials and read the text to the children. Ask them to work in groups to discuss how the author/poet creates particular impact and to identify and record any effective vocabulary. The children then feedback their ideas which might include reference to fronted adverbials. If this is the case, the teacher might take the opportunity to say, 'Ah yes, a useful fronted adverbial – an adverb at the beginning of the sentence! Why do you think the author used this?' If the children do not identify this particular feature, the teacher could include reference to it in the class discussions. It would be important here to discuss what happens if we change the position of the adverb; how does it alter the impact? This activity could then usefully be conducted with sentences in a different language.

Arguably, the third activity will have a more powerful effect, as it aims to support children to consider an author's use of language as a deliberate choice to create a particular impact. A fronted adverbial is a useful tool, but only in the right place for the intended impact, and it can easily be overdone. This needs to be discussed, and dialogue about language use needs to become a regular part of lessons and applied to all different aspects of language – whether English or others.

Consider these two attempts to 'improve' the simple sentence, 'The cat sat on the mat', following a lesson exploring adjectives and adverbs in descriptions:

- The expensive pedigreed cat, washing her velvet paws delicately, sat lazily on the luxury mohair mat.
- The tiger, licking her blood-stained paws, rested in the shade of the cedar tree.

Which sentence do you prefer? Can you explain why? What can you infer from each sentence? What are the words and phrases that describe a story, not just a picture? What feedback might you give the writer of each sentence?

Did you notice the adverbial phrase 'in the shade of the cedar tree' in the second sentence?

Arguably, one of the most powerful ways to raise children's awareness of how very *useful* language can be is by making comparisons with other languages. For example, children could compare the words for the days of the week in languages spoken in the class/school (see Table 1.3). They could look for patterns and organise languages into groups. We share a similar activity using colours in Chapter 9. Children will recognise the usefulness of these words and realise that they are useful *whatever* language one speaks!

A very recent article by Zaidi (2020) discusses a Canada-based project centred around the effectiveness of using dual language texts in the classroom and provides some powerful arguments for promoting this pedagogy in order to raise awareness of linguistic and cultural diversity. Some of the influences on this project came from the Awakening to Languages (AtL) initiative (mentioned earlier in the chapter), which emerged from the Council of Europe and the European Centre for Modern Languages. With the AtL approach, children compare the sounds and written language of different countries and examine how they can use what they know about their own language to help them with other languages. It encourages learners to think about their own and others' identities.

In Zaidi's research, the students were read books in English and then in another language (three languages were focused on, in addition to English, across the project – Spanish, Urdu and Tagalog). It was noted that the students were particularly engaged if the 'other' language was their own L1, and even those pupils who were generally quiet and reluctant to participate were engaging and commenting on links between languages and were keen to share their own ideas. There was a great interest in how words sound, are read and are written, with students drawing comparisons between languages. There were many questions raised, particularly 'why?' and 'how?' questions, demonstrating a real interest in the similarities and differences among languages and a desire to get beneath the surface of these and explore in more depth.

The pupils whose first language was not English became keen to learn about their own first language, use it more and share it with others. There was a sense of pride.

Other benefits of using the dual-language texts and engaging in discussion and activities around these were identified by Zaidi as:

- Enhanced student engagement;
- Enhanced student achievement;
- An awareness of the multidimensionality of language;
- Communicative and intercultural competence;
- The ability to reflect (pupils, teachers and guests);
- Stronger home-school links;
- All children feeling they could participate, contribute and that their contributions were valued;
- Opportunities for teachers to draw on existing knowledge and understanding about language and pupils' backgrounds;
- Promoting curiosity and a desire to learn more about others' languages and lives;
- Freedom for teachers to be creative and innovative change agents;
- A 'heightened literacy learning adventure' (ibid., p. 286).

Table 1.3 How others use languages

English	Monday	Tuesday	Wednesday	Thursday	Friday	Saturday	Sunday
French	lundi	mardi	mercredi	jeudi	vendredi	samedi	Dimanche
Spanish	lunes	martes	miércoles	jueves	Viernes	sábado	Domingo
Italian	lunedì	martedì	mercoledì	giovedì	venerdì	sabato	Domenica
Afrikaans	Maandag	Dinsdag	Woensdag	Donderdag	Vrydag	Saterdag	Sondag
German	Montag	Dienstag	Mittwoch	Donnerstag	Freitag	Samstag	Sonntag
Hungarian	hétfő	kedd	szerda	csütörtök	péntek	szombat	Vasárnap
Slovak	pondelok	utorok	streda	štvrtok	piatok	sobota	nedeľa
Zulu	uMombuluko	uLwesibili	uLwesithathu	uLwesine	uLewishlanu	uMgqibelo	iSonto
Arabic	الإثنين	الثلاثاء	الأربعاء	الخميس	الجمعة	السبت	الأحد

Hopefully the preceding sections have started you thinking about how we might raise our own and our pupils' language awareness – both knowledge about language and how it can be used. The final section examines our role a little more.

The role of the teacher

I think we are all aware that our role as teachers requires us to be flexible, adaptable and open to new ideas, approaches, theories and practices. As part of this, we need to consider our own language awareness and the benefits of promoting a language-aware classroom.

> Do you feel that you are language aware? How does this manifest itself?
> Can you list the benefits of raising our own and others' awareness of the potential and power of language?

As teachers we also have a considerable degree of power and agency over the ethos we promote in our classrooms, and with this comes significant responsibility. Hornberger and Cassels Johnson (2007, in De Angelis, 2011, p. 217) write that teachers have the opportunity to turn their students' multilingualism into 'a useful resource for the entire classroom', or they can maintain a monolingual approach, closing the door to untold possibilities in terms of language. Part of this responsibility, and something that can provide an invaluable starting point, is listening whenever possible to the voices of those we teach. The following case study provides an example.

> Years ago, I (Virginia), worked in a primary school where 25% of the children were Nepalese because the setting was very close to an army barracks that housed a Ghurkha regiment. I was reading the fairy tale 'Cinderella' to my Year 5 class (nine- and ten-year-olds) because we were going to be writing our own tales to share with the four- and five-year-olds in the school. I was a little way into the story when Sunita (name changed) – one of the Nepalese girls – jumped up in excitement and said, 'I know this story, but we call it Soonimaya!' The other children were fascinated by this and wanted to know all about this other version. This led to some wonderful discussion about tales from around the world, and the children undertook online research to locate some examples. We never got to finish the English version that day, but the lesson was much better than anything I could have planned – led entirely by this initial proclamation from Sunita and her classmates' interest!

In this example, the children were made aware – thanks to the intervention of Sunita – that pupils all over the world will be reading books in their own languages. What I was not in a position to do at the time, was to offer the tale in Nepali, but it is now possible to find different versions of the story online (there is a useful audio version here – https://

thefairytellers.podbean.com/e/episode-20-soonimaya-a-nepali-cinderella-tale-support-the-nepal-youth-foundation/). Part of our role as teachers is to recognise opportunities which prompt children to think about language and what they already know about language and to share this with their classmates. This is empowering for all.

Radinger (2018) conducted research examining language awareness of refugees and how this connected with their sense of agency. The participants had a good understanding of themselves as language learners and what worked best for them, and having knowledge of this – by opening conversations and investigations about language – benefits us and the whole school community. We are likely to be more mindful of how important this approach is if we are aware of the benefits of increased language awareness (which is why we asked you to reflect on this earlier). Radinger (ibid.) writes that learners who have experiences in multilingual and multicultural contexts manage social situations more effectively, as they have an explicit knowledge and understanding of the challenges and emotional involvement with communicating in social spaces. Also, raised levels of empathy are common, allowing for altering speech to support others' needs, thereby generally setting a more effective communicative space.

We would argue that being language-aware as a teacher is fundamental to the role and that, ideally, whatever our specific role in educational settings, we would aim to move along a continuum which begins with a broad awareness of the importance of language and works through more specific aspects of language, for example gendered language (the focus of Chapter 5), how language connects to wellbeing (the focus of Chapter 4) and how language can be utilised to best effect across the curriculum (the focus of Chapter 6). So, we need to start with a raising of consciousness around the subject of language and begin to embed ways of thinking and working into our pedagogies and practices. Often, simply by bringing an idea more to the front of our consciousness sets us on the path to transformative practice.

Scarvaglieri's (2017) research project is a good example of this. Scarvaglieri believes that *written* language is an effective medium through which to promote language awareness, as opposed to talking, because there is time to consider, edit, be deliberate, and so forth. He undertook a research study which focused on what he refers to as 'Educational Landscaping' – teachers engaging with the written linguistic landscape (LL) in their setting – signage, displays, posters for example. The teachers attended a workshop which encouraged them to consider the impact of a LL, and then they went away to implement some of the ideas and to create a poster of their findings, which they shared at a final workshop. The author found that there were some significant results, and these included:

- Heightened awareness of language and linguistic diversity leading to a change in behaviours – negative signage removed/altered; more consideration of the learners, with the height of signs being lowered; wider range of signs, e.g. signs on doors in different languages indicating what was in each room;
- The creation of a reading 'cafeteria' where parents and teachers read books in the language of instruction and other heritage languages;
- Teachers being more conscious of the written language around them and seeing the detail in their surroundings, alongside putting time aside to reflect on what they saw;
- Considerable interest from parents.

Scarvaglieri concluded that raising teachers' language awareness has the potential to enable them 'to work with language in a more mindful way that supports the language development, awareness and agency of their students' (ibid, p. 332).

We would argue that a fundamental way to develop our own language awareness is, of course, to learn another language. The following case study and ensuing discussion highlights the challenges and benefits of this.

> I (Virginia) have been learning Portuguese in a haphazard way for over ten years. I now spend most of my life in Portugal and have strong beliefs about the need to learn the language of the place that has welcomed me in and to celebrate and appreciate the new culture and practices. As part of this language-learning process, during the early stages, I enrolled on an evening course at a local university in England for 'Beginner Learners of Portuguese'. We were a group of about 15, and most were students below the age of 20 (I was 42) who, unbeknownst to me, were very confident with languages and already spoke at least three. This was a 'top-up' course for them. Although for the most part enjoyable, I found the sessions challenging in terms of the pedagogies employed and my own lack of confidence.
>
> Much of the session time was spent reading from a text, one student at a time, and answering questions on the text. I would spend most of the time working out which bit I would have to read and which question I would most likely be asked, so that I did not feel stupid. I neither listened to others read nor paid attention to their answers. Most of the other students (aside from myself and two or three others) could read fluently and were able to use their knowledge of Spanish to help with pronunciation and comprehension. I had very little to draw on! There were very few opportunities to practise orally, although when these were presented, they were very useful and a more relaxing way to 'have a go'.
>
> Finishing the course was a relief, and I remember very little of the content.

You might argue that this case study is not the best way to encourage others to learn a new language! However, despite the challenges, there was far more that I learnt about myself and language learning generally which was, arguably, more important than becoming more proficient at the language itself. During those sessions, I 'walked in the shoes' of other learners – particularly children with EAL and those learning a new foreign language. I became aware of the importance of creative, inclusive pedagogies which recognised the diversity of a group of learners and responded to this. I realised how it feels to be the one who cannot access the learning, who feels out of place and marginalised. I recognised the strategies I employed to hide my lack of confidence and competence and became more aware of performance anxiety (something we discuss in Chapter 4). This anxiety about speaking aloud in another language is of course relevant to the children we teach who have English as an additional language. However, this can be equally applicable to those of us who speak using a dialect which is different to what might be most common in a particular setting. This is another important aspect of our role as teachers and something that we are aware many teachers worry about: knowing how to respond to different dialects in the classroom and the potential impact on the children's development of standard English. A conceptual understanding of dialect helps here and is, we believe, an important aspect of language awareness.

A dialect is a form of language spoken by a group of people; although whether a dialect is termed such or becomes known as a language is often a political decision. 'A dialect is a language with an army and a navy' is a saying popularised by sociologist and linguist Max Weinrich (cited in Devlin, 2018, no page) and an argument that can be illustrated with the following examples, which are explained for children in the *Kiddle Encylopedia*'s (2021, no page) 'Dialect facts for kids':

- Catalan and Galician are now recognised as languages but used to be dialects of Spanish;
- Hindi and Urdu used to be the same language, Hindustani. Following Pakistan's separation from India, Hindustani became called Urdu in Pakistan and Hindi in India. Speakers from both countries can understand themselves in everyday speech, although their writing systems are different;
- English was once Anglo-Saxon, a dialect of Old Saxon;
- Chinese is called a language although it has hundreds of dialects, many of which cannot be understood by other Chinese speakers.

In English we might notice differences in dialect in terms of word usage. Consider for instance the name of the shoes worn for physical education in your primary school. Were they 'plimsolls', 'daps', 'gutties' or 'pumps'? Other differences include pronunciation, for example whether you pronounce *scone* as in *gone* or *scone* to rhyme with *bone*, and grammar, for example whether you say, 'I haven't', 'I've not', 'I havnae', or 'I ain't' (Robinson, 2019, no page).

Research by Snell and Andrews (2014, p. 3) asked the question, 'To what extent does a regional dialect and accent impact on the development of reading and writing skills?' They found that although for a minority of pupils, difficulties in understanding the relationship between standard and non-standard English can continue through primary school, in general, dialect does not negatively impact on reading and writing development. All children, regardless of their language or dialect, encounter difficulties in understanding the difference between spoken and written styles since there is no straightforward relationship between spoken and written English. The researchers noticed that children and young people appropriately style-shift between standard and non-standard forms in their speech and writing and are strategic in their language use. A final key finding to consider when responding to children's writing is that the correction of non-standard dialect forms without adequate explanation can lead to 'hypercorrection, confusion and anxiety' (ibid., p. 3).

We recognise that teaching a foreign language or supporting children whose first language is not English is a daunting challenge for teachers who consider themselves to be non-linguists. However, we want to assure you that, even if you are new to teaching languages other than English, throughout this book you will find easy-to-implement activities to encourage language awareness and to help you enjoy learning a language alongside the children. We also want to remind you that, like all teachers, you are a successful linguist in the sense that every day you tune in to patterns of sound and meaning, body language and gesture and symbolic representations, and that you are constantly code-switching between different language systems in different cultural contexts.

Summary

- Building on children's early language knowledge, experience and awareness is essential;
- Knowledge about language is very useful and needs to be explored in creative and playful ways;
- The power and possibilities afforded by language need to be promoted at every opportunity;
- The role of the teacher is vital in developing a language-aware classroom, school and community.

References

Association for Language Awareness (2020) Available at www.languageawareness.org/ (Accessed on 23.01.2021).

Bower, (2017) *Supporting Pupils with EAL in the Primary Classroom*, London: Open University Press.

Cobb, W. (ed.) (2014) *Language Awareness Programme*, Croydon: Accelerated Modern Language Acquisition.

Coelho, D. Andrade, A. I. & Portugal, G. (2018) 'The "awakening to languages" approach at pre-school: Developing children's communicative competence', *Language Awareness*, 27, 3, pp. 197-221.

Corcoll, C. (2013) 'Developing children's language awareness: Switching codes in the language classroom', *International Journal of Multilingualism*, 10, 1, pp. 27-45.

Crystal, D. (1995) *The Cambridge Encyclopedia of the English Language*, Cambridge: Cambridge University Press.

Dabell, J. (2018) 'Why it's important to see maths as a language', *Maths No Problem!* Available at https://mathsnoproblem.com/blog/teaching-practice/maths-as-a-language/ (Accessed 26.02.2021).

De Angelis, G. (2011) '"Teachers" beliefs about the role of prior language knowledge in learning and how these influence teaching practices', *International Journal of Multilingualism*, 8, 3, pp. 216-234.

Devlin, T. M. (2018) 'Is a language a dialect with an army and a navy?' +*Babbel Magazine*, Available at www.babbel.com/en/magazine/yugoslavian-language-dialect (Accessed 28.02.21).

Evans, K. (2016) 'Why it isn't wrong to split the infinitive', *Cell Mentor*, Available at http://crosstalk.cell.com/blog/it-isnt-wrong-to-split-infinitive#:~:text=Infinitives%20are%20the%20verb%20form,writing%20from%20sounding%20overly%20formal (Accessed 28.02.2021).

Freeman, T. (2013) 'To helpfully clarify, to better communicate: A history of the split infinitive', *Stroppy Editor*, Available at https://stroppyeditor.wordpress.com/2013/10/28/to-helpfully-clarify-to-better-communicate-a-history-of-the-split-infinitive/ (Accessed 27.02.2021).

Hornberger, N. H. & Cassels Johnson, D. (2007) 'Slicing the onion ethnographically: Layers and spaces in multilingual language education policy and practice', *TESOL Quarterly*, 41, 3, pp. 509–532.

Karagiannaki, E. & Stamou, A. G. (2018) 'Bringing critical discourse analysis into the classroom: A critical language awareness project on fairy tales for young school children', *Language Awareness*, 27, 3, pp. 222-224.

Kiddle (2021) 'Dialect facts for kids', Available at https://kids.kiddle.co/Dialect (Accessed 28.02.2021).

Koller, V. (2018) 'Language awareness and language workers', *Language Awareness*, 27, 1-2, pp. 4-20.

Merriam Webster (2021) 'To boldly go: Star trek & the split infinitive', *Merriam-Webster*, Available at www.merriam-webster.com/words-at-play/to-boldly-split-infinitives (Accessed 28.02.2021).

Nicholas, H. & Lightbown, P. (2008) 'Defining child language acquisition, defining roles for L2 instruction', in Philp, J., Oliver, R. & Mackey, A. (eds.), *Second Language Acquisition and the Younger Learner. Child's Play?* (pp. 27-51), Amsterdam/Philadelphia: John Benjamins.

Owen, J. (2016) 'To boldly split infinitives', *Arrant Pedantry*, Available at www.arrantpedantry.com/2016/09/08/to-boldly-split-infinitives/#:~:ext=It's%20often%20claimed%20that%20people,split%20them%20in%20English%20either (Accessed 28.02.2021).

Radinger, S. (2018) 'Language awareness and agency in the availability of linguistic resources. A case study of refugees and locals in Austria', *Language Awareness*, 27, 1-2, pp. 61-78.

Robinson, J. (2019) 'Grammatical variation across the UK', *British Library*, Available at https://www.bl.uk/british-accents-and-dialects/articles/grammatical-variation-across-the-uk (Accessed 19.07.2021).

Scarvaglieri, C. (2017) '"Educational landscaping": A method for raising awareness about language and communication', *Language Awareness*, 46, 4, pp. 325-342.

Smith, P. (2016) *Greek and Latin Roots: For Science and the Social Sciences, Part I - Latin*, Victoria, BC: University of Victoria, Available at https://open.bccampus.ca/ (Accessed 16.02.2021).

Snell, J. & Andrews, R. (2014) 'To what extent does a regional dialect and accent impact on the development of reading and writing skills? A Report for the BBC, Report' (Unpublished), Available at http://eprints.whiterose.ac.uk/86129/ (Accessed 01.03.2021).

Uoguelph.ca (no date) 'Bilingualism translates into higher earnings', Available at www.uoguelph.ca/news/2010/08/bilingualism_pa_1.html (Accessed 03.03.2021).

Yamada, M. (2010) 'English as a multicultural language: Implications from a study of Japan's junior high schools' English language textbooks', *Journal of Multilingual and Multicultural Development*, 31, 5, pp. 491-506.

Zaidi, R. (2020) 'Dual-language books: Enhancing engagement and language awareness', *Journal of Literacy Research*, 52, 3, pp. 269-292.

2 Inclusive approaches to language learning

The limits of my language mean the limits of my world.

(Ludwig Wittgenstein, 2001)

Introduction

Sustainable Development Goal 4 (United Nations, no date) states that by 2030, all countries need to: 'Ensure inclusive and equitable quality education and promote lifelong learning opportunities for all'. In this chapter, there will be both an explicit and implicit focus on two key words from this - *inclusive* and *quality* - and a consideration of the more specific goal (4.5) which states that we need to 'ensure equal access to all levels of education and vocational training for the vulnerable, including persons with disabilities, indigenous peoples and children in vulnerable situations'. We would argue that, if children cannot access the curriculum or fully participate in classroom life because account has not been taken of their linguistic abilities (whether native speakers of English or EAL learners), then these goals are unlikely to be met.

With this in mind, the chapter explores two key themes, both of which are central to the idea of an inclusive approach to language learning. The first examines why it is important to maximise children's existing language skills and ensure that we build on these. The second theme puts forward the argument that, by taking a bilingual approach to learning and teaching, planning and resourcing, a more inclusive ethos will be achieved, where a celebration of language and multilingualism is embedded in everyday practices, enhancing the lives of all children.

Maximising home language skills

Maximising home language skills is going to mean two things in this section of the chapter: firstly, examining language skills generally - for example how to capitalise on what children bring to the classroom - and secondly, focusing on children who do not have English as their first language and why it is vital that we build on their first language (L1) to the benefit of all children in the class.

Home language skills

Cremin et al. (2015, p. 14) write that the 'foundations of literacy are laid in the home', and it is essential that this concept underpins our approach to teaching and learning, acknowledging that

DOI: 10.4324/9781003129738-3

Inclusive approaches to language learning 29

children will arrive in school with differing levels of knowledge about language, language use, the power of language, and oral and written skills. The levels will of course be dependent on several factors. These include their exposure to language in both oral and written form; the degrees of interaction they have experienced with other children and adults; the exposure they may have had to literature, rhymes, songs, poems etc.; the opportunities presented for trips, excursions, holidays and so forth and therefore their exposure to a range of environmental print – for example posters, railway timetables, restaurant menus – and access to language in context. Moll's (2019) research over many decades has focused on what he refers to as children's 'funds of knowledge' – the knowledge they have gained and the practices they have been part of within their home communities and, significantly, he challenges the deficit model which sees some children as less likely to succeed because of their family background. Moll (ibid., p. 132), suggests that a better understanding of children's funds of knowledge allows teachers to incorporate into their pedagogies and practices what children bring from home and 'establish the *educational capital* of families often assumed to be lacking any such resources' (original emphasis). This, in turn, provides a more inclusive environment, where children can use their existing knowledge and experience in meaningful ways.

A better understanding of children's home lives and language experiences provides practitioners with the tools to provide a more inclusive approach to language learning, which focuses on meaningful examples (Hayes, 2016). It might be that lessons can be designed around an aspect of environmental print, for example, with which the teacher knows all the children are likely to be familiar – a popular advertisement or road signs specific to the geographical area. The idea of road signs could be taken a step further, in terms of signage which shows the twinning of a town in another country, and this could lead to some exciting links with the foreign language under study (see Chapter 9 for a case study focusing on e-Twinning). In this way, children are making links between their own communities, people and places in other countries and the look and sound of town names in different languages. This in turn, can foster a sense of belonging – a realisation that they are 'on the map' both locally and globally. The following case study provides a powerful example of how a Year 4 teacher promoted an interest in language, using environmental print gathered by the children.

> The teacher, Richard, gave the children an optional homework activity, which was to look around their homes and find something with print on it which was portable and of interest to them. He gave examples of the Argos catalogue, fridge magnets, diaries, calendars and other possibilities and showed them a photograph of a room in his own home. He asked the children to 'spot' any printed material, giving them two minutes to work in groups and record any items. The children then shared their lists and discussion time took place. This gave them some initial ideas for when they returned to their own homes and they were asked to bring in just one example on the Monday (with permission from parents!).
>
> Monday saw an avalanche of contributions, and these were all arranged on a large, central table. Children were given time to explore, share and talk about the different items. There was printed material in different languages, a wide variety of genres and examples of language being used for a multitude of purposes. All of this was of great interest to the children, but it also gave Richard an insight into children's home lives and what they had access to.

In this case study, although the key task was for children to find examples of *written* print, the emerging possibilities in terms of oral interactions and bringing aspects of home into the classroom were infinite. The teacher would have every opportunity to build on their ideas, rather than leading with his own contributions. Children will engage with language in myriad ways outside the classroom, and the key to successful inclusion is to bring these experiences into lessons as starting points where possible. This might include asking children to share poems, stories, word games, songs, favourite song lyrics and so forth from home, rather than always starting with our own examples. Immediately, this ensures a more inclusive approach to language because we begin with the children and their families. Children from different backgrounds may have very different literacy practices, with more of a focus on oral storytelling for example (Bower, 2017), and once we are aware of these it is more likely that we can incorporate them into the school day.

> How might you gain a better understanding of the linguistic experiences of the children you teach and their parents? What activities could you plan that would provide you with a clearer picture of this?
>
> In what ways might this impact on the pedagogies and resources you employ?

Overt promotion of L1 for children with EAL

If we are to see a more inclusive approach to language learning, the status of non-dominant languages needs to be elevated. The positioning of a language affects the way children perceive their home language and, as a result, their willingness to access their existing knowledge and understanding of language within their learning. If home languages and the ability to speak/write more than one language are not valued and receive 'no official support' (Kenner and Kress, 2003, p. 201), children will very soon recognise this and will begin to cast off their L1, in favour of English. Cummins (2005, p. 586) believes that there is a 'rapid loss of heritage language fluency in the early years of schooling when these languages are not reinforced within the school context', and rather than benefitting from the social, cognitive and linguistic advantages of being bilingual, children move towards an 'English-only' mind-set. This has significant consequences, including alienation from wider family, disaffection and confusion relating to identity and the loss of the considerable attribute of being able to speak more than one language.

Overt promotion of L1, maximising children's existing language skills, has the potential to proffer social, cognitive and linguistic advantages – both short- and long-term. In terms of social advantage, research indicates that bilinguals are often flexible, skilled communicators. Ikizer and Ramirez-Esparza (2018) conducted a study which found that bilinguals are more 'socially flexible' than monolinguals, have the ability to adapt to different social environments and are able to 'read' a social situation more effectively. In terms of cognition, bilingual advantages include the likelihood of a strong level of executive functions (see Chapter 6 for more discussion on executive functions), the ability to think about language and make connections, and to have a cognitive flexibility which allows for a more creative approach to problem solving (Antoniou, 2019). Linguistically of course, bilingual learners are adding to an existing language and can use this knowledge and experience to make sense of a new language, both oral and written. When encouraged to do this, it has been found that young EAL learners are very keen to make links between languages. In Kenner's (2007, p. 20) study with British Bangladeshi pupils (second- or third-generation children who were generally more fluent in English than Bangla), all the children declared that they would like to learn in both languages, not just English. They articulated that they were likely to understand more and be able to learn in different ways, and they were cognisant of the fact that, if they learnt solely in English then, 'slowly, slowly we forget Bengali and then we will be like the English people only speaking one language'.

But inclusion of L1 needs to be overt – it is not enough to 'allow' learners to use their L1 in the classroom. If explicit promotion is not in place, pupils will soon realise the status of their own language (perceived as below English) and will begin to discard their L1 in order better to fit in with the dominant classroom practices. They will see any use of L1 as temporary and transitional (Conteh and Brock, 2011), whereby, once an adequate standard of English is achieved, L1 can be abandoned. In her longitudinal study, looking at the life of a very young EAL learner, Day (2002) found that the child went through a series of phases, gradually rejecting his L1. He began by using Punjabi quite happily in the classroom, supporting his peers. He then began to appear embarrassed by his first language and started to mock it. Eventually, he began to 'police' the classroom, ensuring that his peers used English. The class teacher was not aware of discouraging children to use Punjabi within the school day but said that she never *actively encouraged* it. In this way, over time, the English language became the 'most valuable commodity in the classroom' (Flynn, 2013, p. 238). If, instead, children hear the teacher using a range of languages (do not be daunted – this can begin with 'Hello' or 'Thank you' – and there are plenty more examples throughout the chapters), or if they are asked to share what certain words/phrases are in their L1, they will realise that their own language has a place in the rich tapestry of world languages and that it is important, interesting, exciting, desirable and much to be celebrated. Within this classroom ethos, EAL learners will feel comfortable to engage in what Garcia (2009, p. 140) refers to as 'translanguaging', whereby bilinguals use what they know of different languages to 'make sense of their multilingual worlds'.

Virginia: Wendy, what do you feel might be some of the challenges teachers face when attempting to promote children's L1?

Wendy: One of the challenges is parental reluctance, I think. I often hear students of bilingual parents express regret that they were encouraged to use English in the home and therefore have developed only limited competence themselves of their familial L1. What can teachers do to address this parental reluctance to promote L1?

Virginia: I think it is vital to have a whole school/community approach. Everybody involved with the school needs to have the same ethos: that it is essential and beneficial to promote use of L1, both at home and in school. More importantly, everybody needs to understand *why*, otherwise they will not feel invested in this idea. Opportunities need to be built into school life, whereby parents and staff can discuss the benefits of maintaining L1 and what this might look like in practice. This would involve inviting parents into school with the two-fold advantage of proactively developing strong relationships with the community and ensuring that the message about the use of L1 is consistent. These gatherings could involve talks, sharing of resources and ideas and identification of online materials. The Bell Foundation – www.bell-foundation.org.uk/ – whose mission is to promote intercultural understanding through language education – is a great place to start, and this charitable trust runs webinars for teachers and families and provides a range of excellent resources. This type of resource could also be advertised on the school website. As a head teacher, I would be aiming to have the community talking about everything that is positive relating to speaking and learning in more than one language.

Overt promotion of children's L1 is not possible without careful planning. This planning needs to include the use of pedagogies and practices that maximise children's opportunities to bring their existing language skills to the classroom and to use them in ways that benefit them socially, cognitively and linguistically. A key aspect of this is to build in multiple opportunities through the day for genuine dialogic interactions. By 'genuine dialogic interactions', we mean extended opportunities for talk, discussion, debate, argument and questioning. Alexander's (2018, p. 6) principles for dialogic teaching include a focus on 'collectivity, reciprocity and supportiveness', with an emphasis on talk that is cumulative – with children building on their own and others' ideas and contributions – and purposeful, with specific objectives in mind. In their research, Hite and Evans (2006) found that the main voice in the classroom was that of the teacher – to teach either subject content or language. There were far fewer instances of the children having opportunities for extensive discussion, and the authors suggested that this reflects the general trend for the teacher's voice to dominate.

There are, however, many examples where children *are* given time to engage in discussion, and one example of this, often observed in early years and primary classrooms, is 'talk partner' time, when children are instructed to turn to their designated partner and discuss a concept or problem to be solved. These are excellent opportunities for children to share, try out language and co-create meaning, using their L1 if useful. However, in my experience, these times for talk can lack authenticity, as pupils are often given '30 seconds' to engage in discussion. By the time children have turned to each other, settled, thought about what they should be discussing and uttered one sentence, 30 seconds is over. Think about this from the perspective of an EAL learner: having to understand the instructions, think of an idea possibly in your first language, translating it, thinking about how to express it – the list goes on, and 30 seconds will not be of much use!

Earlier I mentioned *extended* and *genuine* opportunities, and this is far removed from 'having a quick chat with your partner'. McNamara and Conteh (2008, p. 204) identify an authentic dialogic approach as one that ensures the 'voices and subjectivities of all participants and the co-constructive nature of the discourses' are recognised – and this requires time planned into a lesson, a flexible approach to how much time children might need and every opportunity incorporated to allow children to have their voices heard. It is important that we also consider whether, during these partner-talk activities, children are at more advantage of sitting with a fellow pupil who has the same L1 (if this is possible) or whether it might be more beneficial for them to sit with a child who has strong English oral language skills and can provide the scaffolding and modelling that might be required.

Another way of promoting authentic opportunities for oral interaction is through group work, with carefully planned activities which encourage/nurture/foster talk and enquiry. A thoughtful approach to seating arrangements is required to ensure that children get the most out of the group work (DfES, 2006), and different groupings can work in distinct ways for different subjects. For example, seating children with others who speak the same L1 during a science investigation lesson enables collaboration, plenty of discussion and the likelihood that the group will be able to access the activity and participate effectively in the same way as their English-speaking peers. If, however, the lesson was focusing on reading comprehension, it might be more useful to have a mixed group of bilingual and monolingual children, whereby the children more proficient in English could support their peers with access to vocabulary. In her research with teachers who were deemed to be particularly effective in supporting EAL learners, Flynn (2007) found that these practitioners ensured a meaningful context for the learning and that there was always a focus on oral language, with specifically planned activities to promote this. Group work allows for this more authentic approach, where there are more opportunities for children to communicate and share ideas.

The next section will examine how we might take the focus on promoting 'more than just English' a step further, perhaps taking you out of your comfort zone! Hopefully, we will convince you that what we suggest is not only possible, but essential for the 'superdiverse' (Vertovec, 2007) world in which we live and teach.

Taking a bilingual approach

By a 'bilingual approach' we do not mean that the curriculum, lesson content, resources and so forth need always to be in more than one language. Instead, the concept is bound up with an overt recognition of, reference to and celebration of language *per se*, and how this has the potential to broaden our own minds and those of the children we teach and to open doors for them to new and exciting worlds.

It is vital that, rather than being influenced by the deficit model, which views anybody who does not speak the dominant language (in this context, English), as 'lacking' (Rodriguez, 2013), we see language, in all its myriad forms and varieties, as a key tool for ensuring a more inclusive, holistic, empowering school experience for all children. With rising levels of mental health issues amongst children and adults (Education Support Partnership, 2018; youngminds, 2018), the wellbeing – both physical and mental – of the children we teach needs always to be at the forefront of our minds (see Chapter 4 for more discussion on this). You might ask what this has to do with a bilingual approach. We argue that the social, cognitive and linguistic benefits of a more flexible approach to incorporating different languages are immeasurable, and they include the potential to increase empathy, raise awareness of difference, support inclusive practices and give children a platform from which to appreciate more strongly the world and its citizens. In this way, we have the capacity to send children out into this world with open but critical minds, well-formed principles and a sensitivity to those they will meet, socialise with and work alongside. So, how would a bilingual approach manifest itself?

We would argue that a bilingual approach can quickly become an integral aspect of everything you do in your classroom, through attention to our version of the 3Rs:

- Routines;
- Resources;
- Role models.

We will discuss each of these in turn.

Routines

Most classrooms – whether early years, primary or secondary – have familiar routines which promote a safe, secure environment for pupils to learn. The predictability of any routine makes it the perfect conduit for a bilingual approach, as the language patterns will be similar each day and can therefore more easily be prepared for in languages other than English (NALDIC, 2015). Table 2.1 shows an example of a typical early morning routine that I (Virginia) observed when collecting data for my PhD in a Reception class. We will use this example to analyse the bilingual approaches already in place and to suggest how these might be expanded on to further enhance practice.

I observed the same routine every morning in this Reception class. The children and parents appeared relaxed, confident and welcomed. The relationship between the teacher and the bilingual teaching assistant, and how they worked together, demonstrated an understanding of the needs of the Nepalese children and their parents and exemplified an ethos

Table 2.1 Early morning routine in a Reception class

Time	Activity
8.35	Children and their parents begin drifting into the classroom, hanging up coats and putting bags in trays. The class teacher (English-speaking) and the teaching assistant (bilingual in Nepali and English) are welcoming the children into the room, using English and Nepali. The Nepalese parents often engage in longer conversations with the teaching assistant, discussing any concerns about their child/homework/events going on in the school.
8.40	The children self-register, moving their names onto the board for that particular day. The days of the week are in English.
8.45	Children move to their group tables where they start 'early morning work', consisting of a range of activities including jigsaw puzzles, building blocks, drawing, matching games etc., and there are a number of picture books available.
9.00	Parents leave the classroom, the children are called to the carpet and the official register is taken. The children respond in English.

of respecting a language other than English. In this way, both the English and the Nepalese parents felt valued, and they were able to communicate any concerns or ask any questions. They were able to feel part of the school community, and they actively engaged in their children's experiences. The role here of the bilingual teaching assistant is clearly extremely valuable. Research indicates that bilingual teaching assistants are often under-utilised, and Baker (2014) suggests that this is in part due to the unfortunate propensity to ignore the indisputable value of maintaining a first language. This in turn negates the significance of bilingual support, and this invaluable asset goes to waste. It was good to see such seamless interactions and effective use of the teaching assistant in the Reception classroom.

Within that early morning routine, whilst the adults were chatting, those children who remembered moved towards the board of names to self-register. Self-registering encouraged the children to find their own names and move them to the relevant day of the week. A small addition to this routine might be to have the days of the week in languages other than English. This could reflect the languages spoken in the class or perhaps the 'language of the month' at that time (see later discussion of this practice). Being immersed in different languages – recognising the patterns of different written scripts and subconsciously absorbing the similarities and differences in how language is presented – is an unobtrusive yet highly effective way of taking a bilingual approach. This immersion needs to become the 'norm' rather than the exception; everyday practice rather than tokenistic one-off incidents. Such a small part of the day – self-registering – and yet part of a powerful ethos that reflects a focus on language.

The children were clearly aware of what was expected next, and they moved without hesitation to their group tables, where the prepared activities were not reliant on children having a strong grasp of written English. One might expect this in a class where the children are five or six years old, but it is something to consider for older pupils also: having activities and resources that can be accessed by all, whilst supporting learning and development. During this 20-minute period in the morning, the teacher and assistant need to be free to talk to parents and prepare for the day, and careful resourcing to enable independence, or activities that are organised so children can support each other, is invaluable. In this instance, it could be seen that children were observing and imitating their peers; they were chattering away, 'translanguaging' to 'maximise communicative potential' (Garcia, 2009, p. 141); and there was a relaxed 'busyness'.

Toohey (2003) undertook research which explored the impact of seating arrangements and the grouping of children with EAL, as well as examining children's mobility around the classroom. All of these aspects were found to be predominantly controlled by the teacher, and opportunities for extended dialogue (see earlier discussion) between children were few and far between. Toohey (ibid) discusses the importance of 'peer talk' because this is the type of language that is useful to children – accessible and relevant to them in that moment in time – whether they be native speakers of English or EAL learners. Leung (2005, p. 249) reinforces this point and emphasises the need for children to engage with 'context-embedded communication': communication that is meaningful and authentic. The early morning activities observed in the Reception classroom embodied this idea and provided opportunities for child-led dialogue. One way to make these activities more language-focused might be to include resources in different languages – books, games, word puzzles – so that children become accustomed to a less Anglocentric setting (regardless of whether or not you have EAL learners in your class). The range of multilingual resources available has increased considerably over the past two decades, and it is worth pushing forward this agenda at staff meetings so that funding can be sought. The section on resources, later in the chapter, provides details of websites where these resources can be found.

The final aspect of this early morning routine was for the children to come together on the carpet for the official registration, taken by the class teacher. In this case, the register was taken in English, and the children responded in English. In many classrooms, I have heard the teacher and the children using a range of languages during registration, whether this was a child's own L1 or a language that the class was focusing on that week/month. Again, using these brief yet regular moments in time has many positive outcomes. Firstly, they celebrate linguistic diversity (this might be generally, or specific to the children in the class). Secondly, they go some small way to redress the balance of an 'English-dominant' society (Kenner and Kress, 2003, p. 201) and raise awareness of other languages. Thirdly, the regularity and repetition involved in registering allows children to absorb and utilise languages other than English, to use their mouths and voices in different ways to make the necessary sounds – something that becomes much more challenging if we become set into monolingual habits.

> You might want to think of more ways that an activity such as registration can support a bilingual approach. What about other routines that happen daily – could these take on a more bilingual aspect?

Another very familiar routine in early years and primary classrooms is the reading of a story near to home time. This is an invaluable opportunity to share stories in languages other than English. This might at first appear to be a strange idea, particularly if all the pupils in your class have English as their first language. I would argue the opposite! All the more reason to share stories in other languages if the children only hear English through their school and home lives. In this way they become accustomed to the rhythms, cadences and patterns of different languages, and their ears are attuned to this when they move into different contexts and environments.

It must be remembered however, that early years and primary teachers are usually generalists; they need to be able to teach at least ten different curriculum subjects and may not be language specialists. In order, therefore, to integrate this activity into a classroom routine, a creative and innovative approach is required, as we may not feel, as teachers, that we have the ability to read stories in different languages (particularly if the alphabet and script is unfamiliar). This can be managed in a range of ways. Parents could be invited in to read to the class in their first language, and a dual-language text could be used so that the children hear English (from the teacher) alongside the other language (from the parent) (see later content for a more detailed focus on dual-language texts). With older children or confident young readers, story time could be undertaken with pupils reading in their first languages. Again, this needs to be managed carefully, as children may not feel comfortable reading in front of the class; but you will know your pupils well and can judge when this might be a successful practice. A final example of how this might be managed is the use of audio books in different languages. The children could listen to the story in English and then listen again in another language (this could be in the language of EAL learners in the class, the foreign language under study or indeed, in any language). The idea here is not necessarily to learn another language; more, it is about recognising that other languages exist and that these have different sounds, rhythms and cadences. It is about raising awareness that children everywhere in the world listen to, read and tell stories and that we are all part of a society which is underpinned by narrative and use of language.

Resources

Hopefully we have convinced you that routines are an excellent way by which a bilingual approach might manifest itself, thereby ensuring a more inclusive approach to language learning. An integral part of a teacher's classroom routines is selecting the most effective resources for what is being taught. The choice of resource can make the difference between an average lesson and a lesson that inspires and motivates children and ensures that they all feel included in the learning. In this section, we are going to examine three examples of resources that could be used across the curriculum and that shine a spotlight on language:

- Multilingual displays;
- Language mats; and
- Dual language books.

Multilingual displays

In my experience, inner city schools have the most wonderful displays around school buildings – often in the entrance to the school – which show all the languages spoken in the setting, frequently with multilingual signage, cultural artefacts, maps and other elements. These are powerful entities, reflective of multicultural communities and a respectful way to acknowledge and celebrate the diversity of the school population. Less common, however, is seeing multilingual displays relating to different curriculum areas in individual classrooms. We would argue that displays – planned and put together in conjunction with the pupils – that reflect the languages spoken in the class are an effective way to promote linguistic diversity and enrich the learning experience for all children.

It is vital to remember, however, that teachers and teaching assistants are often pushed to the limit in terms of time, and multilingual displays might seem an undertaking too far. A way to manage this is by involving the children and their families in the creation of these displays, taking pressure away from practitioners. Planning activities into lessons across the curriculum, whereby the children are learning and creating at the same time, can result in useful displays in which children have an investment and are more likely, therefore, to enjoy and use.

A relatively common multilingual display is to focus on a 'language of the month'. Here are some useful school sites which give examples and ideas for this:

www.millfields.hackney.sch.uk/index.php?page=language-of-the-month
www.rosecroft.school/language-of-the-month/
www.westfield.surrey.sch.uk/news/?pid=3&nid=1&storyid=57

Choosing a language of the month has the advantage of being able to celebrate the range of languages spoken in the class/school or, if the setting is monolingual, to choose any languages and become familiar with the look and sound of both written and oral versions. It could be that the language of the month is linked with a project or theme, and the display reflects both the chosen language and the learning content. An example of this might be children learning about habitats in science, and the display could be very visual with children's drawings and images they have accessed through research, with the key vocabulary being presented in the language of the month and in English. Alternatively, this type of display could be entirely focused on the chosen language with details about where this language is spoken and written examples of the language. If you are working with a class where the children either speak English as their first language or one other language, e.g. Polish, there is no reason why all the displays cannot be bilingual, in terms of key words. This is more difficult if there are many languages spoken and, when this is the case, it is about ensuring that the focus varies.

Language mats

Access to and understanding of the vocabulary associated with a curriculum subject is vital for all children if they are to participate and learn. For EAL learners, the vocabulary may be familiar in their first language, but they need to make the link with English; or they may not be familiar with the words in *any* language. Hashemi and Gowdasiaei (2005, p. 357) found that opportunities were required for EAL learners 'to study vocabulary systematically and in meaningful contexts' and one way to support this, whatever the individual's level of understanding – and whether they are EAL learners or native speakers of English – is through the use of language mats. Most of us are familiar with monolingual language mats (see Figure 2.1), where there is usually a picture and a word, so that children can more easily read the word and understand its meaning, supported by the visuals. Bilingual/multilingual language mats merely add a further layer by including another language as well as English. Language mats are available to purchase online, but I would argue that personalised mats, created, where possible, by the children, are far more useful (and definitely cheaper!).

Imagine you are about to embark on a topic in the early years focusing on the seaside. Generally, a topic starts by finding out what the children already know. After initial discussion, you could ask them to draw pictures showing what they might see at the seaside, giving the children pieces of A4 paper divided into four squares as shown in Figure 2.2. Each square has space for a picture and has two lines at the base where, eventually, words will be added to the appropriate pictures in English and in another language. This activity can be used with children of all ages, adding more boxes for older children and putting the onus on them to find out the word in English, how to spell it and then the word in another language. If you have a large number of children with EAL in the class, you could sit children in pairs – one English, one Portuguese, for example – and they could work together on translating.

Inclusive approaches to language learning 39

Figure 2.1 Monolingual language mat

Figure 2.2 Language mat template

Alternatively, if you do not have EAL learners in the class, all the children could create their word mats with English words and then, as a class, using shared writing, the language of the month could be utilised or perhaps the foreign language they are studying that year and the words translated for the word mats (see Figure 2.3).

The advantage of any or all of these methods is that the children are immersed in language and problem solving – finding the most appropriate words to fit the images and the

40 *Inclusive approaches to language learning*

Figure 2.3 Bilingual (Portuguese/English) language mat

topic. They are working together, discussing language, maybe 'translanguaging' (Garcia, 2009), recognising similarities and differences between languages and undergoing a learning experience which has a focus on both content and language. See the following case study, which shows how one teacher chose to take this project forward.

> Michael (a Key Stage 2 teacher) was very familiar with using monolingual language mats to support the development of vocabulary across the curriculum. Up to this point, these had tended to be examples purchased from online resource companies. Michael felt, however, that the children were not sufficiently invested in these resources, as they had not been involved with choosing or buying them. The resources were also very expensive. He decided therefore that he wanted to involve the children with the creation of language mats, particularly as he was about to embark on a new topic, centred on Mexico. He gave the children a partly filled-in language mat (four squares completed out of nine on an A4 sheet) with an image, the word in English and the word in Spanish. The class then discussed general background information about Mexico, and the children spent some time researching the country, its language, culture and people. Along the way, they began completing the word mats with any images and vocabulary they felt would be useful, but there was no rush to do these – they were organic and individual to each child. Children shared mats, made additional examples, did more for homework, created a bilingual display and used the class laptops to generate more sophisticated resources using Google Translate and programs that allowed them to be more creative with their use of images. Some of the children went on to create digital language mats, with hyperlinks to other websites, images etc.

> Can you think of other ways that you might use language mats to ensure an inclusive approach to language learning? What might be the cognitive, linguistic and social benefits of making and using these resources?

Dual language books

Dual language books – particularly picture books – are a powerful and inclusive resource, whether you have children with EAL in your class or not. These resources have become more numerous, varied and of a much better quality over the past few decades and are easily located online. Using dual language texts allows children to make 'global connections' (Leaman, 2008) and transfer their knowledge of one language to their developing knowledge of another (Chen, 2019). This makes the texts invaluable to enhance the experience of EAL learners, but also for all children during foreign language lessons and across the curriculum. They provide authentic, meaningful contexts for culturally based conversations and activities (Rowe and Fain, 2013), and they are an effective way to forge links between home and school.

There are many ways that these texts might be used to ensure a more inclusive approach to language learning. Dual language picture books can be used in whole-class sessions, perhaps using a visualiser to show the book as it is read. Initially, before starting to read the text, you might promote a discussion about how the two languages are displayed on the page, whether the script is different and why this might be. Are there any words in the language other than English that children recognise? Does anyone recognise the second language, or can they read any of it? This should ignite conversation, and time needs to be given for children to discuss and share their ideas, promoting an interest in language and opening up possibilities beyond what the children are accustomed to.

Gordon (2018), in her master's research, used a bilingual version (Polish and English) of the picture book *Not Again, Red Riding Hood!* Initially, she found that the Polish children were reluctant to talk about their first language and how it might be used – for them, Polish was for home and English for school. However, as the project continued, and the status of the Polish language was raised through the use of the book, the children started to enjoy using their L1 for reading, and 'the languages ended up complementing each other' as children realised that 'Polish literacy could help form a bridge between their two linguistic worlds' (2018, no page).

The text could then be read in English, asking the children to note any similarities between words in the two languages or any other observations about what they saw and heard. This whole-class session might lead to children creating their own dual language picture books. These can be very basic, with single sentences on the page (rather like *Rosie's Walk* by Pat Hutchins, www.youtube.com/watch?v=rYuINILGW1A), and children can take time illustrating and translating, using online resources. If possible, focusing on a language spoken by a child/children in the class, would be powerful and potentially make translating easier (depending on the age and reading and writing ability of the children). Parents might be invited in for this activity to support with translating.

Another way to use dual language books is with individual children or pairs. This works particularly well if you have audio versions, so that children can listen to the book in either language, whilst following the story and enjoying the pictures. Children could be paired up in different ways – a native English speaker with an EAL learner or two EAL learners together or two native English speakers together. It really does not matter – there are benefits to all of these. The main thing to remember is that these are not for the exclusive use of the pupils who speak the non-English language of the book. Instead, it is about raising the status of different languages for *all* children and celebrating the diversity of language and culture in our school, our country and our world (Leaman, 2008).

Role models

So far, we have examined the use of routines and resources to promote inclusive approaches to language learning. The final one of our '3Rs' is role models, and by this we mean ensuring that by our actions, our words, our thoughts and our philosophies, we embody an ethos which celebrates language, its power, its beauty and its utility. If this philosophy is at the heart of all that we do in the classroom, every subject and every child will benefit. Bourne (2001) notes that simply because a school and an education system recognise and value linguistic diversity, this does not challenge a monolingual ideology. Similarly, research conducted by Karabenick and Clemens Noda (2004, p. 69) found that although teachers who were interviewed believed diversity within a community had the potential to enrich the lives of those residing within it, there was 'ambivalence in their beliefs that people of different cultures can work and socialise together'. These examples might indicate that while the concept of diversity is accepted and celebrated, this is not necessarily reflected in everyday practice.

Bourne (2001) recognises that the rhetoric of valuing children's languages is not easy to make a reality within the confines of an English curriculum and assessment system. We would agree but would assert that it is essential and that there are many ways by which we can make the rhetoric more of a reality and 'walk the talk' in everyday practice. One way to start this is to commit to learning a language yourself (see the case study in Chapter 1 for a detailed example). Even if you are already multilingual, take on the challenge of a new language. There are numerous benefits to this, but most importantly you are putting yourself in the shoes of any EAL learners in the class and you are a role model in terms of your own interest in languages other than English. Share your experiences with the children – the challenges, the frustrations and the mini-victories as you master aspects of this new language. Have a go at using in the classroom words and sentences that you are learning and – if you have children whose L1 is that which you are learning – encourage them to correct you and help with pronunciation. There is nothing so empowering for children than to become the teacher themselves!

As a role model, take every opportunity to introduce a focus on and a discussion of language across the curriculum. Make links between words, noting when words arise which are the same in different languages. Knowing the different languages spoken in your classroom helps you to draw attention to them, for example: 'If we were counting to ten in Polish, it would sound like this. . . .'

Ask children to find the etymology of words – this often helps them to remember what words mean (see Chapter 1 for a range of ideas on this). Imagine you are teaching geography with older children, exploring rivers. You are likely to come across the word *meander*, and this might be difficult for children to remember. Discuss the etymology of the word:

> Meander, which comes from Greek Maiandros – an old name for a river in Asia Minor that is now known as the Menderes – implies a winding course and lazy movement, and it is still sometimes associated with rivers (as in, 'the river meandered through the town'). Meander can also be used as a noun meaning 'a winding path'.
>
> (Merriam-Webster Dictionary)

You only have to model this a few times, and children soon start to enquire for themselves and want to find out where words come from and what they mean.

If you have EAL learners in your class, ask them, 'How would you say that in Polish/Punjabi/Bulgarian? How would you write it?' In her study, Gordon (2018) encouraged children to create Venn diagrams and sound charts, comparing and contrasting the phonemes and graphemes in Polish and English – easy and powerful strategies whereby you are championing linguistic diversity and acting as a role model for the children and your colleagues. This latter point is an important one. Not only do we need to be role models for the children we teach, but it is important to convince colleagues of the benefits of an approach which prioritises language in all aspects of classroom life.

Summary

- Finding out as much as possible about children's existing knowledge and understanding about language and the languages they speak is a priority for all teachers;
- It is essential to build on children's existing language skills, and this requires research into languages/dialects spoken at home and in the local community;
- Promotion of L1 needs to be overt so that children feel comfortable and confident with using all their language skills across the curriculum;
- If we have a more bilingual ethos in our classrooms, we can seize every opportunity to celebrate, explore and utilise languages;
- Routines, resources and role models are essential in an inclusive, language-focused classroom.

References

Alexander, R. (2018) 'Developing dialogic teaching: Genesis, process, trial', *Research Papers in Education*, pp. 1–38.

Antoniou, M. (2019) 'The advantages of bilingualism debate', *Annual Review of Linguistics*, 5, pp. 1.1–1.21.

Baker, F. S. (2014) 'The role of the bilingual teaching assistant: Alternative visions for bilingual support in the primary years', *International Journal of Bilingual Education and Bilingualism*, 17, 3, pp. 255–271.

Bourne, J. (2001) 'Doing "what comes naturally": How the discourses and routines of teachers' practice constrain opportunities for bilingual support in UK primary schools', *Language and Education*, 15, 4, pp. 250–268.

Bower, (2017) *Supporting Pupils with EAL in the Primary Classroom*, London: Open University Press.
Chen, X. (2019) 'Selecting and using dual language books in classrooms and beyond', *NABE Journal of Research and Practice*, 9, 3-4, pp. 191-197.
Conteh, J & Brock, A. (2011) '"Safe spaces"? Sites of bilingualism for young learners in home, school and community', *International Journal of Bilingual Education and Bilingualism*, 14, 3, pp. 347-360.
Cremin, T. Mottram, M. Collins, F. M. Powell, S. & Drury, R. (2015) *Researching Literacy Lives Building Communities Between Home and School*, London: Routledge.
Cummins, J. (2005) 'A proposal for action: Strategies for recognizing heritage language competence as a learning resource with the mainstream classroom', *The Modern Language Journal*, 898, 4, pp. 585-592.
Day, E. M. (2002) *Identity and the Young English Language Learner*, Clevedon: Multilingual Matters.
Department for Education and Skills (DfES) (2006) *Raising the Achievement of Bilingual Learners in Primary Schools: Evaluation of the Pilot/Programme*, Nottingham: DfES.
Education Support Partnership (2018) *Teacher Wellbeing Index 2018*, London: Education Support Partnership.
Flynn, N. (2007) 'Lessons from effective literacy teachers in inner-city primary schools: Good practice for pupils learning English as an additional language', *Journal of Early Childhood Literacy*, 7, 2, pp. 177-198.
Flynn, N. (2013) 'Linguistic capital and the linguistic field for teachers unaccustomed to linguistic difference', *British Journal of Sociology of Education*, 34, 2, pp. 225-242.
Garcia, O. (2009) *Bilingual Education in the 21st Century: A Global Perspective*, London: Wiley-Blackwell.
Gordon, D. (2018) 'Using dual language story books to foster biliteracy', *NALDIC*, Available at https://ealjournal.org/2018/11/12/using-dual-language-story-books-to-foster-biliteracy/ (Accessed on 29.08.2020).
Hashemi, M. R. & Gowdasiaei, F. (2005) 'An attribute-treatment interaction study: Lexical-set versus semantically-unrelated vocabulary instruction', *RELC Journal*, 36, 3, pp. 341-361.
Hayes, C. (2016) *Language, Literacy and Communication in the Early Years*, Northwich: Critical Publishing.
Hite, C. E. & Evans, L. S. (2006) 'Mainstream first-grade teachers' understanding of strategies for accommodating the needs of English language-learners', *Teacher Education Quarterly*, 33, 2, pp. 89-110.
Ikizer & Ramirez-Esparza (2018) 'Bilinguals social flexibility', *Bilingualism, Language and Cognition*, 21, 5, pp. 957-969.
Karabenick, S. A. & Clemens Noda, P. A. (2004) 'Professional development implications of teachers' beliefs and attitudes toward English language learners', *Bilingual Research Journal: The Journal of the National Association for Bilingual Education*, 28, 1, pp. 55-75.
Kenner, C. (2007) *Developing Bilingual Learning Strategies in Mainstream and Community Contexts: Full Research Report ESRC End of Award Report*, RES-000-22-1528, Swindon: ESRC.
Kenner, C. & Kress, G. (2003) 'The multisemiotic resources of biliterate children', *Journal of Early Childhood Literacy*, 3, 2, pp. 179-202.
Leaman, H. (2008) 'One world, many languages: Using dual language books', *Social Studies and the Young Learner*, 21, 1, pp. 29-32.
Leung, C. (2005) 'Language and content in bilingual education', *Linguistics and Education*, 16, pp. 238-252.
McNamara, O. & Conteh, J. (2008) 'Teaching and learning as socio-cultural processes', *Education 3-13: International Journal of Primary, Elementary and Early Years Education*, 36, 3, pp. 203-205.
Moll, L. C. (2019) 'Elaborating funds of knowledge: Community-oriented practices in international contexts', *Literacy Research: Theory, Method and Practice*, 68, pp. 130-138.
NALDIC (2015) 'Supporting bilingual children in the early years', Available at www.naldic.org.uk/eal-teaching-and-learning/outline-guidance/early-years/ (Accessed 19.08.2020).
Rodriguez, G. M. (2013) 'Power and agency in education: Exploring the pedagogical dimensions of funds of knowledge', *Review of Research in Education*, 37, 1, pp. 87-120.
Rowe, D. & Fain, J. G. (2013) 'The family backpack project: Responding to dual-language texts through family journals', *Language Arts*, 90, 6, pp. 402-416.
Toohey, K. (2003) *Learning English at School Identity, Social Relations and Classroom Practice*, Clevedon: Multilingual Matters.
United Nations (no date) 'Sustainable development goals', Available at www.un.org/sustainabledevelopment/education/ (Accessed 31.01.2021).

Vertovec, S. (2007) 'Super-diversity and its implications', *Ethnic and Racial Studies*, 30, 6, pp. 1024-1054.
Wittgenstein, L. (2001) *Tractatus Logico-Philosophicus*, Oxon: Routledge.
youngminds (2018) Available at https://youngminds.org.uk/blog/new-figures-show-a-rise-in-young-peoples-mental-health-problems-since-2004/ (Accessed 28.08.2020).

3 Language, culture and identity

I wonder if I've been changed in the night. Let me think. Was I the same when I got up this morning? I almost think I can remember feeling a little different. But if I'm not the same, the next question is 'Who in the world am I?' Ah, that's the great puzzle!

(Lewis Carroll, *Alice in Wonderland*)

Introduction

This chapter is written at a turning point for England in relation to its departure from European Union (EU) involvement and the potential for movement across EU borders. The referendum in 2016 split the country almost equally – in terms of votes – but into splinters that reflected devastating differences of opinion, leaving families divided by conflict, politicians scrabbling for position and power, and minority groups looking fearfully towards a future of uncertainty and displacement.

It can be argued that there has never been a more important time to consider the concepts of language, culture and identity, and within this chapter we hope to highlight certain key messages and reinforce the connections between these three concepts, all of which combine to make us who we are. Rather than examining each in turn, the chapter covers a range of themes, within which language, culture and identity are examined, sometimes overtly whilst at other times it is down to you as the reader to make the links. This approach has been adopted because of the interdependence of this triumvirate (see Figure 3.1) when we are considering what makes us human and how this links to learning, teaching and educational life.

Initially, it might be assumed that these words and concepts are most likely to be discussed in relation to children and families from different countries and cultures, as educators consider aspects relating to integration, inclusion, communication and language and learning support. We would suggest however, that a school ethos which puts language, culture and identity at the forefront of its considerations for *all* staff, children, their families and the local community, will provide a more safe, supportive, nurturing, creative, inclusive, innovative and forward-thinking environment, where learners thrive and flourish.

As you read the chapter, allow your ideas to form and revise in relation to the complexity of the relationships between language, culture and identity and how they apply to your own personal and professional life.

DOI: 10.4324/9781003129738-4

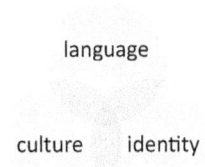

Figure 3.1 Interdependence between language, culture and identity

What is culture?

This section begins by considering the question, 'What do we mean by culture?' Until we have a grasp of this, it is difficult to make the connections between culture and identity and culture and language. Here are some quotes from writers in this field. Which of these seems to resonate with your own beliefs about culture? 'Culture reflects the totality of our being, our values and our beliefs' (Mercuri, 2012, p. 14). 'A *'road map'* through our lives' (Kumaravadivelu, 2008, p. 10). 'The integrated pattern of human behaviour that includes thoughts, communication, actions, customs, beliefs, values and instructions of racial, ethnic, religious, or social groups' (Hanley, 1999, p. 2).

You may have heard of the 'iceberg model' relating to culture which emerged from the work of Hall in 1976. It is a powerful metaphor to enable a better understanding of the complexity of the notion of culture, positing that the more obvious aspects of someone's culture, for example their behaviour/traditions/music/art (often known as 'Big C' culture) are merely the tip of the iceberg. As you travel down the iceberg (into 'Little c' territory), culture involves more of an awareness of others' beliefs; and what lies completely below the surface are people's values and thought patterns – much more difficult to access and understand. Hall believed that the only way to explore beneath the surface is through immersion in other cultures and having a deeper understanding of the lived experiences of others. Weaver (2001) built on the analogy of the iceberg and noted that, although cultural aspects at the 'tip' are fairly easy to navigate – being more overt and visible – those beneath the surface can cause a 'real collision' (ibid, p. 3) of cultures, as they are inherent, less easily explained and relate to our innermost values.

From this complex notion of culture, many offshoots have emerged, including the terms *pluricultural* and *intercultural*, and an appreciation of these enables us better to understand our educational settings and those we teach. The European Centre for Modern Languages (ECML) produced, in 2007, a training kit entitled, 'Plurilingual and pluricultural awareness in language teacher education', and this document provides a useful explanation of how these terms and others relate to individuals, groups and communication. We have represented this in Figure 3.2. *Pluricultural* relates to the self and how we, as individuals, learn to live within different cultural environments – our national culture, our family culture, our school culture – and 'actively interact to produce an enriched, integrated pluricultural competence' (Bernaus et al., 2007, p. 11). According to Bernaus et al. (in the ECML training kit), *multicultural* is more connected with groups in society – 'culture as nation state', 'culture as religion' and 'culture

48 *Language, culture and identity*

Figure 3.2 Understanding terminology

as ethnic groups'. *Intercultural*, on the other hand, is more focused on communication, where 'the people involved use all their capacities to interact with each other' and use 'a set of communicative strategies for that interaction' (ibid., p. 12). Suffice it to say that whole books have been written on these concepts, and there is only scope here to touch on key ideas. But simply a consideration of these terms, and what they might mean to you and those you teach, raises an awareness of the complexity of the idea of culture.

Cultural and intercultural competence

To avoid the 'collision of cultures' described by Weaver (2001), we require a degree of cultural and intercultural competence, an understanding of both 'Big C' and 'little c' culture within and outside our day-to-day experiences and the ability to build this understanding into our personal and professional lives. We say 'degree' because there are stages to this, some easier to navigate than others and which are fluid in terms of our levels of competence depending on the setting and situation. Mason (1993) presented the idea of a continuum of competence, which Stein (no date) illustrates in a useful way (see Figure 3.3).

The terminology here is relatively self-explanatory, but you may want to look at Stein's definitions: – http://intranet.dragon.k12.pa.us/about/Presentations/culturalcompetencelewisburg.pdf.

Holliday (2016) uses the terms *blocks* and *threads* to conceptualise the challenges that might emerge with intercultural competence and how we might work through these. The 'blocks' are essentialist assumptions; for example, 'All English people are very polite and drink tea.' This is a fairly harmless and potentially amusing example, but if we replace this with an example relating to Islamophobia and the consequences of thinking about others as a homogeneous 'mass', this is far from amusing. Holliday then introduces the idea of 'threads' which 'we can pull through from our previous experience to find and engage with the threads of other people's experiences' (ibid., no page). He writes that we are all involved with intercultural understanding and competence from an early age, but that at times there might be impediments; times when 'searching for openings and possibilities for connections' (ibid., no page) is an essential part of what we do as responsible humans – and these are the threads.

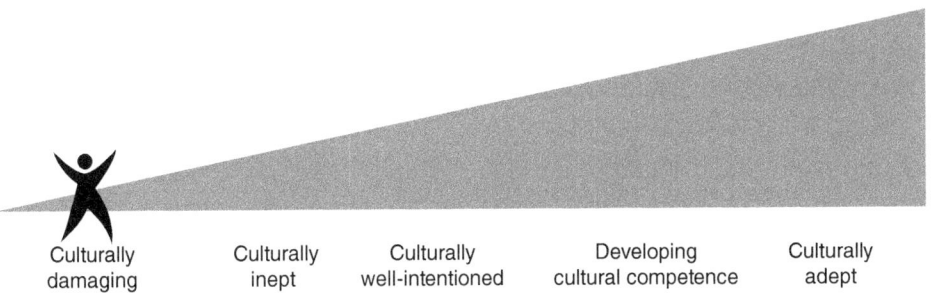

Figure 3.3 A continuum of competence

> Take a moment to think about your own experience of a school – whether from the perspective of pupil or practitioner – and place the setting on the continuum in Figure 3.3 with regards to its ethos and practices. When we consider this continuum, in relation to the constant ebb and flow and flux of our lives, it is clear that the nexus between culture and identity will be strong. A lack of cultural and intercultural competency may result in a failure truly to understand the lives and actions of the pupils we teach and our own decision making, affecting the way that both teachers and pupils come to terms with and celebrate their own identities.

Shared and individual identity

When considering culture and identity, we need to think about both the 'shared identity of the group and the felt identity of the individual' (Fanshawe and Sriskandarajah, 2010, p. 9). As we go through the following examples, which focus more on the development of a shared identity, keep in mind what the 'felt identity of the individual' might be at any moment. A shared identity might relate to identifying as a family member, a school pupil, a Girl Guide or Boy Scout, for example. It could relate more to a national identity – being British or Polish or Australian. Each of these identities will have a cultural element, in which we embed ourselves – to a greater or lesser extent – in order to 'fit'. Let us first consider the example of a shared identity within the school culture, as that is the main focus of this book. To identify as a pupil might mean to wear a certain uniform, to follow particular rules and routines, to have access to certain resources and activities, to speak the language of that particular school. It is important to consider the implications of 'fitting in' with the aim of assuming a shared identity. Lankshear and Knobel (2003) recognise that children might experience a 'double loss' as they attempt to be assimilated within the dominant culture by shedding the skin of their known identity but failing to fully take on the mantle of and feel comfortable within the new. What of shared or individual identity now?

It might be argued that, for those working in schools, the challenge is to encourage pupils to share their own cultural experiences, thereby protecting their individual identity, whilst supporting them to align themselves with the school culture in order to be academically successful and avoid marginalisation (Janks, 2000). Remember, we are not necessarily talking

50 *Language, culture and identity*

here about pupils with non-native backgrounds and languages. For many children, despite being perceived as sharing a national language and culture, school can be an alien and alienating place. Gregory and Williams (2000, p. xvii) suggest that we need to develop practices that enable pupils to 'syncretise or blend home, community and school language and cultural practices' so that children feel comfortable within both their 'inherited' culture and their 'learned' cultural experience (Kumaravadivelu, 2008, p. 2).

Tensions relating to culture and identity are inevitable, and Nieto's seven characteristics of culture (2010, cited in Mercuri, 2012) help to identify why this might be the case (see Figure 3.4).

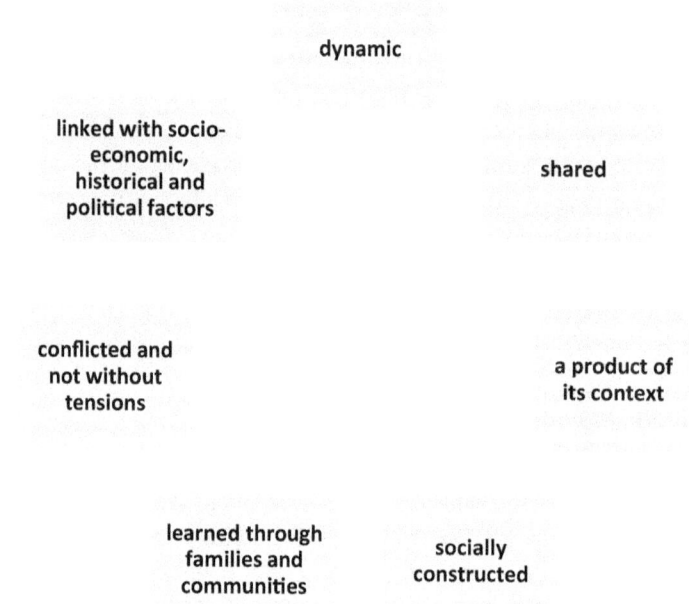

Figure 3.4 Seven characteristics of culture

Take a look at Figure 3.4 and think for a moment about your own identity. Do the words and statements resonate with how you have developed that identity? Have a go at answering these questions:

- Does your identity change with the context you are in?
- Is it shared with others?
- To what extent is your identity influenced by your family and the community in which you live/work?
- Do you ever feel conflict or tension between the identities you assume in different contexts?
- To what extent is your identity influenced by your social habits, your political affiliation and your economic status?

> Thinking about these questions enables us to empathise with the pupils we teach and the colleagues we work alongside. It makes us more aware of difference, diversity, opinion and perspective – to consider the submerged elements of the iceberg. Hopefully, it enables us to sustain 'intercultural sensitivity' (Nieto, 2008) and make this the foundation for our planning, teaching and the resources we use.

Let us now consider the idea of a *national* identity. To assume a national identity is to take on aspects – again, to a greater or lesser extent – of the national culture. Hall (1992, p. 292-293) describes a national culture as 'a *discourse* – a way of constructing meanings which influences and organises both our actions and or conception of ourselves'. A national culture endures through stories, repeated events, traditions and practices. Hall goes on to say that myths become enshrined in truth over time, making what has come before more 'palatable' and acceptable for the time in which we live. When we sometimes look to the past and identify what we consider to be great moves for the nation, this may well be hiding a desire to 'mobilise "the people" to purify their ranks, to expel the "others" who threaten their identity, and to gird their loins for a new march forwards' (ibid, p. 295) – what Holliday (2016, no page) refers to as 'rallying their membership to partisan action'. Does this sound familiar?

To contextualise the concept of national identity, the focus is going to turn briefly to the subject of migrants and asylum seekers, as this provides a useful example of how meanings are constructed (in this case, through the media), which organise our actions and how we think about ourselves and others and influence our attitudes towards our national identity.

Here are some newspaper headlines from the past few years:

ILLEGAL MIGRANTS FLOOD IN. 500,000 MIGRANTS GET SOCIAL HOUSING
ASYLYM SEEKERS FERRIED AROUND IN STRETCH LIMO. AND GUESS WHAT, YOU'RE PICKING UP THE £3000 BILL! 40% SURGE IN ETHIC NUMBERS
MIGRANT CHAOS ALL SUMMER
MIGRANTS ROB YOUNG BRITONS OF JOBS

Greenslade (2020), writes that between 2016 and 2020, many newspapers were selling the idea of a migrant 'crisis' through the types of headlines and articles shown here. He notes that this extended focus on migrants has now died out, having run its media course. He asks, so where is that crisis now? He answers his own question by saying that it never existed – it was purely a media campaign, designed to push readers towards particular attitudes and discourses. This example has not been presented with a particular political persuasion in mind; rather it is to demonstrate the potential effect on our sense of national identity, from different sources – in this case, the media. Other evidence also exists of how a media approach can impact on a population's national identity. In 2016, Berry et al. published their findings into press coverage of the refugee and migrant crisis in the EU. This was no small study – it involved an analysis of five European countries and was prepared for the United Nations High Commission for Refugees. One of their key conclusions was that:

coverage in the United Kingdom was the most negative. Despite the presence of newspapers such as the *Guardian* and *Daily Mirror*, both of which were sympathetic to refugees, the right-wing press in the United Kingdom expressed a hostility towards refugees and migrants which was unique. Whilst newspapers in all countries featured anti-refugee and anti-migrant perspectives, what distinguished the right of centre press in the UK was the degree to which that section of the press campaigned aggressively against refugees and migrants.

(Berry, Garcia-Blanco, and Moore, 2016, p. 10)

A national identity – and the cultural aspects which form part of that, what Holliday (2016, no page) describes as 'big culture framing' – has the ability to bring people together; to strengthen in order to do good; to overcome challenges, natural disasters, political and economic turmoil. It has also however, the potential to antagonise, alienate, divide and, in extreme cases, provoke racist and dangerous reactions. This is why we have broached the subject within this chapter – because there is much that schools can do to promote both a shared and an individual identity which gives pupils a platform to challenge information presented to them and to make their own decisions.

Classroom activities have the potential to support children with both their group and individual cultural identity and to provoke a curiosity, excitement and sense of community through the exploration of difference. However, this comes with a 'health warning' as we remember that we are competing with a *National* Curriculum, a *national* assessment system, *national* testing and *national* reporting of results, with, arguably, little recognition of other cultures, languages and practices (Kumaravadivelu, 2008). To counteract this, we suggest that a teacher with an intercultural mindset does not plan for activities such as those described in the following examples, as 'bolt-on' additions to the language curriculum (DfES, 2005a), but instead recognises both the communal and personal aspects of language learning and how the development of intercultural understanding is integral to both. The Key Stage 2 Framework for Languages (DfES, 2005b) promoted intercultural understanding as a core component of the languages curriculum, having equal weighting with literacy and oracy (see Chapter 9 for more discussion on this). However, although intercultural understanding is clearly implicit in the purpose of the 2014 curriculum, it is completely absent from the subject content. It is our job to bring it to the fore. The following section explores how a focus on names is one way to go about this.

A focus on names

Getting to know each other is an important part of establishing a group entity at the start of a new year or when working for the first time with a new class, and there are many games and activities that teachers can use involving children's names to establish a collaborative learning culture. An internet search for 'icebreakers and name games' will bring up a wealth of ideas that teachers can adapt for the primary classroom.

A focus on names can support children's developing concepts of identity. The British Council's (2015) Connecting Classrooms project 'Identity and Belonging' enables children to explore their social identities and develop intercultural competence through knowledge of social groups and their cultures, and through sharing their work with children in partner schools. Children can be given a template, to which they then add or create symbols for the different groups (when we did this, we encouraged children to add group names). After the classes have exchanged their 'identity and belonging' illustrations, they can be challenged to create a symbol that represents both classes. This helps them to see the aspects of their own cultures that unite them as members of a wider, global community.

Our names are bound up in notions of identity and culture, and understanding cultural approaches to choosing names, family naming traditions and the meaning of names can transform our understanding of who we are and provoke an interest in the names of others. Names can indicate gender, marital status, birthplace, nationality, religion and position in the family. For instance, in English-speaking countries the father's name is usually passed to the children as a surname and, traditionally, it is the women who change their surname from that of their father to that of their husband when they marry.

Within the classroom, there may be instances which cause us some discomfort, for example when we discover that the name we have been using for a child is not in fact their birth name. The Anglicisation of people's names was a consequence historically of a determination by many immigrant communities to avoid discrimination after arriving in English speaking countries. Peterson et al. (2015) posit that renaming practices by either parents or teachers (such as Giovanni to Joe), which still often occur when children start school, can be detrimental and have the potential to undermine a child's self-esteem and cultural identity. The following case study provides a powerful example, albeit in a different type of context.

> ### Who am I?
>
> Erika Piazzoli describes her experiences at eight years old when she started to learn English at her school in Milan. In the very first lesson, the English teacher told the class that she was going to change their names to English ones as a first step to learning the language. So 'Angelo' became 'Angel'; 'Davide' became 'David'; 'Daniele' became 'Daniel'. When it came to Piazzoli's, turn the teacher explained that there was no English translation of her name. Piazzoli describes anxiety kicking in as the teacher 'rebaptised' her as 'Heather'.
>
> I still remember the feeling of displacement as she addressed me by my new name. I was alarmed by this new identity. Little did I know that the plant 'heather' is translated as 'erica' in Italian. Instead, the obvious connection for me and my classmates was Heather Parisi, a voluptuous Italian showgirl in the 1980s. This was definitely too much of an identity stretch for an eight-year-old introverted child. All through primary and middle school I disliked English. I remember a vague sense of confusion mixed with shame, not understanding what I had to say, what the right answer was. Classes were a blur. My name didn't make sense. I didn't make sense (Piazzoli, 2018, pp. 1-2).

Piazzoli relates these early experiences to Van Lier's (2004) argument that as learners our sense of identity is tied to our motivation to learn a foreign language, as 'we can only speak the second language when thoughts, identities and self are aligned' (cited in Piazzoli, 2018, p. 2). Despite the teacher's best intentions, this mismatch between the teacher-assigned name and Piazzoli's eight-year-old developing self-concept ('Who am I?') impacted negatively on the child's engagement with the English curriculum over several years.

Of course, we are not suggesting that the teacher was wrong to introduce a focus on names. As Piazzoli suggests, if the children were given the opportunity to investigate the meanings of their names and choose their identities, thereby 'gifting them the agency to reinvent themselves', we can imagine that the young Erika may have developed earlier both motivation and perseverance for language learning.

We may feel uncomfortable navigating these situations, and of course teachers are not in a position to argue this highly sensitive issue with parents. However, teachers are not powerless, and Petersen et al. (ibid) suggest that the teacher is in a unique position to impact children's perceptions and developing identities, positively or negatively, by taking on the role of 'culturally responsive educators' who value each child. Learning about children's names is one way to respect their cultures and identities:

> Culturally responsive instruction in the early childhood classroom can meaningfully focus on names and social identity during curricular explorations of self, family, friendships, school, and community. Multicultural literature that celebrates the diversity of children's names or presents social conflicts surrounding names can contribute to these explorations.
>
> (Peterson et al., 2015, p. 40)

Virginia: Wendy, how would you manage a situation where you were engaged in a game or activity involving names and a child said, 'Well that's not my real name anyway' and other children appeared astonished and questioning about this?

Wendy: That's an interesting question, because in my experience most children and older learners tend to accept (and this makes me a little sad) their Anglicised or abbreviated name as a way of fitting in, so I wonder how often this scenario would arise. Of course, we all have the right to decide what name we choose to be called in different contexts, but no one should have to accept a name just because it is easier for others to say or identify with. So, I think it is important that whenever we meet a new class or welcome a new child (or older learner) that we take time to find out how to say each learner's name. We can ask children what they prefer to be called, and we can encourage everyone in the class to tune into and practise unfamiliar sounds. By modelling this interest in names and naming traditions, we can help children recognise the uniqueness of different language sound systems and begin to understand and celebrate the cultural heritage intertwined with the names we are given.

Petersen et al. (ibid) researched and evaluated a range of available multicultural literature focusing on names and naming traditions. Their recommendations for texts for the primary classroom include the following titles:

- *Rene Has Two Last Names/Rene Tiene Dos Apellidos* (Colato Lainez, 1996): a bilingual picture book which can be used from Key Stage 1 onwards to stimulate discussions around naming traditions, 'All about me' topics and family heritage investigations.
- *My Name is Sangoel* (Williams and Mohammed, 2009): Sangoel and his family are refugees from Sudan and face major adjustments to life in the United States. When no one seems to be able to pronounce Sangoel's Dinka name he designs a name rebus so teachers and classmates will say his name correctly.

A useful resource for finding out about naming practices around the world is the UK government's publication 'A Guide to Names and Naming Practices'. Table 3.1 shows an example, relating to the Yorùbá language, that has been adapted from this resource (2006, p. 5).

Word-level name investigations could include a focus on:

- Directionality (e.g. left to right or right to left depending on the script);
- Rhyme;
- Rhythm;
- Stress;
- Accents;

Table 3.1 Names and naming practices

Yorùbá – South Western regions of Nigeria
Names are usually a personal name followed by a family name e.g. **Oluwole Ransome-Kuti** Many Yoruba names are compound words, with the following elements frequently occurring in some part of the name: **ade, ayo, fe, ifc, ire, oba, omo, ola, olu, oluwa** e.g. **Olatunde** *Familial relationships* Women typically take their husband's family name upon marriage. Children traditionally take their father's family name. In Yoruba culture, personal names often reflect the circumstances under which a child was born: • **Sunday**: some children are named after the day of the week on which they were born (in English), particularly used for children born on a Sunday; • **Taiwo**: 'pre-tasted the world', given to the first of a set of twins; • **Kehinde**: 'the one who lagged behind', given to the second of a set of twins; • **Idowu**: this is given to the child born after a set of twins; • **Alaba**: this is given to the child born after Idowu; • **Tokunbo**: this is given to a child born outside of Nigeria. **Unique Characteristics** Long Yoruba names are often abbreviated: '**Wole**' for **Oluwole**, '**Tai**' for **Taiwo**. Some Yoruba names are not gender specific: **Kehinde**. Individuals may also have a Western nickname or an additional Western personal name. These are quite often biblical names, such as Joseph, Samson or Moses, but they can be other Western names e.g. **Austin Babatunde OLALEGBIN**. Some Yoruba individuals add a Muslim title to their name e.g. **Al-Hajj(i)/Haxjj(i)** indicates that the person has undergone the Muslim pilgrimage to Mecca.

56 *Language, culture and identity*

- Sound symbol relationships (e.g. children could create phonetic cues to help pronounce children's names);
- Words within words;
- Capital letters;
- Consonants and vowels;
- Alphabetical order.

(Cobb, 2014)

Teachers can discuss with their classes formal and informal ways to address people; the closer we are socially to the person we are speaking to, the more likely we are to use the less formal version of a name, such as a nickname or term of endearment. Discussions can be had with the children about appropriate ways to ask a question of a friend, a teacher or a member of the Royal Family in English and compare to polite and informal modes of address in other cultures (e.g. *tutoyer* v. *vouvoyer* – using *tu* or *vous* in French).

You might want to read or search for an audio version of the poem 'Isn't my Name Magical?' by James Berry (2004) (https://childrens.poetryarchive.org/poem/isnt-my-name-magical/). Then challenge the children to find their name in their home environment or the school grounds and take pictures to illustrate name poems. In Figure 3.5 there is an example Wendy created at home to illustrate this activity for her students.

Children could create name poems using a template as a guide. They might write these in English, home languages, the target foreign language or in a mixture of languages. Here is an example Wendy wrote to share with her class:

Wendy [your name]
It means hidden, silent, wild, [3 adjectives that describe you]
It is the number *quatre-vingt douze*, [your favourite number – Wendy wrote her favourite French number]
It is like the iris of a mysterious eye, [describe a colour without using the name for the colour]
It is little red wellies splashing through puddles, a hand in a hand, [describe the memory of an experience important to you]
It is the memory of Uncle Leslie, [name someone significant to you]
Who taught me joy and adventure, [2 abstract nouns]
When he flew to Australia at 90, [something that person did]
My name is Wendy, [your name]
It means live and love. [2 adjectives or a sentence about something that is important to you]

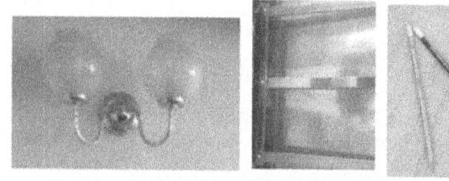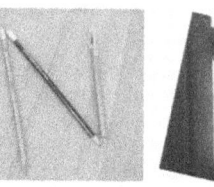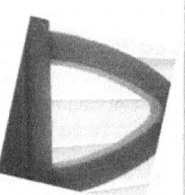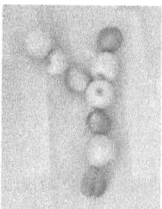

Figure 3.5 Finding names in the home environment

These are easily implemented, powerful and empowering pedagogies and practices, which put language and identity at the heart of our teaching and learning. The following section looks at language and identity in a little more depth.

The role of language within our identity

We would like to begin by asking you a question: What is the singular most important thing that makes you who you are?

At times, people identify themselves or are identified by their ethnicity, their gender, the job they do, their place in the family and so forth. Nazroo and Karlsen (2003, p. 904) write that 'ethnicity is only one element of identity', and we would agree, arguing that the makeup of a person's identity is unique and deeply personal. In her research study into children whose parents were of different nationalities, Sousa (no date) found that *place of birth* and *language* were the two points of reference when the children were required to describe themselves and others, characteristics tightly bound up with their identities.

Language is intimately bound up with identity in that it allows us to make sense of how we 'fit' into overlapping social contexts and to cultivate a sense of belonging (Conteh, 2012). Language allows us to express ourselves, to share ideas and to make sense of 'the vast range of meanings which are already embedded in our language and cultural systems' (Hall, 1992, p. 288). Pupils may find that their sense of identity is challenged when they enter a school setting, particularly where their first language (L1) is not the main language spoken or where their accent or dialect differs from that of their fellow pupils and teachers. Whilst taking on an 'acceptable' classroom identity and becoming a functioning member of that community, the learner has also to feel that their home identity, their language and the way they speak is not threatened and is respected and acknowledged (Gee, 2014) and, hopefully, celebrated and capitalised on.

Alongside this, however, is the need to use the language and lexicon appropriate to different activities, functions and contexts. School is a social community wherein learners are immersed for long periods each day and, inevitably, they will begin adopting that vernacular – to varying extents – developing what Gee (2014, p. 21) refers to as a new 'socially situated identity' (Gee, 2014, p. 21). This can be problematic, as Day (2002) found in her longitudinal study of one particular EAL learner (you may remember discussion about this from Chapter 2). Day observed through the year the changes that took place as the child struggled with coming to terms with his own linguistic identity. Although the child began the school year happily using his first language – Punjabi – in addition to English, helping his fellow pupils by translating at times, he gradually made less and less use of Punjabi and actually began to mock his home language. The child began to chide others for using Punjabi, and he and others could be seen rejecting L1. Speaking with the child's mother, she confirmed that her child preferred watching films and television programmes in English but was still fluent in oral Punjabi in the home environment.

Pinter (2011, p. 32) argues that children's language learning is 'embedded in their emotional development' and suggests that learning a new language can involve negotiating new identities: 'It is bound up with who we are, who we would like to become, how we feel about ourselves and how we form social relationships'. However, because of the linguistic capital invested in being able to speak and use the English language effectively (with, arguably, decisions about curricula and assessment made predominantly by White, middle class power-holders), this is what becomes most valued in the classroom (Flynn, 2013). Day's example demonstrates some of the issues that might occur in relation to this linguistic capital and how this might pose problems for children as they begin to find an identity for themselves and fit into the different worlds that make up their lives. You might also want to explore Mercuri's (2012) compelling research into a particular individual who was forced to shed her language and identity at a very early age and what she experienced in her life (see reference list for link).

In America there has been a steady move in the past decades away from a celebration of bilingualism and a bilingual approach, where the benefits of maintaining L1 and building on this were at the forefront, to an 'English-only' diktat. In England, this attitude is not so overt, and there is research, literature and government publications which champion the use of L1. In reality, however, a transitional approach to language learning exists, whereby L1 is acceptable but only until the 'real' goal is achieved – becoming proficient and literate in English. And not just any English – but Standard English – with implications for native speakers and EAL learners.

The dangers of losing a sense of identity because one's language and culture are disregarded, disrespected or discarded – by implication or more overtly – are manifold and deleterious and include the following:

- Lack of self-worth and self-esteem;
- Inability to communicate successfully with wider family members and community;
- Loss of a sense of who you are and your place in the world;
- Little or no opportunity to build on existing linguistic or cognitive skills.

The post-modern view of identity is that we have 'no fixed, essential or permanent identity' (Hall, 1992, p. 277); identity is reformed to fit the situation or time or cultural setting. Think about this in relation to language and how our linguistic identity forms and reforms according to context, environment, audience. It could be argued that the child in Day's study has reformed his identity to 'fit' the new setting of school. The issue of course is children retaining a sense of *themselves* within the different identities they might assume, and this could be said to rely on finding a way to bridge the gap between languages and cultures. Moje et al. (2004, p. 43) refer to Bhabha's idea of the 'third space' as a means to bridge this gap. The first and second spaces are home and school, whereas:

> third space is produced in and through language as people come together, and particularly as people resist cultural authority, bringing different experiences to bear on the same linguistic signs or cultural symbols and, likewise, different signs and symbols to bear on the same experiences.

Moje et al. (ibid) present three different views of how the third space might work in reality:

1. A place wherein connections can be made and bridges built between marginalised and privileged discourses;
2. A 'navigational space' within which learners can draw on existing experience – from home, popular culture and so forth, enhancing their participation;

3   A space from which the privileged and the marginalised discourses can be challenged, enabling children to find a 'way of being' in the classroom which meets their own very individual needs. For some children, this might be seen in their use of home languages (either explicitly or secretly), using silence, disengaging from the dominant discourse or code-switching (Park, 2013).

> Think about how you might facilitate this 'third space' in the classroom and which of the three examples listed might help learners to retain a sense of linguistic and cultural identity, whilst being given every opportunity to fulfil their potential in school.

One way to really focus your mind on how your classroom practices can reflect learners' needs is to prioritise the social side of learning. Liddicot and Scarino (2013, p. 15) make specific reference to this in relation to using language:

> If language is viewed as a social practice of meaning-making and interpretation, then it is not enough for language learners just to know grammar and vocabulary. They also need to know how the language is used to create and represent meanings and how to communicate with others and to engage with the communication of others.

The extent to which children decide to engage is of course variable. A useful example is given by Souza (2008) in her research into how linguistic and cultural identities are affected by migration, where she uses the ideas of Hannerz to present possible categories into which migrants might fall:

- Those who shed their origins and 'go native' (Hannerz, 2000);
- 'Tourists' – those who retain their culture, language and so forth, and reject the majority culture;
- 'Cosmopolitans' – those who do a little of both – assimilating to a point, but retaining a sense of being different, whether that be regarding language, culture, traditions – or all of these. In this way, they are involved with a 'plurality of different cultures' (Souza, 2008, p. 37).

Similarly, Kumaravadivelu (2008) describes three different levels of assimilation:

- Those who try to be fully assimilated and reject their own cultural beliefs;
- Those who move to 'ethnic ghettoes' in inner cities;
- Those who strive for 'educational and economic advancement' (p. 81), whilst retaining the values and beliefs of their own culture.

> Think for a moment about how this might relate, beyond migrants and minority groups, to the pupils and families in your class. Although the example of migrants here is powerful, the points made are equally applicable to any children and families joining the culture of school.

Whilst accepting these categories exist, Souza suggests that there is a continuum, rather than a limited number of groups, and that positioning is dynamic: 'The notion of a continuum is important in that it allows for the visualisation of the fact that these identifications are not static and can move along between the two extremes' (Souza, 2008, p. 37).

If we think about children in school – there are some who fully immerse themselves in school life, shedding their home 'skins' and adopting the lexicon of school, the rules, the patterns, the routines without question. Then there are those who happily accept school life but bring elements of home with them – some rogue trainers on their feet/a handheld electronic game in their bags/inserting home examples into their writing tasks. And there are those who refuse to 'fit' into school life and reject the rules, the curriculum, the impositions, the uniform and so forth. But, like Souza, I would argue that each child is somewhere on a continuum, always in flux. Where they sit on that continuum at any one time depends on the identity they choose to adopt maybe for that year, that lesson, that playtime. We would argue, however, that planning activities which are underpinned by a fundamental belief in the importance of intercultural understanding will be more likely to engage learners who might otherwise decide that school 'is not for them'. In the next section we demonstrate how games are an important part of this.

A focus on games

In an increasingly digital age and with media headlines which suggest the demise of traditional games – 'Parents outraged as school bans "tag" children's game for bizarre reason' (Mirror Online, 2016) – we might be led to believe that traditional forms of playground games are a thing of the past. Research suggests, however, that they are continuing traditions and that children are the experts in their cultural practices as game players (Marsh, 2012). Playground games have many cultural and linguistic – not to mention cognitive and social – benefits in addition to the promotion of a healthy and active lifestyle. Among the extensive outcomes outlined in the Game on Scotland (the official education programme around the Glasgow Commonwealth Games in 2014) introduction to their 'Learning Journey – Our Games' project, are the descriptions of outcomes for 'successful learners' and 'responsible citizens' which include:

- Promoting collaborative and open-ended inquiry;
- Providing an opportunity for children to become social researchers investigating games and play;
- Children asking questions based on their own experiences of outdoor games and link[ing] their understanding across historical periods and cultures with information they have gathered from friends, parents, grandparents and teachers;
- Developing and demonstrating respect for others and making informed choices and decisions based on . . . values and principles of inclusion, equality, fairness and generosity.

(Education Scotland n.d., p. 2)

It is difficult to argue, from this, against the promotion of games at every opportunity.

One such popular game, which could be expanded/altered is 'Rock, paper, scissors', which many of you may be familiar with. This game, which is often used as a choosing activity, is usually played in pairs with each player simultaneously forming one of three shapes with an outstretched hand:

- Rock (a fist);
- Paper (a flat hand);
- Scissors (a fist with the index and middle fingers together forming a V).

There are four possible outcomes to the most commonly played English version of the game.

- Rock crushes or blunts scissors – rock wins;
- Paper covers rock – paper wins;
- Scissors cut paper – scissors wins;
- A tie when both players make the same shape.

An internet search will bring up various unverified suggestions for the historical origin of the game. Historian John Buescher (n.d.) presents his own perspective, which he admits is based on circumstantial evidence and suggests a link to the Japanese game of 'Janken'. He notes the discrepancy in the English-speaking Wikipedia pages which refer to the French version of the game on one page as 'Rochambeau' (*ro-cham-beau*) and on another, lists Francophone country names for the game as 'Pierre-feuille-ciseaux', 'Papier-caillou-ciseaux', 'Roche-papier-ciseaux', 'Pierre-papier-ciseaux', and 'Feuille-caillou-ciseaux'.

The most common Spanish version of the game appears to be 'Piedra' – rock, 'papel' – paper, 'o tijera' – scissors, although suggestions for Spanish versions from Latin America include 'Cachipún' (Mexico) and 'Jan-quen-po' (Peru). Children could certainly enjoy finding out whether there are other versions played across the world, strengthening their intercultural understanding and piquing their curiosity about other people, places and languages.

Mama Lisa's World (www.mamalisa.com/?t=eh), an online repository of songs and rhymes from across the globe, includes an Indonesian version of the rock, paper, scissors game with three signs – ant (little finger), elephant (thumb) and person (index finger). The game is started by brushing the two opponents' palms against each other and throwing one of the three signs.

- The elephant squashes the person – elephant wins;
- The person squashes the ant – person wins;
- The ant crawls inside elephant's ear and drives him crazy – ant wins.

> Wendy introduced the Indonesian version of the game to one class which included a child of Indonesian heritage. A discussion ensued, which verified the local nature of games; game adaptations may be cultural or personal variations. Children offered various versions of the game, with several children mentioning a fourth weapon (water) to the traditional English version of the game. This led to further discussion about the probability of winning with different numbers of weapons and children creating their own versions of the game.

Class-initiated discussions such as these are inevitably continued in the playground and brought into the home, with the opportunity for children to explore their family heritage through the history of traditional play forms. If your school has an international-link partner school, an investigation into playground games and rhymes in both cultures could be carried out. If you do not have a partner school, there are several videos available online of playground games from other cultures, including a large number of different clapping games.

The role of the teacher and the school

Meaningful learning needs to draw on children's 'funds of identity' (Moises and Moll, 2014, p. 76) – their knowledge and experiences from outside school – in order to make connections with their lives. Funds of identity move beyond funds of knowledge (Moll et al., 1992) – the latter implying a focus on family life, whereas the former encompasses what children know from other areas of their lives, for example social networking, gaming, popular culture, as well as the political and economic circumstances of their lives. We would expand on Moll et al.'s concepts of funds of knowledge and funds of identity to add 'funds of language' and 'funds of culture'. As teachers, if we can take every opportunity to put children's existing linguistic and cultural knowledge and experiences at the forefront of every lesson, we can draw on these 'funds' to the benefit of all children. Here are three ways that this might be implemented:

- Set up a language investigation, perhaps similar to that mentioned earlier in the chapter, where Wendy encouraged the children to share different versions of 'Rock, paper, scissors'. Give children time to research, to gather ideas from family members at home, to share in class and discuss in depth.
- Focus all subjects on the languages spoken in your school. For example, if you were looking at data in mathematics, ask children to conduct research on the number of languages spoken in the school; in art, examine the beauty of written scripts and their differences; in language lessons, even if the target language is, say, French, bring in the other languages spoken in the classroom.
- Ask children and their families to share oral stories which may have been passed down from one generation to the next and which reflect the cultural traditions of that family. Stories in different languages and from different cultures often share themes and focal points, and identifying these similarities promotes intercultural understanding.

Berumen and Silva (2014) argue that if, as Erickson (2010) suggests, 'everything in education is culture', teachers must be responsive to cultures within their classrooms because this will have an ongoing influence on the learning that takes place. However, given the increasing diversity of classroom cultures, being culturally responsive is not always easy, particularly given the wide and varied expectations placed on the primary class teacher. There are, though, some freely accessible reference sources that will support teachers' professional development, some of which we have already mentioned. Another example is the UNICEF resource (2016) 'In search of safety: Children and the refugee crisis in Europe', which will support planning to mark World Refugee Day, which takes place on or around the 20th of June each year, and the United Nations World Refugee Day site contains links to various videos telling the stories of child refugees (https://www.un.org/en/observances/refugee-day). The British Council's 'Connecting Classrooms' is a global education programme which offers a free learning journey to help teachers improve their classroom practice and develop their ideas with like-minded teachers internationally (https://schoolsonline.britishcouncil.org/about-schools-online/about-programmes/connecting-classrooms).

UNICEF UK also provides chargeable training for schools to support their Rights Respecting Schools Award that recognises a school's achievement in putting the United Nations Convention on the Rights of the Child (CRC or UNCRC) into practice within the school and beyond. These rights are expressed in a series of Articles which include:

- The protection and preservation of a child's identity. Article 8 states that governments must respect and protect the right of every child to an identity and prevent the child's name, nationality or family relationships being changed unlawfully;
- Goals of education. Article 29 refers in Part C to the school's responsibility for the development of respect for the child's parents, his or her own cultural identity, language and values, for the national values of the country in which the child is living, the country from which he or she may originate and for civilizations different from his or her own (UNICEF, 1990, p. 9).

The Council of Europe suggests that teachers need to consider 'how to fit learning concerned with a particular language or culture coherently into an overall curriculum in which the experience of several languages and several cultures is developed' (2014, p. 176.) This implies that teachers need to consider where cultural learning fits across the curriculum and how they can build cultural learning in a range of contexts and learning opportunities. It also implies that teachers need to be aware of the cultural element involved in how a subject is learned and how it is taught in other countries. For instance, globally there are a wide variety of culturally different numerical systems and mathematical calculation strategies. The Yorùbá culture, for example, uses a counting system based on 20 (ogún), with other numbers worked out using extensive subtraction:

- 15 = 5 from 20 = àrún-úndínlógún
- 16 = 4 from 20 = ẹrindínlógún
- 17 = 3 from 20 = ẹtadínlógún

(Akinadé & Ọdẹjọbí, 2014, p. 174)

The English system may be less complicated but not necessarily always logical. For instance in English we say 'fourteen, sixteen, seventeen, eighteen and nineteen', so one would think that we would also say 'one-teen, two-teen, three-teen and five-teen', but instead we represent these numbers in a different form – 'eleven, twelve, thirteen and fifteen'. For numbers above 20, we put the decade first, but for 'teens' numbers we do this the other way round. China, Japan and Korea appear to have a more logical counting system. Eleven is 'ten one'. Twelve is 'ten two'. Twenty-four is 'two ten four', and so on. Comparing the complexities of different counting systems may help children (and teachers) understand why children speaking some languages may find counting more difficult than children from other cultures, and it is just one example of how we, as teachers, can promote intercultural understanding.

Perhaps we, as teachers, also need to see our schools and classrooms as 'small cultures', which, according to Holliday (1999) are any cohesive social grouping. Although children will arrive in the classroom from different backgrounds and experiences, they will create their own classroom culture from commonalities of experience and collaborative activities. Perhaps what we need to aim for is Kumaravadivelu's beautifully expressed ideal, wherein 'each ethnic group can preserve and protect its own integrity and identity yet produce harmonious music with other groups' (2008, p. 99).

Summary

- The idea of culture is complex, and we need to think about what this means to us;
- An understanding of the terms *pluricultural*, *multicultural* and *intercultural* will enable a better understanding of how to support the children we teach;
- We are all on a continuum of cultural competence, and recognising this can raise awareness of how we can move forward;
- A consideration of both shared and individual identity enables us to develop more inclusive learning environments where children can develop a sense of themselves within the diverse contexts of their lives;
- Our names are an important part of our identity, and activities to explore this will support intercultural understanding;
- Games and investigations are useful pedagogies to employ to raise awareness of different languages and cultures;
- The role of the teacher is essential in developing a classroom ethos which celebrates diversity and provides opportunities for children to find an identity for themselves and feel proud of who they are.

References

Akinadé, O. O. & Ọdẹ́jọbí, O. A. (2014) 'Computational modelling of Yorùbá numerals in a number-to-text conversion system', *Journal of Language Modelling*, Available at http://jlm.ipipan.waw.pl/ojs/index.php/JLM/article/view/83 (Accessed 02.08.2016).

Bernaus, M. Andrade, A. I. Kervran, M. Murkowska, A. & Saez, F. T. (2007) *Plurilingual and Pluricultural Awareness in Language Teacher Education*, Strasbourg: Council of Europe Publishing.

Berry, J. (2004) *Only One of ME: Selected Poems (Pick a Poem)*, New York: MacMillan Children's Books.

Berry, M., Garcia-Blanco, I. & Moore, K. (2015) *Report Prepared for the United Nations High Commission for Refugees*, Geneva: UNHCR.

Berumen, F. C. & Silva, C. (2014) 'A journey with a refugee family: Raising culturally relevant teaching awareness', *New Directions for Teaching and Learning*, 140, pp. 51–67.

British Council (2015) 'Identity and belonging teachers notes 7–14. Connecting classrooms', Available at https://schoolsonline.britishcouncil.org/sites/so/files/identity_and_belonging_teachers_guide_0_0.pdf (Accessed 01.08.2016).

Buescher, J. (n.d.) 'Rock paper scissors', Available at http://teachinghistory.org/history-content/ask-a-historian/23932 (Accessed 01.08.2016).

Cobb, W. (ed.) (2014) *All About Me Planning Guide Stage a French and Spanish*, Croydon: AMLA.

Colato Lainez, R. (1996) *Rene Has Two Last Names/Ren e tiene dos apellidos*, Houston, TX: Arte Publico. 32.

Conteh, J. (2012) *Teaching Bilingual and EAL Learners in Primary Schools*, Exeter: Learning Matters Ltd.
Council for Europe (2014) *Common European Framework of Reference for Languages; Learning, Teaching and Assessment*, Cambridge University Press, Available at www.coe.int/t/dg4/linguistic/Source/Framework_EN.pdf (Accessed 28.07.2016).
Day, E. M. (2002) *Identity and the Young English Language Learner*, Clevedon: Multilingual Matters.
Department for Education and Skills (2005b) *The Key Stage 2 Framework for Languages*, London: HMSO.
Department for Education and Skills (2005a) *Aiming High: Meeting the Needs of Newly Arrived Learners of English as an Additional Language*, Nottingham: DfES.
Education Scotland (n.d.) 'Learning journey – our games', Available at www.educationscotland.gov.uk/Images/LearningJourneyOurGames_tcm4-749024.pdf (Accessed 01.08.2016).
Erickson, F. (2010) 'Culture in society and in educational practices', in Banks, J. A. & Banks, C. A. M. (eds.), *Multicultural Education: Issues and Perspectives* (7th ed., pp. 33–56), Hoboken, NJ: Wiley-Blackwell.
European Centre for Modern Languages (2007) 'Plurilingual and pluricultural awareness in language teacher education', Available at http://archive.ecml.at/documents/B2_LEA_E_web.pdf (Accessed 14.02.2021).
Fanshawe, S. & Sriskandarajah, D. (2010) *'You Can't Put Me in a Box' Super-Diversity and the End of Identity Politics in Britain*, London: IPPR.
Flynn, N.(2013) 'Linguistic capital and the linguistic field for teachers unaccustomed to linguistic difference', *British Journal of Sociology of Education*, 34, 2, pp. 225–242.
Gee, J. (2014) 'Decontextualized language: A problem, not a solution', *International Multilingual Research Journal*, 8, 1, pp. 9–23.
Greenslade, R. (2020) 'Migrants are off the agenda for the UK press, but the damage is done', Available at www.theguardian.com/media/2020/jan/26/migrants-are-off-the-agenda-for-the-uk-press-but-the-damage-is-done (Accessed 10.02.2021).
Gregory, A. & Williams, A. (2000) City *Literacies Learning to Read Across Generations and Cultures*, London: Routledge.
Hall, E. T. (1976) *Beyond Culture*, New York: Doubleday Publishing.
Hall, S. (1992) 'The question of cultural identity', in Hall, S. Held, D. & McGrew, T. (eds.), *Modernity and its Futures*, pp. 274–316, Cambridge: Polity Press/Open University.
Hanley, J. (1999) 'Beyond the tip of the iceberg', Available at www.aacu.org/sites/default/files/files/hips/Beyondthetipoftheiceberg.pdf (Accessed 15.01.2021).
Hannerz, U. (2000) *Transnational Connections*, London: Routledge.
Holliday, A. (1999) 'Small cultures', *Applied Linguistics*, 20, 2, pp. 237–264.
Janks, H. (2000) 'Domination, access, diversity and design: A synthesis for critical literacy education', *Educational Review*, 52, 2, pp. 175–186.
Kumaravadivelu, B. (2008) *Cultural Globalization and Language Education*, New Haven and London: Yale University Press.
Lankshear, C. & Knobel, M. (2003) *New Literacies: Changing Knowledge and Classroom Learning*, Buckingham: Open University Press.
Liddicot & Scarino (2013) *Intercultural Language Teaching and Learning*, West Sussex: Blackwell Publishing.
Marsh, J. (2012) 'Children as knowledge brokers of playground games and rhymes in the new media age', *Childhood*, 19, 4, pp. 508–522.
Mason, J. L. (1993) *Culturally Competence Self-Assessment Questionnaire*, Portland, OR: Portland State University, Multicultural Initiative Project.
Mercuri, S. P. (2012) 'Understanding the interconnectedness between language choices, cultural identity construction and school practices in the life of a latino educator', *Gist Education and Learning Research Journal*, 6, pp. 12–43.
Mirror Online (2016) 'Parents outraged as school bans "tag" children's game for bizarre reason', Available at www.mirror.co.uk/news/uk-news/parents-outraged-school-bans-tag-7527073 (Accessed 01.08.2016).
Moises, E-G. & Moll, L. C. (2014) 'Lived experience, funds of identity and education', *Culture and Psychology*, 20, 1, pp. 70–81.
Moje, E. B. McIntosh Ciechanowski, K. Kramer, K. Ellis, L. Carrillo, R. & Collazo, T. (2004) 'Working toward third space in content area literacy: An examination of everyday funds of knowledge and discourse', *Reading Research Quarterly*, 39, 1 pp. 38–70.

Moll, L. Amanti, C. Neff, D. & Gonzalez, N. (1992) 'Funds of knowledge for teaching: Using a qualitative approach to connect home and classrooms', *Theory into Practice*, 31, 2, pp. 132-141.

Nazroo, J. & Karlsen, S. (2003) 'Patterns of identity among ethnic minority people: Diversity and commonality', *Ethnic and Racial Studies*, 26, 5, pp. 902-930.

Nieto, C. P. (2008) 'Cultural competence and its influence on the teaching and learning of international students', MA thesis.

Nieto, C. P. (2010) *Language, Culture and Teaching*, New York: Routledge.

Park, M. S. (2013) 'Code-switching and translanguaging: Potential functions in multilingual classrooms', *TESOL & Applied Linguistics*, 13, 2, pp. 50-52.

Peterson, B., Gunn, A., Brice, A. & Alley, K. (2015) 'Exploring names and identity through multicultural literature in K-8 classrooms', *Multicultural Perspectives*, 17, 1, pp. 39-45, DOI: 10.1080/15210960.2015.994434.

Piazzoli, E. (2018) *Embodying Language in Action. The Artistry of Process Drama in Second Language Education*, London: Palgrave Macmillan.

Pinter, A. (2011) *Children Learning Second Languages (Research and Practice in Applied Linguistics)*, Basingstoke: Palgrave Macmillan.

Souza, A. (2008) 'How linguistic and cultural identities are affected by migration', *Language Issues*, 19, 1, pp. 36-42.

Stein, M. (no date) 'Cultural competence', Available at http://intranet.dragon.k12.pa.us/about/Presentations/culturalcompetencelewisburg.pdf (Accessed 14.02.2021).

UK Government (2006) 'A guide to names and naming practices', Available at www.fbiic.gov/public/2008/nov/Naming_practice_guide_UK_2006.pdf (Accessed 01.08.2016).

UNICEF (1990) 'The united nations convention on the rights of the child', Available at www.unicef.org.uk/ (Accessed 02.08.2016).

UNICEF (2016) 'In search of safety. Children and the refugee crisis in Europe. A teaching resource', Available at www.unicef.org.uk/ (Accessed 29.07.2016).

Van Lier, L. (2004) 'The semiotics and ecology of language learning', *Utbildning and Demokrati*, 13, NR 3, pp. 79-103.

Weaver, G. R. (2001) 'American cultural values', Available at www.airuniversity.af.edu/Portals/10/AFNC/documents/Negotiationsectionstef/American%20Cultural%20Values.pdf (Accessed 30.10.2020).

Williams, K. L. & Mohammed, K. (2009) *My Name is Sangoel*, Grand Rapids, MI: Eerdmans Books for Young Readers.

4 Language and wellbeing

Give sorrow words; the grief that does not speak knits up the o-er wrought heart and bids it break.

(William Shakespeare - *Macbeth,* Act iv, Scene iii)

Introduction

If, like us, you have ever agonised over the right words to say to a bereaved friend, rewritten an email to a work colleague 20 times before pushing 'send' and immediately regretted sending it or panicked after accidently clicking 'like' on a provocative post on social media, you will already have a clear sense of the link between language and mental wellbeing. Trying to find the right 'heart' words in challenging times is always tricky; for children from the early years into adolescence struggling to find their place in the world to adults looking to lead flourishing and fulfilling lives, having the right words to be able to express ourselves is crucial.

In other chapters we have highlighted the importance of building inclusive classrooms that encourage a sense of belonging and connectedness, which are key protective factors for positive mental health. We believe that learning communities that are built on healthy relational cultures are foundational to both staff and child wellbeing. In this chapter we develop these ideas further and explore what we mean by wellbeing and why a focus on child mental health is so important, suggesting that using our own experiences and autobiographical insights can enhance our support of children and their learning. We examine the idea of language development as an indicator for wellbeing and how language play is a potentially powerful aspect of this. The importance of choice of lesson content is presented and how social and emotional learning are closely bound up with the teaching and learning of language. The chapter ends with a consideration of how we might limit performance anxiety in terms of language teaching, thus further supporting wellbeing.

What do we mean by wellbeing, and why is child wellbeing so important?

Evidence suggests that child mental health is strongly associated with both wellbeing and future life chances, by which we mean the opportunities people have to improve the quality of their lives. Specifically, findings from Goodman et al.'s (2015) review into social and

DOI: 10.4324/9781003129738-5

emotional skills in childhood and their long-term effects on adult life suggest that emotional health at age 16 is a stronger predictor of mental health and life chances at age 30 than either demographic or socio-economic factors.

Wellbeing is an elusive construct; it is something we all strive for, but which has many different perspectives (Seligman, 2011; Huppert and So, 2013; Diener, Helliwell, and Kahneman, 2010), and perceptions of health and wellbeing for children and families will differ according to where they live and their available resources (Underdown, 2007). However, most definitions refer to the presence of positive emotions (for instance an understanding of happiness in terms of pleasant/unpleasant feelings) and often include concepts of human flourishing (Grant, 2012) (achieving self-actualisation and fulfilment).

Contemporary theoretical perspectives outline a range of indicators for positive wellbeing, typically organised into objective measures – such as health, education and poverty – and subjective measures such as a person's sense of happiness with different aspects of their life for instance linked to a sense of agency as we have discussed. Findings from the Good Childhood Report (Children's Society, 2019, p. 9), which prioritise children's views of what makes a good childhood, suggest children's overall life satisfaction is similar on different days of the week and therefore relatively stable, while feelings of happiness and sadness vary (the report found that generally children are happier at the weekend).

All models of wellbeing cite the importance of relationships or social connectedness, and children can develop strong social networks through positive family relationships and opportunities to build relationships with others both at school and within the wider community. Research suggests that social connectedness plays a key role in alleviating suicidal thoughts and behaviours among adolescents (Gunn, Goldstein, and Gager, 2018) and is therefore vital when we know that suicide is a major health issue and the second leading cause of death for those in the 15 to 24 age range (Gunn, 2020). A comprehensive national multi-agency study of suicide in people under 20 in England (Rodway et al., 2016) reported a number of key antecedents for the individuals for whom the researchers had report data including academic (especially exam) pressures (27%), bullying (22%) and social isolation or withdrawal (25%). Research suggests that suicide attempts and ideation is significantly higher among lesbian, gay, bisexual and transgender (LGBT) youth than the general population (Ream, 2018; Bachmann and Gooch, 2018).

These statistics are clearly extremely worrying. However, the development of pro-social behaviours such as empathy and concern for the welfare and rights of others has been linked to a reduction in depression and anxiety, conduct disorders, violence, bullying, conflict and anger (Sancassiani et al., 2015). Positive classroom environments, established by teachers who understand the impact of trauma on children's wellbeing and who have built trusting reciprocal relationships, are safe spaces where children are able to share their emotions and concerns. We would argue that the language classroom which prioritises intercultural understanding, communication, self-awareness, student voice and agency has a significant role to play in promoting social and emotional health and thereby enhancing children's future life chances.

Using autobiographical insights as educators

In order to develop this inclusive, safe language learning environment, which places children's wellbeing at the forefront of our actions, we can usefully tap into our own lives and use our experiences to support the children we teach. Like us, you might link your own sense of wellbeing to positive memories and emotions. For instance, here is an autobiographical note taken from Wendy's master's research on leadership resilience and wellbeing (Cobb, 2015, p. 41):

> I wrote a large part of the methodology sitting beside the blue sea on a warm day in June while on holiday with my husband in Madeira. I have a picture of a sunny Madeiran plateau, taken high above the cloudy hills, on my laptop display. I finished the methodology at home on a hot day in July. I went into the garden and spread my arms, feeling the warm sun on my back and the soft grass beneath my feet.

I (Wendy) am lucky to have a small, secluded garden edged by three beautiful oak trees, and my sense of wellbeing here is partially linked to a mindful awareness of my place within the natural world. In this memory, wellbeing for me is also closely associated to a sense of agency and ownership of my writing. I chose not to share my dissertation drafts with anyone prior to submission (other than family members who proofread the final multi-edited version). Although I talked regularly with my research supervisor about what I was writing, the actual content I kept to myself. This ownership of my writing was hugely important to me at the time as I began to dip my toes into autobiographical and reflective writing. Clearly, I have moved on since then and now happily share very sketchy drafts in the initial stages of collaborative writing – a regular activity with this co-authored book.

However, it is worth remembering the mental processes we struggle through and the emotional encounters we face as we tackle challenges such as these. In this way, we can recognise what children might be experiencing and better support their wellbeing. The case study that follows provides an example of a writing activity between adults. As you read this, think about similar classroom scenarios where children tackle writing and the emotional and cognitive challenges these tasks present. We have chosen this particular example because writing is difficult, overwhelming at times, and yet we expect children to take this day-to-day practice in their stride. Drawing on our own experiences can allow for a more empathic response to children's efforts.

Adults writing together

My (Wendy's) confidence to share in this way is partly an outcome of an iterative journal-writing research study I took part in with two colleagues exploring the emotional aspects of academic writing for publication (Beighton, Cobb, and Welland, 2021). Iterative journal writing is a 'repeated process of writing, exchanging, responding, and exchanging written responses to a particular topic . . . an "open loop" which allows change and development to happen' (ibid, p. 3); much like the process of writing this book. What was important in the study was that we felt comfortable to be honest and open about our feelings and emotions, questions and expectations about the writing process, particularly as two of us were quite novice writers in comparison with the more experienced other.

There are a lot of parallels between the writing for academic publication study and the writing of this book. For instance, there were no expectations about how we would write our first iterations. For our initial attempts at writing (both in the journal exchanges in the study and our first drafts for this book) we used quite different writing styles, and we found that 'we tuned to each other's ... style in subsequent iterations – a common form of code-switching in communication' (ibid, p. 5). The sharing of our iterations and our discussions in the study were carried out under a set of guiding principles, much like the unwritten principles we have adhered to when writing this book:

- Trust: we agreed not to share our writing with anyone else without prior agreement;
- Validity: we deemed all writing as worthy of sharing;
- Parity: despite our different levels of experience, our approach to writing and publishing was deliberately non-hierarchical.

Consider the key principles of choice, agency, trust, validity and parity, which we have linked in the case study to the emotional aspects of writing development. To what extent are they important to you, not just as a writer but as a person? To what extent are these aspects embedded in your classroom, in writing activities and beyond? How might you draw on your own autobiographic insights (relating to language and beyond) to support children's wellbeing?

Language development as an indicator for wellbeing

Language development and wellbeing are intrinsically linked from the early years, tied up in the inherent need for humans to be able to understand and express themselves. Communication and language is one of three prime areas highlighted in the 2017 review of the Early Years Foundation stage (DfE), the other two being physical development and personal, social and emotional development. All three are interrelated and integral to a sense of personal wellbeing:

Communication and language development: giving children opportunities to experience a rich language environment; to develop their confidence and skills in expressing themselves; and to speak and listen in a range of situations;

Physical development: providing opportunities for young children to be active and interactive; . . . to understand the importance of physical activity, and to make healthy choices in relation to food;

Personal, social and emotional development: helping children to develop a positive sense of themselves, and others; to form positive relationships and develop respect for others; to develop social skills and learn how to manage their feelings; to understand appropriate behaviour in groups; and to have confidence in their own abilities (DfE, 2017, p. 8).

The Early Intervention Foundation Report (Law, Charlton, and Asmussen, 2017, p. 5) highlights the fundamental link between language and social, emotional and learning outcomes which makes early language development a primary indicator of child wellbeing. You might want to return at this point to examine the examples from research presented in Chapter 1, exploring how we can build on children's early language awareness.

Research evidence linking early language development and later-life outcomes has led to several recommendations to prioritise early language skills, building on the initial conclusions of the 2008 Equality and Human Rights Commission Report, 'Early years, life chances and equality' (Johnson and Kossykh, 2008). A study following over 17,000 children born in Britain in 1970 through to adulthood found that those with poor vocabulary skills at age five were four times more likely to have reading difficulties in adulthood, three times as likely to have mental health problems, and twice as likely to be unemployed when they reached adulthood (Law et al., 2009). Additionally, Save the Children's (2012) Scottish report, Thrive at Five, reported that children who grow up in poverty are twice as likely to face difficulties with their communication development when they enter school as other children and more than three times as likely as children in the most affluent households to face such difficulties.

Arguably, young children who grow up in language-rich environments are well equipped to express themselves as they enter school; however expensive resources are not pre-requisites for language-rich classroom environments. Instead, language teachers require a good understanding of child development and awareness of effective strategies for developing children's communicative competences. These include teaching, practising and role modelling the language of clarification and polite requests, in English and in the target language (see French examples in Table 4.1). This repetitive and reciprocal rehearsal process enables children to become familiar with routine structures that they can manipulate to express what they know and what they need. For instance, the question structure 'Est-ce que je peux?' can become 'Est-ce que je peux m'assoir/lire?' (Can I sit down/read?).

Language play and wellbeing

Multiple studies suggest that play, which Goldstein (2012, p. 5) refers to as 'any activity freely chosen, intrinsically motivated and personally directed', improves the cognitive, physical, social and emotional wellbeing of children and young people (Ashiabi, 2007; Brockman, Fox,

Table 4.1 Polite classroom responses and language of clarification

S'il vous plaît	Please
Merci	Thank you
Je sais/Je ne sais pas	I know/I don't know
Je comprends/Je ne comprends pas	I understand/I don't understand
Est-ce que je peux... (plus infinitive)?	Can I...?
Comment dit-on... en français/anglais?	How do you say... in French/English?
Pouvez-vous répéter, s'il vous plaît?	Please can you repeat that?
Pouvez-vous m'aider?	Can you help me, please?

and Jago, 2011; O'Connor and Stagnitti, 2011). Young children naturally play with language. Sometimes language play is used as a tool to facilitate another form of play, and at other times the manipulation of the language becomes the play activity itself.

Language play allows children to be inventive, to break language rules and take risks with the grammar and pronunciation of the language system. Of course, in order to deliberately and purposefully break rules (Can you see what we have done here with the split infinitive? See Chapter 1 for more discussion.), we need to be aware of both the rules and the intended outcome. Unfortunately, at times, we find some students are worried about experimenting with language in case they get it 'wrong'. Education systems that focus heavily on test and exam accountability encourage a sense of following rules, of getting it 'right', and this can discourage risk-taking and creative experimentation (Sahlberg, 2008). Sometimes, however, students will break rules unconsciously, for instance by inadvertently creating a new word, and in so doing they can produce language forms that have more powerful impact than the 'correct' words. This accidental language is useful because it provides an opportunity to unpick the rules whilst highlighting the benefits of purposeful play and authorial choice. The following case study provides some examples of how language play might be promoted.

> ### Noun play
>
> Wendy delivers a sequence of poetry seminars to her English language group. Language play features predominantly through the three sessions. A number of poetry activities focus on different noun types, and for one activity, the students are asked to gather lists of common nouns (for instance *bottle, carpet, juggler*) and abstract nouns (such as *excitement, fear, anticipation*) linked to ideas and emotions emerging from a reading of a story. Before they gather their lists, students discuss patterns of word endings when changing verbs to abstract nouns (for instance *excite – excitement, disappoint – disappointment, anticipate – anticipation, attract – attraction*). The students then write nouns on two differently coloured piles of self-adhesive notes, and then randomly turn the notes over in pairs to create collective nouns such as 'an excitement of bottles' or 'an attraction of carpets'. Much giggling ensues, and the students talk about their favourite pairings and the impact of a word order that implies a personification of inanimate objects such as bottles. They ask questions such as, 'Why are the bottles excited? Are they recycled soda bottles about to be filled with champagne?' Their choices are used to create a class poem, which students subsequently perform, often with some difficulty due to the degree of suppressed laughter prompted by mental images of the randomly created personified objects.

During these relaxed, fun activities, inevitably some students will inadvertently invent new words by trying to follow the rules. A call for a list of random abstract-noun and common-noun pairings might elicit a suggestion of 'a worriment of rabbits' and a discussion around the fact that the verb and the abstract noun are in this instance the same word: *worry* rather than *worriment*. However, *worriment* is in fact an archaic or humorous form of *worry*, not commonly used today, so in this instance is not a newly invented word (and often what seems to be a new word, has already been created by another author having fun with language). We personally prefer *worriment* to *worry* in this context, and even if it were a made-up word, we would encourage the student to use it if they liked it too. This might seem obvious, but we have known teachers in training to ask, 'Are we *allowed* to encourage children to make up words?', so worried are they about teaching their classes incorrect grammar.

> Where are the opportunities for playful use of language in your classroom?
> How important to you is it that children always follow the grammatical 'rules'?

Wendy: Poetry lessons are such wonderful contexts for playing around with language and seeing things empathically from different perspectives. The strange combinations that emerge from the abstract noun/noun activity, such as an 'excitement of bottles', can elicit some powerful mental images. This can lead to a poetry-writing activity where children question inanimate objects, for instance, 'Ceiling, do you ever get fed up with looking down at noisy children?', 'Pencil, what does it feel like to be sharpened?' and 'Carpet, do you mind being trodden on?'. Virginia, do you have any favourite language play activities that you recommend that would be particularly useful for children with English as an additional language?

Virginia: Definitely, Wendy! One of the challenges when learning a new language is when a word sounds the same as another word but has a different meaning and/or spelling (homophones) – *hare* and *hair*, for example. Language investigations are useful and fun here. I gave children a list of words, and they would undertake research using a range of resources to find out whether there were other words that sounded the same but meant something very different. The task was then to put these words into a humorous sentence – 'I tried to pour the water over the poor cat's paw but instead spilt it on the pores on my hand'. These also make great tongue twisters and lead to interesting discussions about spelling rules, phonics, comprehension and effective word use. You cannot go wrong!

Chukovsky refers to 'the inexhaustible need of every healthy child of every era and of every nation to introduce nonsense into his small but ordered world, with which he has only recently become acquainted' (Chukovsky, 1963 cited in Crystal, 1996, p. 330). The language classroom is a good place to feed this need for nonsense through a range of language play activities that will also help children understand and play with grammar rules, including through the introduction of word games, rhymes and riddles. A good place to start is the website www.

mamalisa.com/?t=eh where you will find songs, rhymes and playground games from around the world, with many examples also including audio files, videos and sheet music.

Examples of tongue twisters are also readily found online in many languages and are great for practising pronunciation, for instance these two French examples:

- Cinq chiens chassent six chats. (Five dogs hunt six cats.)
- Je suis ce que je suis, et si je suis ce que je suis, qu'est ce que je suis? (I am what I am, and if I am what I am, what am I?)

Another way to use word play to explore grammar is through jokes. You can rarely go wrong in the classroom with some good old-fashioned jokes! These are particularly useful when they involve a play on words or use grammar as the foundation of the pun. Here is an example:

TEACHER: Can someone give me a sentence starting with "I"?
STUDENT: I is . . .
TEACHER: No. Always say, "I am."
STUDENT: All right, if you say so. I am the ninth letter of the alphabet.

(Nordquist, 2019, no page)

This joke could be the starting point for a discussion about 'subject'. The 'subject' is a grammatical term used to describe a part of the sentence, which could be a noun, pronoun or noun phrase that contains the person or thing performing the action (or verb) in the sentence. Identifying the subject of a sentence is important because in many languages verbs are conjugated according to the number, person and gender of the subject noun or subject pronoun. This is relatively easy when there is one subject and one verb, although see the example where the word *I* can be used to represent either a first-person subject pronoun or a proper noun (here the name of a letter requiring third-person agreement); so be wary about saying 'always' when introducing any grammar 'rule'. A simple illustration of subject/verb agreement in French is shown in the following sentences in which the verb ending changes to agree with the subject (which is singular in the first sentence and plural in the second):

Je mange une pomme. (I eat an apple.)
Elles mangent des pommes. (They eat some apples.)

Once the children are confident with identifying the subject of the sentence, you might introduce the following French joke and ask:

Dans la phrase *le voleur a volé une télévision*, où est le sujet?
(In the phrase *the thief stole a television*, where is the subject?)
The answer is of course 'En Prison!' (In prison!)

An online search will find many grammatical jokes that will enhance social connectedness through shared laughter and at the same time prompt metalanguage discussions (see Chapter 9 for more ideas about this). Of course, as a trauma-aware school, you might worry about the possible insensitivities of using the earlier French joke in the classroom. According to the National Information Centre on Children of Offenders (2018) an estimated 310,000 children have a parent in prison every year in England and Wales, and every day 10,000 visits are made by children to public prisons. We do need to be mindful of our topic and language choices, and sometimes, despite our best intentions to create engaging and inclusive lessons, we present ideas that are difficult for some children (see also the Toby and Lina case study that follows). However, within the pro-social classroom, supportive student-teacher and pupil-pupil relationships enable children to develop the resilience and behaviours to self-regulate in challenging situations, to voice their emotional responses and for these voices to be actively listened to.

Content matters for wellbeing in the language classroom

In Chapters 6 and 7 we posit the benefits of cross-curricular approaches to language learning, and the power of this approach is undeniable. However, the choice of content to be covered needs to be carefully thought through as we ensure consideration of the impact of the topic on the social and emotional wellbeing of the students. For example, in the following case study we illustrate how a teacher's well-intentioned choice of context for teaching a grammatical structure has the potential to impact in a negative way on the emotional wellbeing of some students.

Toby and Lina

In a school-based teacher training programme, trainees are asked to observe expert colleagues, develop teaching sequences and then engage in peer observations which include opportunities for narrated observations with their mentor. Parental consent is obtained for the lessons to be videoed to allow follow-up discussions to take place within a primary language seminar group.

Toby and Lina jointly develop a languages lesson adapting pedagogical approaches they have observed being used by expert practitioners. For the narrated observation, Toby leads a Spanish language lesson with a Year 4 class during which the children are introduced to the first-person verb form *soy* ('I am') and descriptive adjectives including *alto* (tall), *bajo* (short), *gordo* (fat) and *delgado* (thin). The lesson activities have been carefully planned to help the children develop good pronunciation and read, write and translate descriptive structures with correct adjectival agreement. To help illustrate the latter, the class are initially divided into boys and girls to practice reciting adjectival agreement ('Soy alto/Soy alta').

Lina and the mentor carry out a narrated observation and identify language learning approaches incorporated in the planning which include:

- Songs
- Actions

- Visuals
- Repetition
- Emphasis on key sounds e.g. 'y', 'ba**jo**'
- Tongue twisting translation practice 'Soy, soy, I, I, soy, I, soy'/'I, I, soy, soy, I, soy, I'
- Pupils micro-teaching
- Group sorting activities

By the end of the lesson most children are able confidently to write and translate a range of extended structures to describe themselves, with some of them also drawing on prior learning:

- 'Soy alta y delgada y tengo el pelo corto.'

In the subsequent tutor group seminar, the tutor prompts discussion around content, intercultural understanding and classroom ethos for wellbeing. Toby and Lina agree with their colleagues that although the chunked learning enabled the children to build structures and demonstrate progress within the lesson, intercultural understanding, cross-curricular links and creative thinking opportunities are targets for future planning. However, Toby and Lina are initially surprised when some of the trainees express a sense of unease about the sensitivities of expecting children to describe themselves using adjectives such as **fat/thin** and of dividing the children into gender groups. Subsequent discussions explore alternative approaches to teaching adjectival agreement to avoid gender stereotyping as well as opportunities for developing the language of emotions.

There is much to be learned from this case study, not least of which is the importance of thinking carefully about what we decide to teach (content) and how we decide to teach it (pedagogy). There are also important points to draw out in terms of gender and language, and you may want to read Chapter 5 where we explore these issues further.

If you were asked to describe yourself, what would be the first adjectives you would use?

Are the adjectives mostly negative or positive?

Would your choice of adjectives depend on who you were talking to?

To what extent do you think your language choices might be linked to gender or cultural stereotypes?

How does your choice of language to describe yourself relate to your own sense of wellbeing?

Language and social and emotional learning

In the case study, Toby and Linda initially used descriptions of appearance as a context for teaching the structure *Soy* ('I am') from the verb *ser* (which, in Spanish is used to describe a permanent state, for example 'I am tall/he has blue eyes/the sun is round') and adjectival agreement. The verb *ser* is also used for descriptions of character traits. For example:

- Soy timido. (m.) (I'm shy.)
- Soy timida. (f.) (I'm shy.)

Of course, character traits are not exactly permanent, and our actions may be impacted by our emotional state. Therefore, after their post-lesson discussions with the tutor, the students in the case study might have decided to continue practising adjectival agreement using *Estoy* from the verb *estar* – used to describe temporary states such as locations, actions and emotions; for example, 'Estoy feliz' ('I'm happy'). Attention to details such as these can have a considerable impact on children's social and emotional wellbeing.

Many primary schools use circle time strategies and the language of emotions to support children's social and emotional development and to develop a positive whole-class ethos, and you might want to explore Jenny Mosley's circle time resources (2015) and the Responsive Classroom programme's morning meetings (Responsive Classrooms, 2020). The following case study examines how circle time might be used to teach about emotions in the language classroom.

Teaching emotions during circle time

The Sonrisas Spanish (2018) elementary school programme incorporates circle time into its curriculum. Every lesson follows the structure of circle time followed by story time and then art time. During circle time the children sing songs, play games and do introductory activities in Spanish, with circle time lasting anywhere from five minutes to half an hour. A typical lesson from the curriculum would begin with the class sitting in a circle and the teacher conducting the register in Spanish.

- ¿Maria, dónde estás?   (Maria, where are you?)
- Aquí.   (Here.)
- ¿Leo, dónde estás?   (Leo, where are you?)
- Aquí.   (Here.)

Children then sing a greeting, asking each other how they are and responding with different emotions words. Here is an example of a greeting song that can be sung to the tune of 'Frère Jacques'. The children perform different actions to match the emotions words.

- Buenos días, Buenos días (Good morning, good morning)
- ¿Como estas como estas? (How are you?, How are you?)
- Muy feliz, muy feliz/Muy triste, muy triste (Very happy,/very sad)
- Gracias, gracias (Thank you, thank you)

78 Language and wellbeing

This daily structure enables the teacher to start the lesson with an emotional check-in, which in turn can help them gauge how ready children are to learn. Understanding how the children are feeling at the start of the lesson enables teachers to modify their responses to classroom incidents appropriately. Circle time also provides children with a safe space where they can attune with their own and each other's emotions. They can also explore language to describe how they are feeling, which in turn supports their own self-regulation and consequently their wellbeing.

Take a look at Table 4.2 which lists examples of phrases describing emotions in French and Spanish.

Evidence suggests that creative activity can boost wellbeing (see for instance Galton and Page's 2015 review of the Creative Partnership programme activities in primary schools) and provide the perfect vehicle for social and emotional learning. When these activities can also be linked to language, the potential for powerful experiences and long-lasting impact is considerable.

The charity Paper Boat has worked with local experts and grassroots community-based partners for over 50 years, focusing on innovative education projects designed to unlock children's potential including through the setting up of Children's Hubs – community-owned spaces where children come to learn and play after school. Much of the charity's work has been based in Tamil Nadu in India, working with children at risk of exclusion because they have lost their parents, are living on the streets or living with HIV/AIDS, and young people from Dalit (former untouchable) and tribal communities rejected by some as impure or unclean (Shaheen, 2020). The following case study provides an example of what the charity Paper Boat does and how a creative approach can support emotional and social learning whilst raising an interest in language.

Table 4.2 French and Spanish emotion words

French	English
Je suis heureux(se)	I'm happy
Je suis en colère	I'm angry
Je suis nerveux (se)	I'm nervous
Je suis inquiet(e)	I'm worried
Je suis gêné(e)	I'm embarrassed
Je suis calme	I'm calm
Je suis triste	I'm sad
Spanish	English
Estoy feliz	I'm happy
Estoy enojado/enojada	I'm angry
Estoy emocionado/emocionada	I'm excited
Estoy asustado/asustada	I'm frightened
Estoy aburrido/aburrida	I'm bored
Estoy contento/contenta	I'm content
Estoy nervioso/nerviosa	I'm nervous
Estoy preocupado/preocupada	I'm worried

> ### Paper Boat
>
> Guna is a community leader and inspirational artist who paints alongside the children, inviting them to join in. Paper Boat director, Shaheen, describes Guna at work in the hub:
>
> > Guna delights in helping children to use art so that they can 'discover their passion' early. Something that he was not able to do because there was no one to similarly inspire him as a child struggling to give voice to his creativity. He holds up a brightly coloured and vibrant piece of art that the children have collaborated on in a Children's Hub recently. The beautiful looping swirls are Tamil letters – vowels to be precise. Vowels are 'magic letters' he tells us – known as 'soul letters' because they give life to 'body letters' (consonants) – through them words take shape as letters collaborate to carry and convey meaning. 'Soul letters' help to unlock the latent potential of words just as Guna uses art to unlock the unique and creative potential of every child.
> >
> > (Shaheen, 2020)
>
> Guna's community leadership reminds us that teaching language is much more than memorising words and learning about culture and language systems. It is a heart and soul activity, best practised by language teachers who are attuned to their own emotional wellbeing in order to support the emotional health of their classes.

> How might your existing language-teaching routines be adapted to develop further opportunities for creativity and social and emotional learning?
>
> How attuned are you to your own emotional health? What/who can support you?

Limiting performance anxiety in language learning

In Chapter 7 we discuss and contrast the fearless experimentation of children's language acquisition during the early years with the often-painful process of learning a new language. If you are not a language specialist, you may be very aware of your own anxiety in presenting new vocabulary and structures in the target language or responding to student questions. Anxiety in language learning can be particularly evident in any situation where we sense a perceived threat (Convington, Omelich, and Schwarzer, 1986), and research suggests anxiety can have a particularly significant impact on speaking in the target language (Aida, 1994; Matsuda and Gobel, 2003; Horwitz, 2001; Oya, Manalo, and Greenwood, 2004). We need, therefore, to consider different approaches that can help to limit performance anxiety in the language classroom, and the following case study includes an example of how this might be accomplished through the use of drama techniques to create safe environments for learning.

> ### Creating safe environments for learning
>
> Wendy enjoys using drama with her primary classes across the curriculum. At the beginning of a new academic year, she is aware that the children are more open to unfamiliar teaching and learning approaches. During the initial weeks of term, she introduces creative approaches to lessons, inviting children to experience arts, drama, languages and divergent thinking (for example, 'What if. . . ?') to explore the curriculum and confound gender and cultural stereotypes. Wendy encourages children during role-play activities to choose to be characters who are very different to what other children might think to be closer to their own identity. For instance, when reading a class book, she asks the children to role play and then freeze frame a character from the story. 'If you are tall, perhaps you will trick us and choose to be the mouse. If you are a girl, you might choose to be the big scary mayor'. Wendy asks the children to think about how to express the emotion and body language of a character who is very different to themselves and asks other children to guess which character in the story each child is. She finds that doing this activity early in the school year means that children are less inclined to stereotype what other children should be doing in the classroom. For instance, boys are happy to come to the front of the room and sing to their peers, when in other classes it may be more likely for the girls to volunteer to sing.

> Revisit the Toby and Lina case study. How might they incorporate role play and cross-curricular planning to avoid gender stereotyping and identity issues in teaching children language structures to describe themselves and others (see Chapters 5 and 6 for more suggestions)?

The next case study illustrates how teaching a language through the context of sport had a positive impact on reducing performance anxiety in a French language classroom. Embedding language learning within a subject context in this way is an example of Content and Language Integrated Learning (CLIL). We explain more about this approach in Chapters 6 and 7.

> ### French and PE CLIL research
>
> A study by Lamb and King (2020) investigated the impact of adopting a CLIL approach in secondary PE with the aim of improving students' spontaneous speaking in French. The study's stimulus was the 2016 changes to England's General Certificate of Secondary Education (GCSE) French specifications, in which the highest mark band requires the speaker to 'react naturally to the questions asked [with] an air of spontaneity' and to respond promptly with some fluency 'though not necessarily with that of a native speaker' (AQA, 2016). Students aged 13-14, soon to embark on GCSE French, were introduced to a 10-week handball scheme of work that included learning associated key French vocabulary and students communicating with each other and the teacher in French.

Data from the study indicated that during classroom lessons, students' least favourite activities were speaking and reading out loud. The researchers noted that a dominant factor in student responses was anxiety and a fear of 'getting it wrong':

> 'I can't always pronounce words right'.
> 'It's bad when I get it wrong'.
> 'Sometimes I feel people might laugh at me'.
> 'Sometimes it is embarrassing'.
> 'Sometimes I don't feel confident'.
> 'I don't like being corrected in front of my peers'.
>
> (Lamb and King, 2020, p. 522)

The students' expressions of anxiety in the French classroom were similar to other studies exploring students' attitudes to PE, 'which also requires students' abilities and physical competencies to be 'on display'' (Carlson, 1995, cited in Lamb and King, 2020, p. 522). This fear of failing can lead to students opting out or hiding themselves behind more skilled peers. However, in their study Lamb and King found that the physical education lesson appeared to create a non-judgemental learning environment where students were happy to experiment with the French vocabulary: 'In PE everybody is shouting French all over the place – it is a lot more fun than in the class' (p. 523).

The researchers concluded that the outcomes of the study suggest the importance of an 'applied and collaborative working environment' (p. 529) that emphasises working in a group and has a potential to increase a willingness to take risks.

Review your current classroom environment for language learning. To what extent do the classroom ethos and context encourage children's willingness to take risks with the language and provide a safe, collaborative environment for learning?

Summary

- Wellbeing is a complex concept with many perspectives;
- Children's wellbeing is a key indicator of future life chances;
- Protective factors for wellbeing include positive relational cultures, social-connectedness, belonging, a sense of agency and communicative competences;
- Creativity, language play and emotional awareness can enhance wellbeing;
- Teaching language is a heart and soul activity best practised by language teachers who are attuned to their own emotional wellbeing in order to support the emotional health of their classes.

References

Aida, Y. (1994) 'Examination of Horwitz, Horwitz, and cope's construct of foreign language Anxiety: The case of students of Japanese', *Modern Language Journal*, 78, 2, pp. 155–168.

Ashiabi, G. S. (2007) 'Play in the preschool classroom: Its socioemotional significance and the teacher's role in play', *Early Childhood Education Journal*, 35, pp. 199–207.

Bachmann, C. L. & Gooch, B. (2018) 'LGBT in Britain health report', Available at www.stonewall.org.uk/lgbt-britain-health (Accessed 28.07.2020).

Beighton, C. Cobb, W. & Welland, H. (2021) 'Autoethnographic approaches to academic writing development: Dialogue as a research tool', in *SAGE Research Methods Cases*, SAGE Publications Ltd, https://dx.doi.org/10.4135/9781529762044.

Brockman, R. Fox, K. R. & Jago, R. (2011) 'What is the meaning and nature of active play for today's children in the UK?' *International Journal of Behavioural Nutrition and Physical Activity*, 8, 15, pp. 1–7.

Carlson, T. B. (1995) 'We hate gym: Student alienation from physical education. Journal of Teaching in Physical Education', 14, 4, pp.467–477.

Children's Society (2019) 'The good childhood report', Available at www.childrenssociety.org.uk/sites/default/files/the_good_childhood_report_2019.pdf (Accessed 28.07.2020).

Cobb, W. (2015) *A Tale of Leadership Resilience and Wellbeing*, Boston, MA: Leadership and Management for Learning, Canterbury Christ Church University.

Covington, M. V. Omelich, C. L. & Schwarzer, R. (1986) 'Anxiety, aspirations, and self-concept in the achievement process: A longitudinal model with latent variables', *Motivation and Emotion*, 10, pp. 71–89.

Crystal, D. (1996) 'Language play and linguistic intervention', *Child Language Teaching and Therapy*, 12, 3, pp. 328–344.

Department for Education (DfE) (2017) 'Statutory framework for the early years foundation stage Setting the standards for learning, development and care for children from birth to five', Available at www.gov.uk/government/publications/early-years-foundation-stage-framework – 2 (Accessed 27.07.2020).

Diener, E. Helliwell, J. F. & Kahneman, D. (eds.) (2010) *International Differences in Wellbeing*, Oxford: Oxford University Press.

Galton, M. & Page, C. (2015) 'The impact of various creative initiatives on wellbeing: A study of children in English primary schools', *Cambridge Journal of Education*, 45, 3, pp. 349–369.

Goldstein, J. (2012) 'Play in children's development, health and wellbeing', Available at www.ornes.nl/wp-content/uploads/2010/08/Play-in-children-s-development-health-and-well-being-feb-2012.pdf (Accessed 19.07.2020).

Goodman, A. Joshi, H. Nasim, B. & Tyler, C. (2015) 'Social and emotional skills in childhood and their long-term effects on adult life: A review for the early intervention foundation', Available at www.eif.org.uk/report/social-and-emotional-skills-in-childhood-and-their-long-term-effects-on-adult-life (Accessed 03.08.2020).

Grant, C. A. (2012) 'Cultivating flourishing lives: A robust social justice vision of education', *American Educational Research Journal*, 49, 5, pp. 910–934.

Gunn, J. F. (2020) *Social Connectedness and Suicidal Thoughts and Behaviors Among Adolescents*, The Association for Child and Mental Health, Available at www.acamh.org/research-digest/social-connectedness-and-suicidal-thoughts-and-behaviors-among-adolescents/ (Accessed 27.07.2020).

Gunn, J. F. Goldstein, S. E. & Gager, C. T. (2018) 'A longitudinal examination of social connectedness and suicidal thoughts and behaviors among adolescents', *Child and Adolescent Mental Health*, 23, 4, pp. 341–350.

Horwitz, E. K. (2001) 'Language anxiety and achievement', *Annual Review of Applied Linguistics*, 21, pp. 112–26.

Huppert, F. A. & So, T. T. (2013) 'Flourishing across Europe: Application of a new conceptual framework for defining well-being', *Social Indicators Research*, 110, 3, pp. 837–861.

Johnson, P. & Kossykh, Y. (2008) *Early Years, Life Chances and Equality: A Literature Review*, Equality and Human Rights Commission, Available at http://cdn.basw.co.uk/upload/basw_25807-5.pdf (Accessed 27.07.2020).

Lamb, P. & King, G. (2020) 'Another platform and a changed context: Student experiences of developing spontaneous speaking in French through physical education', *European Physical Education Review*, DOI: 10.1177/1356336X19869733.

Law, J. Charlton, J. & Asmussen, K. (2017) *Language as a Child Wellbeing Indicator*, Early Intervention Foundation, Available at www.eif.org.uk/report/language-as-a-child-wellbeing-indicator (Accessed 27.07.2020).

Law, J. Rush, R. Parsons, S. & Schoon, I. (2009) 'Modelling developmental language difficulties from school entry into adulthood: Literacy, mental health and employment outcomes', *Journal of Speech, Language and Hearing Research*, 52, pp. 1401–1416.

Matsuda, S. & Gobel, P. (2003) 'Anxiety and predictors of performance in the foreign language classroom', *System*, 32, 1, pp. 21–36.

Moseley, J. (2015) *Circle Time for Young Children* (2nd ed.), London: Routledge.

The National Information Centre on Children of Offenders (2018) Available at www.nicco.org.uk/ (Accessed 28.07.2020).

Nordquist, R. (2019) *Grammar Crackers: Jokes, Riddles, and Word Play: The Lighter Side of the English Language*, Available at www.thoughtco.com/grammar-jokes-riddles-and-word-play-1688753 (Accessed 04.08.2020).

O'Connor, C. & Stagnitti, K. (2011) 'Play, behaviour, language and social skills: The comparison of a play and a non-play intervention within a specialist school setting', *Research in Developmental Disabilities*, 32, pp. 1205–1211.

Oya, T. Manalo, E. & Greenwood, J. (2004) 'The influence of personality and anxiety on the oral performance of Japanese speakers of English', *Applied Cognitive Psychology*, 18, pp. 841–55.

Ream, G. L. (2018) 'What's unique about lesbian, gay, bisexual, and transgender (LGBT) youth and young adult suicides? Findings from the national violent death reporting system', *Journal of Adolescent Health*, 64, 5, pp. 602–607.

Responsive Classrooms (2020) 'What is morning meeting?' Available at www.responsiveclassroom.org/what-is-morning-meeting/ (Accessed 29.07.2020).

Rodway, C. Tham, S. Ibrahim, S. Turnbull, P. Windfuhr, K. Shaw, J. Kapur, N. & Appleby, L. (2016) 'Suicide in children and young people in England: A consecutive case series', *Lancet Psychiatry*, Available at http://dx.doi.org/10.1016/S2215-0366(16)30094-3 (Accessed 27.07.2020).

Sahlberg, P. (2008) 'Rethinking accountability in a knowledge society', *Journal of Educational Change*, 11, pp. 45–61.

Sancassiani, F. Pintus, E. Holte, A. Paulus, P. Moro, M. F. Cossu, G. Angermeyer, M. C. Carta, M. G. & Lindert, J. (2015) 'Enhancing the emotional and social skills of the youth to promote their wellbeing and positive development: A systematic review of universal school-based randomized controlled trials', *Clinical Practice & Epidemiology in Mental Health*, 11(Suppl 1 M2), pp. 21–40.

Save the Children (2012) 'Thrive at five: Comparative child development at school-entry', Available at https://resourcecentre.savethechildren.net/node/6842/pdf/6842.pdf (Accessed 27.07.2020).

Seligman, M. E. P. (2011) *Flourish: A Visionary New Understanding of Happiness and Well-being*, New York: Free Press.

Shaheen, K. (2020) 'Paper boat: Working towards a future that unlocks the infinite potential in every child', Available at www.paperboatcharity.org.uk/what-we-do/thought-leadership/ (Accessed 24.02.2021).

Sonrisas Spanish (2018) 'Sonrisas Spanish PreSchool and elementary Spanish curriculum', Available at www.sonrisasspanishschool.com/ (Accessed 28.07.2020).

Underdown, A. (2007) *Young Children's Health and Wellbeing*, Berkshire: Open University Press.

5 Language and gender

All human beings are born free and equal in dignity and rights. They are endowed with reason and conscience and should act towards one another in a spirit of brotherhood.
  (Article 1 of the Universal Declaration of Human Rights, United Nations, 2020)

Introduction

The Universal Declaration of Human Rights (UDHR) was drafted by cross-cultural legislative representatives from around the world and endorsed by the United Nations General Assembly in Paris on 10 December 1948. Motivated by the devastating global consequences of the two preceding world wars, the Declaration was the first time that countries had united to agree on a statement about universal human rights, including an entitlement to all declared rights and freedoms 'without distinction of any kind, such as race, colour, sex, language, religion, political or other opinion, national or social origin, property, birth or other status' (Article 2). Sadly, today we are still far from achieving global equity. Critiques of the UDHR include the argument that the document is predicated on Western biases and fails to account for the cultural norms and values of the rest of the world (Willmott-Harrop, 2003; O'Connor, 2014).

Language is a primary means by which discrimination of all types reproduces and perpetuates within and across cultures (Van der Bom and Paterson, 2017), and it plays a major role in how we perceive the world. For instance, recent research reveals that sentences that frame one gender as the standard for the other, such as 'Girls are as good as boys at maths', can unintentionally perpetuate biases (Chestnut and Markman, 2018). As we will discuss later in the chapter, gender bias is evident in the language used in Article 1 of the UDHR and, like us, you may be conscious of how other forms of discriminatory language, intentional or otherwise, continue to persist in different forms across the world today.

Despite this rather gloomy start to the chapter, we would like to emphasise that language can also be a transformative tool for the greater good. Like us, you will have experienced the considerable potential for classroom language transactions to open mindsets and change negative self-concepts. Teachers should not underestimate the power of their language interactions to change children's and parents' lives in hugely positive ways. Sometimes, we are not aware until many years later of the little changes that our words and actions have instigated on a child's journey towards a more positive future. Like us, you may be lucky to receive a letter, an email or a spoken 'thank you' at some point in the future which will make you pause, reflect and be thankful that you took the time to listen and respond to that challenging child or despairing parent. Or in the case of teachers in Wendy's language network, look back in satisfaction at the time when they spent hours over the holiday transforming their classroom into an aircraft and learning farewell messages in 20 unfamiliar languages so that they could fly the Year 6 'leavers' away on a multicultural adventure.

In this chapter we consider how the pro-social and language-aware classroom can mitigate the potentially damaging impact of gender discrimination, bias and gender stereotyping on a child's developing sense of identity. We begin by discussing what we mean by *grammatical gender*, *gendered language*, *gender-inclusive language* (including *false gender-neutrality*) and *gender as a social construct* and then explore potential issues and the impact of misgendering. Within this, we examine practical responses to these issues viewed through the lens of classroom scenarios and provide opportunities for readers to reflect on their own experiences and classroom practice. Finally, we present a set of prompts to support gender-inclusive teaching.

Grammatical gender

Grammatical gender refers to a noun class system (which could be composed of two, three or more classes) in which the division of noun classes forms an agreement system with another aspect of the language, for example adjectives, articles, pronouns or verbs. The classes are often linked to biological sex, which is why many languages, for instance French and Spanish, refer to masculine (m.) and feminine (f.) forms. However, it is more helpful to think of grammatical gender as relating to language *patterns* rather than biological sex, and there are many different patterns of noun classes and associated agreements across languages. For instance, the German language has three noun classes: masculine, feminine and neuter. If you have never studied German, you may be surprised to learn that the word for girl, *das Mädchen*, is an example of a neuter noun. In German, nouns that are diminutives and end in *chen* are always neuter:

die Maus (mouse), das Mäuschen (little mouse)
das Brot (bread) das Brötchen (bread roll)

Mädchen is a diminutive of *Madg*, although this archaic base word has fallen out of use.

The Polish language has the same three main noun classes as German but also sorts nouns into animate and inanimate things. In the Polish language system, people and animals (things that move around) are animate, but other things (including plants) may be either animate or inanimate (Swan, 2008).

In Spanish, all nouns are either masculine or feminine. However, although there are some language patterns (note the endings of the masculine and feminine forms), it is not possible to predict the gender of all Spanish nouns:

- el gato (m.), la gata (f.)/the male cat, the female cat
- el chico (m.), la chica (f.)/the boy, the girl

Table 5.1 Exceptions to the Spanish *o/a* gender rule

Masculine nouns	Feminine nouns
el aroma – scent	la foto – photo
el dilemma – dilemma	la mano – hand
el Canadá – Canada	la radio – radio
el clima – climate	la moto – motorcycle
el diagrama – diagram	
el drama – drama	
el día – day	
el idioma – language	
el mapa – map	
el poema – poem	

For instance, we might assume that the word for 'dress' would be feminine, when in fact it is masculine:

- el vestido

For this reason, children need to learn the article (*el/la*) when a new word is introduced.

In general, Spanish nouns that end in o are masculine, and those that end in a are feminine, although there some exceptions including those listed in Table 5.1. A useful activity is to provide children with a list of Spanish words, some of which break the gender rule. Ask the children to order the list into masculine and feminine words using their knowledge of grammatical patterns, and then provide dictionaries so that they can check their responses. Allow time for lively discussion as the children discover the exceptions to the gender rule, and remind children of the principle that grammatical gender is about patterns (and exceptions) of agreements rather than about biological sex.

A similar activity that further illustrates this point is to provide a list of words in English and ask children to guess the grammatical gender of each word in Spanish before sorting the words into groups according to whether they think they are masculine or feminine. This second activity is also likely to generate some interesting debates and surprises when they subsequently check the words in the dictionary. For example, they may suggest that *dress* is a feminine word, although as we have highlighted, in Spanish *el vestido* is a masculine word. The following case study illustrates how useful such activities can be for confounding gender stereotypes.

Courage is a feminine word!

Language teacher Rachel Cunning (2018) explains that when we learn a new language with gendered nouns, we learn a new way to look at the world. She cites the example of her students learning that, although gendered masculine in the French language ('le courage'), the Spanish translation of *courage* is in fact feminine ('la valentía') (see also the 2018 article by Mangis, 'Courage is Feminine – and It's for All of Us).

> The explosion of sound in class is cacophonous when students learn that courage is feminine. Some students groan, 'No way!' as others declare, 'I knew it!' Still more say nothing because they are either too shocked or too delighted. It is telling of our own biases today that no other word in the activity elicits such a reaction as a feminine courage.
>
> (Cunning, 2018, no page)

The English language does not have grammatical gender in the way that other languages do, and consequently native English speakers often find it challenging to grasp the concept of gendered nouns and associated agreements when learning a second language. This is particularly the case if the language learner interprets grammatical gender primarily in terms of biological sex. As suggested earlier, it is more helpful to understand grammatical gender as referring to patterns of agreement between nouns and other elements of language and apply a 'best bet' approach (similar to the approach used in the English phonics classroom where spelling rules are only ever a best guess), by which we mean the learner should accept that there are likely to be exceptions to any language system 'rules' and/or new patterns emerging as language evolves over time.

Gendered language

Prior (2017) explains gendered language as language that has a bias towards a particular sex or social gender. Examples include gender-specific terms referring to professions or people, such as *fireman* or *waitress*, or using the masculine pronouns (*he, him, his*) to refer to people in general, for instance in the following statement: 'A footballer should know how to communicate with his team.'

The use of masculine forms in language, when referring to people in general or where the gender is unknown – for instance in phrases such as 'the common man' – has long been considered sexist in feminist philosophy since it leads to the invisibility of women (Weatherall, 2002). Furthermore, Saul and Diaz-Leon (2017, no page) highlight feminist objections to even gender-specific occupational terms like *manageress* and *lady doctor*, since these terms appear to presuppose maleness as a norm.

Gendered language is also evident in the previously mentioned sentence taken from the title of Chestnut and Markman's (2018, p. 2229) research study:

Girls are as good as boys at maths. (A)

The subject of the sentence is the noun *girls*, and if we take the boys out of the picture, the redacted statement has a complete meaning on its own:

Girls are good at maths. (B)

However, in sentence A the noun *boys* takes the form of the complement in the sentence, by which we mean it provides additional information to complete the intended meaning (i.e. the initial assumption that boys are better than girls at maths). It is when we compare both sentences and notice the function of the word forms in each that we highlight the subtle gender bias which is easy to miss (or unconsciously accept) on a first reading of the text.

Chestnut and Markman's (2018) research involved presenting adults with summaries of actual scientific evidence for gender equality in maths or verbal ability. However, the researchers manipulated whether the reference point in the statements of equality in the summaries was *girls* or *boys* and found adults attributed more natural ability to each gender when it was in the complement rather than subject position in the sentence.

Compare for example the following two statements and note the subtle change in gender bias as you read each one:

Boys' verbal ability is as good as girls'.
Girls' verbal ability is as good as boys'.

Consider your own experience of education. Were there any situations where you were consciously aware of gender biases or where, on looking back, you now recognise that biased perspectives were taking place? Is there any danger that any similar situations could arise in your current or future classes? How might you address/prevent these issues?

Can you think of other examples where common phrases are used which contain gender bias? How might you introduce this concept to your class? Or in a staff meeting?

Gender-inclusive language

The phrase *gender-inclusive language* is defined by the United Nations (no date) as 'speaking and writing in a way that does not discriminate against a particular sex, social gender or gender identity, and does not perpetuate gender stereotypes'. It provides its staff with a set of guidelines for using gender-inclusive language, which it recommends as a powerful tool to promote gender equality and eradicate gender bias in social and cultural attitudes. An example in the classroom could mean choosing to use gender non-specific terms to replace gendered nouns, which in turn avoids gendered future possibilities (the idea that certain professions are better suited as aspirations for either boys or girls). Table 5.2 gives some examples.

Table 5.2 Gendered and gender-neutral nouns

Gendered noun	Gender-neutral alternative(s)
man	person, individual
mankind	human beings, people, humankind
policeman	police officer
bin man	refuse collector
chairman	chairperson
air hostess/steward	flight attendant
fireman	fire fighter

The three aspects of gender that we are exploring here – grammatical gender, gendered language and gender-inclusive language – can be illustrated through revisiting Article 1 of the UDHR which we used as an opening quotation for this chapter: 'All human beings are born free and equal in dignity and rights. They are endowed with reason and conscience and should act towards one another in a spirit of brotherhood.'

In this quotation, the word *they* at the start of the second sentence has the function of a gender-neutral pronoun because its referent (the thing that the pronoun *they* stands for) is the plural noun phrase *human beings*, which is a gender-neutral noun. The noun phrase *human beings* is an example of a gender-inclusive term, whereas the word *brotherhood* is an example of gendered language since it implies a social and cultural masculine bias.

Another way of analysing the language of Article 1 is to note that although the use of the noun phrase *human beings* and its pronoun *they* seems to suggest that the statement applies to all genders equally (given that they are apparently used here as gender-neutral terms), the subsequent use of the term 'brotherhood' presents a male-biased perspective that appears to position 'mankind' before 'humankind'. This may in turn shift the balance of the degree of gendered equity towards the male in the unconscious mind of the reader. It could be argued, therefore, that the language in Article 1 is an example of what feminist philosophers would call 'false gender-neutrality' (Saul and Diaz-Leon, 2017). An encultured acceptance of such male-biased language traditions led to Mercier's feminist war cry, 'It is high time to let go of the illusion that "man" and his accomplice "he" are equitable representatives for women' (1995, p. 18).

The UDHR has been translated into 500 languages, and these translations can be found on the United Nations website. Article 1 in French reads as follows: 'Tous les êtres humains naissent libres et égaux en dignité et en droits. Ils sont doués de raison et de conscience et doivent agir les uns envers les autres dans un esprit de fraternité' (United Nations, 2020).

In this translation the pronoun *they* is translated as 'ils'. In French, *ils* is used for men, masculine nouns, and mixed gender groups and is the default pronoun for any plural groups, implying a linguistic and cultural male gender bias (although see also our earlier cautionary note about the danger of interpreting grammatical gender as relating to biological sex). In French, unlike the male plural pronoun *ils*, which can refer to mixed gender groups, the plural pronoun *elles* can only be used for a group of women and/or feminine nouns.

An interesting cross-curricular classroom activity would be to discuss the use of gendered language in Article 1 of the UDHR and consider alternative words or phrases to remove the gender bias. Possible examples for discussion might include *community* and *kinship*. Some other alternatives retain a gender bias, for example *fellowship* and *fraternity*. You may find in your discussions that you and the children are not satisfied with any of the available alternative words, and you might then prompt students to invent a new word to express the intended meaning. As we discuss in Chapter 4, we believe that teachers should encourage children to play with language to explore new ways of thinking and communicating. For these language creation/manipulation opportunities to be effective, teachers need to be building into their curriculum regular spaces for language-awareness discussions.

Gender as a social construct

Sunderland (2010) proposes two models of social gender: a people-based model and an ideas-based model. In the first model, people are socially shaped. For instance, this social shaping might relate to literacy practices within and outside school, including what adults read and write for children, what boys and girls read and write, and any differences in the way adults communicate with individuals or groups of children or other adults (2010, p. 23). In recent years several of our student teachers have shown an interest in a people-based construct of social gender and have conducted research projects around gendered literacy practice in schools, for instance evaluating the diversity of books available in the school library. Their interest stems from evidence from existing research suggesting that there has been a clear gender bias in children's books, as the following case study illustrates.

> McCabe et al. (2011, p. 197) analysed the representation of males and females in the titles and main characters of over 5,500 children's books published in the United States throughout the 20th century. They found that males were represented nearly twice as often as females in titles and 1.6 times as often as central characters. The authors describe these disparities as 'symbolic annihilation'. Interestingly, although the gender disparity came close to levelling out in the 1990s in books with human characters, the imbalance remained for books with animal characters with a significant disparity of nearly two to one. These findings clearly have implications for children's understanding of gender.

In their second model, Sunderland describes gender as 'an idea (or set of ideas) about men/women, boys/girls and gender relations' (2010, p. 29). Sunderland argues that this construct shifts the emphasis from biological sex to a focus on language discourse (*what* is said as opposed to *who* said *what*). The following case study provides an example in the form of a teacher research project that focuses on a study of gender in language discourse.

> *Farah's project*
>
> Farah decides to carry out an investigation into children's perceptions of gender through the reading of a gender typical and a gender atypical picture book. She starts with the gender typical text – *Cinderella* – and after the reading, records children's discussions, noticing that the language includes examples of gender bias and stereotyping. Farah then reads an atypical picture book – which she classifies as a text which redefines gender roles. This chosen text is *The Paper Bag Princess* by Robert Munsch (2009) whose main character, Princess Elizabeth, does not fit the perfect picture of a princess. Princess Elizabeth is about to marry Prince Roland when a dragon

captures him, destroys her castle and burns all her clothes. The princess rescues the prince dressed only in a paper bag. The prince is unimpressed with her un-princess-like appearance, but Elizabeth makes it clear that she really does not care!

After the reading of the second text, Farah again encourages discussion. When she analyses the children's responses, she notices that this time there are some shifts in the children's response to gender representations in the story with some children openly challenging gender stereotypes.

As we have established, language is a primary means by which sexism and gender discrimination can perpetuate within and across cultures. Gender stereotypes are reflected in the lexical choices of everyday communication (Menagatti and Rubini, 2017) and internalised by children from a young age. As teachers, we all bring both conscious and unconscious biases to our classrooms, but pro-social and language-aware learning settings can help to uncover and avoid the gender stereotypes that have the potential to impact in a negative way on a child's developing sense of identity. Picture books are a powerful way of challenging bias and gender stereotypes, because they tend to provoke interest and discussion.

Can you think of other pedagogies, practices and resources that might be used to get children thinking and talking about these issues? Are there scenarios that you could set up across the curriculum subjects to promote these ideas?

The impact of misgendering

Often, a key concern of those working in education is making mistakes about gender which might be considered insulting or sexist or insensitive. This would obviously never be deliberate, and we need to keep in mind that we will not get everything right all of the time! It is more about keeping our minds open to possibilities and listening to the voices of others. We start with a case study which provides a powerful example of how we can learn from others and move our thinking forward.

Meera

Meera is a transgender teacher trainee on an undergraduate teaching programme. Meera is a popular member of the tutor group and has developed a trusting relationship with the English tutor, contributing enthusiastically to class discussions. Meera attends a preparation for placement grammar workshop led by the English tutor, during which the class explore subject/verb and noun/pronoun agreement. Students look at and critique examples of grammar test questions where pupils are expected to tick the correct answer and then apply these to their own assignment writing. For instance, they consider the common error of using a singular verb after the use of *et al.* when referring to more than one author. For example, 'Cobb et al. (2020) suggests' is an example of incorrect subject/verb agreement. The phrase is better expressed as 'Cobb et al. (2020) suggest'.

Students give examples from their own assignments where they have assumed a female writer was male, admitting that this is usually because they have not read the original text and do not, therefore, know the author's first name(s). The feedback from the marker has highlighted that they have used the wrong pronoun (*he* instead of *she*) or that their use of *et al.* requires the plural pronoun *they*.

At the end of the workshop, Meera approaches the tutor, apologises for not engaging in the noun/pronoun discussion and talks about feeling awkward during the last part of the workshop. Meera sensitively explains to the tutor that some people prefer to use the pronoun *they* to refer to themselves, and Meera is uncomfortable about any assumptions of an author's preferred gender. The tutor thanks Meera for sharing these feelings and immediately reflects on her own assumption that Meera is a feminine name and therefore that Meera would choose to use a feminine pronoun. She also considers her own marking comments and resolves to review the language feedback she gives.

> Review the case study. Consider the use of gendered pronouns and gender-neutral language and the relationship between the tutor and trainee. What impact might this have on your own practice?

In this case study, if the term 'transgender' had not been used in the first sentence, you might have made an assumption about Meera's gender based on your cultural understanding of common patterns of girls' names ending in *a*. There are in fact many male names ending in *a* (examples include Joshua, Hosea, Ezra and Mustafa). In India, Meera is a girl's name (Meera Bai was a popular Hindu mystical poet) and has the meaning 'prosperous' in Sanskrit. Of course, you do not have to be of Indian heritage to choose to call your child, or yourself, a name of Indian origin.

In this case study, the tutor has made what Brookfield (1995) would term a 'paradigmatic assumption'. Paradigmatic assumptions are the structuring assumptions we use to order the world into fundamental categories, and Brookfield suggests they are the hardest of all assumptions to uncover. Such assumptions can lead to misgendering, whereby we refer to someone using a word (typically a pronoun or form of address) that does not correctly reflect the gender with which they identify.

The mental health charity Young Minds (2020) points out that gender is a spectrum rather than a binary concept and that people may express themselves in different ways. They might self-identify as male or female, or in the middle (non-binary) and for others, where they are on this spectrum may change or fluctuate at different times. Other terms used by people who identify as non-binary include 'gender fluid' or 'gender queer'.

The solution to avoid misgendering is not as simple as just removing all gendered word forms. I (Wendy) am a cis-gendered female. By this I mean I have a sense of gender which corresponds with my birth sex, and being a woman is an important part of, but does not wholly define, my identity. Some schools have taken to removing gendering labels, for instance by replacing signs for boys and girls toilets with labels that say, 'gender neutral', sometimes with additional signage to indicate accessible facilities. This is a well-intentioned decision but could be considered misgendering, alienating and unnecessary. If the intention is to provide facilities that everyone can use, then it could be argued that a sign identifying the space as a toilet should suffice within an inclusive setting.

As Young Minds (2020) points out, having a sense of identity helps children to be resilient. Children who are resilient are better equipped to self-regulate and less likely to suffer from mental health issues. However, while people may identify with either 'she', 'he' or 'they' pronouns, these labels alone should not define us. As we have already considered, there is much more to our identity than a grammatical label.

What can language teachers do to avoid the use of discriminatory language and behaviours in the classroom?

Boroditsky's (2018) TED talk 'How Languages Shape the Way we Think' is a thought-provoking overview of some of the interesting findings of research data collected from around the world that suggest that the languages we speak shape the way we view our world. Boroditsky's own studies – including research with the Australian aboriginal group Kuuk Thaayorre who, instead of using the equivalent of 'right', 'left', 'front', 'back' to define space relative to the observer, use cardinal direction forms (north, south, east, west) – suggest that people who speak different languages think differently and that grammar can profoundly affect how we see the world and how we reason about events (Boroditsky, 2009). To illustrate these cultural differences in perception, consider how easy you would find it to describe that itch on your lower left leg: the one north, northeast of your ankle bone!

Unless orienteering is your obsession and/or you live in a transparent tent under the stars, you are unlikely to feel a permanent sense of East-West orientation like the Kuuk Thaayorre people. However, the more we are aware of how language – and for the purpose of this chapter, specifically gendered language – can shape our perceptions, the more able we are to make our classrooms fully inclusive. Establishing a classroom ethos that is open to different preferences and cultural perceptions, that acknowledges that sometimes we all make mistakes and that promotes active listening is a good place to start. We can see, for instance, in the Meera case study, that the tutor had clearly established a positive classroom ethos built on trusting relationships. This safe learning environment in turn enabled Meera to express her emotions, and both the tutor and the other students to uncover their own paradigmatic assumptions.

Virginia: You mention here the importance of a positive classroom ethos, Wendy, and how this needs to build on trusting relationships. Are there any specific activities you use to create this ethos, when you first meet a group of children or university students?

Wendy: One of the first things I try to do is to get to know the group and help them to get to know each other – even if they have been learning as a group for some time, I do not assume that they know everyone's name or anything about each other's strengths. For instance, on a postgraduate professional studies programme, I mix up my students on the first day and ask them to talk to their new partners to find out something that they are good at so that they can introduce each other to the class. Everyone is usually really humble, so I model something simple that I am good at, like rolling my tongue from side to side – which apparently is quite rare and gets the class laughing as they all have a go! Everyone then introduces their partner in a positive way – usually students 'big up' their partners' skills, and we quickly find out who will be bringing in homemade cakes, fixing computer glitches, offering personal fitness training and who will help them organise their lives during a very hectic year's teaching and assessment schedule. We also uncover some truly impressive talents, such as the knife-thrower, the student who speaks seven languages and the amazingly flexible trapeze artist – the latter being one of my co-tutors!

At the start of the second session, I describe to the group different facets of my character using phrases in the form of 'I'm a tongue twisting night owl', 'I'm an accident-prone runaway', 'I'm a rainbow-salad-loving mum', 'I'm a posh friend' – I explain that the latter phrase is how a child in my last class described me to his mum after the many chats we had outside the classroom – the only time to my knowledge that I have been called 'posh'! We then go round the room with the students describing a facet of themselves in the same way, and as they call their phrases out, I capture words on a flip chart and sort these into related categories such as 'family', 'nature', 'adventure' and 'food/drink'. The students then use the categories to organise themselves into similarity groups (although there are of course often quite contrasting interests within each group – for instance the lovers and haters of marmite!), and together they then agree upon a set of group working rules. We compare each group's rules and make sure that words and phrases such as 'encourage one another', 'actively listen', 'be brave' and 'laugh' are positively framed, celebrated and remembered across the year. Sadly, some students reveal that this is the first time they have had the opportunity to co-create their own working-together rules.

Virginia: Some great ideas there, Wendy – thank you. I have had experiences where both young children and university-age students have commented on their peers' behaviours – both positively and negatively – with specific reference to gender e.g. 'We never get a word in edgeways because boys' voices are louder, and they dominate' and 'It's always good to be in a group with girls because they are kinder and more caring'. How would you tackle this Wendy, to address gender bias without restricting their right to have opinions and feelings?

Wendy: I think there are two responses to this, one that is proactive and the other reactive. The proactive response is being prepared for the fact that learners are likely to enter the class with some gendered and other assumptions and to respond to this by establishing from the beginning an ethos aimed at confounding these potential stereotypes. For instance, by introducing some of the things we have mentioned earlier, such as encouraging learners to step into completely different shoes through drama and role-play activities, selecting gender atypical class story books that promote non-gendered possibilities and providing ample opportunities for learners to get to know each other and work with different people.

An example of a reactive response would be to listen for the emotions behind the statement and help the learner to reframe the situation with an empathic response. For instance, with young adults I might respond to the first example with:

> I am sorry to hear that you are feeling frustrated today. Thanks for letting me know how things are going for you. I noticed myself that a couple of students in one group were a bit loud today too, and I have some ideas for mixing everyone up next week. Let me know how they work out. Interestingly, I have the opposite situation in another class where there are a group of boys who tend to sit together and are really quiet. It's strange how every group is so different; hopefully mixing up the students will work in that class too!

For the second example, in a primary class I might say:

> It sounds like you are really happy with the group you are working with this lesson. It is great that we have so many kind and caring children in the class. Foysal was really kind in maths too, wasn't he when he showed everybody how to [describe specific instance]. I wish I had someone like Foysal in my group when I was learning maths at school.

So, I do not think you always have to be confrontationally reactive about gendered statements; in these kinds of situations, persistently reframing/helping learners to reframe statements can be a powerful strategy for encouraging everyone to view things from different perspectives.

Virginia: Many thanks, Wendy – such useful suggestions.

96 Language and gender

You may find the following prompts helpful in checking that you are using gender-inclusive language in your transactions with children, parents and colleagues.

1. *Be language-aware*
   - Notice when you are using gendered language;
   - Check whether your language choices exclude any groups or individuals.
2. *Reverse the gender*
   - When using gendered phrases, try reversing the gender. Does a change of term from masculine to feminine change the meaning or emphasis of the sentence? Does the sentence sound strange? For example, as a child learning to read music Wendy was taught a mnemonic, 'Every Good Boy Deserves Football' (EGBDF), to help her remember the notes on the lines of the treble clef stave. Back then, only boys were expected to try out for the school football team. How might changing the masculine term **boy** to the feminine noun **girl** change the meaning or emphasis of the statement? In this instance, the power of the mnemonic to help with reading music would be lost, but it would take very little effort to change the two nouns in this example.
3. *Recognise and avoid making assumptions*
   - Family and marital relationships: If you think you are making assumptions, use **partner** instead of **husband** and **wife**, **parent** instead of **father** or **mother**;
   - Pronouns: If you are not sure of a person's pronoun preference, make gender-neutral choices, such as making nouns and pronouns plural.
4. *Avoid the gender-binary*
   - As we have uncovered, many languages and cultures are rooted in a gender binary system which can lead us to develop binary assumptions about people and things (assuming that they are either this or that). Research the history and language of gender diversity. See for instance the Stonewall Getting Started Toolkits for Early Years, Primary and Secondary LGBT Inclusive Education (Hall, 2016).
5. *Promote possibilities not determined by gender*
   - Help children to see that possibilities in life are not determined by gender, for example by using gender-neutral language for professions.

How do you explain grammatical gender to your classes?

Does any of the language you currently use reinforce gender bias or stereotypes?

How gender-inclusive are the literacy practices in your school? For instance, how are diversity and non-gendered possibilities represented in the stories you use?

Summary

- *Grammatical gender* refers to a noun class system and is best understood as referring to patterns of subject and other word-form agreement rather than biological sex;
- *Gendered language* is language that has a bias towards a particular sex or social gender;

- *Gender-inclusive language* is speaking and writing in a way that does not discriminate against a particular sex, social gender or gender identity;
- Attempts at *gender-neutrality* can be exclusive, for instance when they perpetuate an encultured gender bias;
- Pro-social classrooms which are founded on trusting relationships are safe places for children to explore their identity, emotions and gender-related language questions;
- Teachers who are language-aware, conscious of human bias and who promote possibilities not determined by gender are well prepared to establish gender-inclusive classrooms that can literally transform children's lives.

References

Boroditsky, L. (2009) 'How does our language shape the way we think?' Available at www.edge.org/conversation/lera_boroditsky-how-does-our-language-shape-the-way-we-think (Accessed 07.08.2020).

Boroditsky, L. (2018) 'How language shapes the way we think', Available at www.youtube.com/watch?v=RKK7wGAYP6k (Accessed 28.07.2020).

Brookfield (1995) *Becoming a Critically Reflective Teacher*, San Francisco: Jossey-Bass.

Chestnut, E. K. & Markman, E. M. (2018) '"Girls are as good as boys at math" implies that boys are probably better: A study of expressions of gender equality', *Cognitive Science*, 42, 7, pp. 2229–2249.

Cunning, R. (2018) 'Engendering inclusivity in a language class', Available at www.tolerance.org/magazine/engendering-inclusivity-in-a-language-class (Accessed 28.07.2020).

Hall, F. (2016) 'Getting started a toolkit for preventing and tackling homophobic, biphobic and transphobic bullying in primary schools', Available at www.stonewall.org.uk/system/files/getting_started_toolkit_-_primary.pdf (Accessed 05.08.2020).

Mangis, K. (2018) 'Courage is feminine – and it's for all of us', Available at https://goodmenproject.com/featured-content/courage-is-feminine-and-its-for-all-of-us-chwm/#:~:text=Courage%20is%20faith%2C%20discipline%2C%20thoughtfulness,It's%20within%20all%20of%20us (Accessed 28.07.2020).

McCabe, J. Fairchild, E. Grauerholz, L. Pescosolido, B. A. & Tope, D. (2011) 'Gender in twentieth-century children's books: Patterns of disparity in titles and central characters', *Gender & Society*, 25, 2, pp. 197–226.

Menegatti, M. & Rubini, M. (2017) 'Gender bias and sexism in language', *Oxford Research Encyclopedias*, Available at https://oxfordre.com/communication/view/10.1093/acrefore/9780190228613.001.0001/acrefore-9780190228613-e-470 (Accessed 05.08.2020).

Mercier, A. (1995) 'A perverse case of the contingent a priori: On the logic of emasculating language (A reply to Dawkins and Dummett)', *Philosophical Topics*, 23, 2, pp. 221–259.

Munsch, R. (2009) *The Paper Bag Princess*, Toronto: Annick Press.

O'Connor, T. (2014) 'Debating human rights – universal or relative to culture?' Available at https://developmenteducation.ie/ (Accessed 05.08.2020).

Prior, J. (2017) 'Teachers, what is gendered language?' Available at www.britishcouncil.org/voices-magazine/what-is-gendered-language#:~:text=Does%20'gendered%20language'%20mean%20words,e.g.%2C%20'air%20hostess'%3F&text=So%20gendered%20language%20is%20commonly,particular%20sex%20or%20social%20gender (Accessed 28.07.2020).

Saul, J. & Diaz-Leon, E. (2017) 'Feminist philosophy of language', *Stanford Encyclopedia of Philosophy*, Available at https://plato.stanford.edu/index.html (Accessed 05.08.2020).

Sunderland, J. (2010) *Language, Gender and Children's Fiction*, London: Continuum.

Swan, O. E. (2008) *Polish Verbs and Essentials of Grammar*, New York: McGraw Hill.

United Nations (2020) 'Universal declaration of human rights', Available at www.un.org/en/universal-declaration-human-rights/ (Accessed 05.08.2020).

The United Nations (n.d.) 'Gender inclusive language guidelines', Available at www.un.org/en/gender-inclusive-language/guidelines.shtml (Accessed 28.07.2020).

Van der Bom, I. & Paterson, L. (eds.) (2017) *Journal of Language and Discrimination*, Available at https://journals.equinoxpub.com/JLD/index (Accessed 07.08.2020).

Weatherall, A. (2002) *Gender Language and Discourse*, London: Routledge.

Willmott-Harrop, E. (2003) 'The universal declaration's bias towards Western democracies', Available at https://libertyandhumanity.com/themes/international-human-rights-law/the-universal-declarations-bias-towards-western-democracies/ (Accessed 05.08.2020).

Young Minds (2020) 'Supporting your child with gender identity issues', Available at https://youngminds.org.uk/find-help/for-parents/parents-guide-to-support-a-z/parents-guide-to-support-gender-identity-issues/ (Accessed 28.07.2020).

6 Languages across the curriculum

To have two languages is to possess a second soul.

(Charlemagne)

Introduction

When I (Wendy) started working as a tutor on a pilot language-specialist primary-teacher education programme, I was also employed as a local authority cross-phase languages advisor. At my university end-of-year appraisal, when we reviewed my achievements across the year, my appraiser encouraged me to separate the different aspects of my working lives, but I simply could not. Most achievements in one role were interdependent with the other, and during the working week I would regularly switch focus as I made links between the two complementary jobs. Since then, I have never been able to settle with one employment, and although juggling too many roles at once is not good for our mental health, I am a strong advocate for the wellbeing benefits of being able to switch focus in times of stress. Of course, juggling different roles only works well when you have an adequate degree of skills and knowledge in each area and can make valid connections.

Evidence from neuroscience suggests that most people are not actually multi-tasking when they think they are (Crenshaw, 2008) and are more likely to be switching quickly between tasks. You may have noticed yourself poorly 'multi-tasking' if, like me, you have ever found yourself the only one left in a virtual meeting room when you were trying to engage in the conversation while responding to some urgent emails! Numerous business guides warn that mind-switching distractions can have a negative impact on workplace productivity (Mackay, 2019; Toren, 2017; Yang, 2019), and many of my colleagues find their homes are full of distractions and prefer to work in the office. I, however work best at home in my study, where I can avoid noise and other office interruptions, and I am particularly good at forgetting to take the washing out of the machine! Unlike some of my colleagues who have diary days and specific times for writing and seem to stick to their schedules, I am more likely to switch to other work (or the gardening) on planned writing days while I mull over my thoughts, gradually making connections until finally the spark ignites, usually around mid- to late evening when at last I find my creative all-absorbing flow (Csikszentmihalyi, 1988).

You may well ask how these introductory autobiographical mullings (Wendy thinks she may have invented a new noun, 'a mulling', although we expect it has been 'thunk' before) fit

DOI: 10.4324/9781003129738-7

with the chapter title! The answer is that the ideas of multi-tasking and combining activities lead us to some questions about the best way to structure language teaching and learning. For instance:

- Which works best, discrete or embedded language teaching?
- What are the cognitive and wellbeing impacts of multi-tasking in the bilingual classroom?
- How can the language teacher make connections with the wider curriculum?

Before exploring these questions, we begin the chapter by positing that a positive pedagogue is essential in a classroom that promotes a cross-curricular approach to language learning. Next, we explore Content and Language Integrated Learning (CLIL) theory to provide a rationale for embedding the target language across the curriculum. We then move on to explore the three questions listed here, beginning by considering some findings from cognitive science, including the benefits of interleaving content and the impact of effective use of practice strategies to enhance learning. The idea of linguistic multi-tasking is introduced and the effect of this on bilinguals' wellbeing and executive functioning skills. We end the chapter with examples of simple ways to embed language learning across the school day in language-aware classrooms, including in the maths classroom.

The positive pedagogue and the cross-curricular classroom

In previous chapters we have made a case for positioning emotional health at the heart of language learning and teaching, and we have highlighted links between language and wellbeing. Yet, prior to the millennium, applied linguistic research paid scant regard to the role of emotions in the language classroom, with Swain describing them as 'the elephants in the room – poorly studied, poorly understood, seen as inferior to rational thought' (2013, p. 195). However, since 2000, an increasing focus on emotions in language learning has led to a better understanding of the impact of the positive and negative teacher and learner, and recently Dewaele et al. (2019) reviewed what they describe as a 'flowering of positive psychology' in research into foreign-language teaching and acquisition. In the conclusion of their research, the authors adopted interesting language choices in capturing the research 'landscape' by describing their findings through the emotion-bound lens of a photographer who selects pictures for a unique album of images framed by personal, in-the-moment preferences.

Positive psychology (PP) is not about blotting out parts of the landscape and denying that problems exist. Our classrooms will not always be the positive places we hope them to be, and language subject leaders face many challenges in developing and delivering an effective and positive languages policy, which we explore in Chapter 9. However, PP shifts the focus away from the negative to positive topics such as hope, courage, wellbeing, creativity, flourishing, possibilities; and in the classroom this relates to the goals of a positive pedagogy.

We relate Dewaele et al.'s emotion-bound photographer metaphor to Barnes' (2018) emphasis in his book *Applying Cross-Curricular Approaches Creatively* on the unique nature of the physical, emotional and relational environment within which we alone exist. In co-authoring our book, we are aware that we are like-minded teachers and writers; yet we inhabit our own unique worlds. The sense of knowing ourselves and understanding how our own autobiographies shape our perspectives, values and beliefs is one of three issues which Barnes (ibid.) argues feed into a positive pedagogy. In his book he refers to the positive pedagogue: one who 'encourages children . . . to draw positive messages from their interactions with ideas, others, subjects and experiences' (ibid., p. 18). We believe that much of what we are arguing for throughout this book is linked to this concept of the positive pedagogue.

The positive pedagogue thinks innovatively about using language across the curriculum and goes beyond setting grammar sentence practices or worksheets that hint at creative writing but are in reality more focused around the teacher's ideas or are, as Didau (2012) argues, simply something for the children to do. Instead, the positive pedagogue builds 'a positive social, emotional and physical environment in class' (Barnes, 2018, p. 18), linking positivity, creativity and cross-curricularity in the 'connecting curriculum'.

Throughout this book we hope that you will find some examples of simple activities that might trigger those wonderful learning experiences where either enthusiastic group chatter or the silence of attentive thinking and writing are signs that the sparks are alight and the children are absorbed in their own worlds and purposes. We suggest that these motivating opportunities do not require linguistic expertise, nor do they need extensive resourcing, although they often involve taking risks and moving beyond usual language-topic contexts. To illustrate this point, we include a case study which illustrates the motivating power of choice and challenge in the language learning classroom.

In their first undergraduate year of a three-year primary teacher education course, students attend four seminars on languages teaching. Most of the students have not participated in or observed languages teaching in the classroom. Some are unsure whether languages are even taught in their placement schools. Most describe themselves as monolinguists despite many having studied one or more languages at their secondary schools. Their tutors work hard to help them see the value and importance of language teaching and their own language strengths and to engage them in fun, practical activities with the hope that they will try them out with their classes.

The final seminar looks at progression in language learning during which the students are given examples of simple creative writing activities they might do with their pupils and are told at the beginning of the session that their 'exit ticket' for this final seminar will be to produce some writing of their own in a foreign language. Most look dubious and some even sigh.

Towards the end of the session, the tutor explains the writing task. The expectation is simple: write something, anything, and in any language other than their L1. Students are told that they can use any of the ideas that have been shared in the lesson or they could create wordsearches, write shopping lists, love letters (lots of giggles!), acrostic poems or concrete (shape) poetry. They can use their phones, iPads, laptops and online dictionaries or just their notes from language activities during any of the seminars.

Students are reminded of the exit ticket – their only means of escape! There is a momentary pause, a few blank looks and stares at the clock as lunch time approaches, but many students are already underway. Others are sharing blank pieces of paper,

> coloured pens and rulers and frantically searching back through their notes. Never have the students looked so focused, absorbed and excited about languages. Some write Spanish chat-up lines to try out on their planned summer holiday; others create shopping lists in Portuguese for a student party. Some work together; some on their own. One student attempts a love letter in Chinese, switches to Italian and his female peers whisper, 'Aw!' when he happily reads it out to the tutor. While some proudly share, others prefer not to but assure the tutor they are writing. When lunch time arrives, some students appear not to notice and carry on; others say they want to finish theirs later. All leave smiling.

In the case study, the tutor demonstrates characteristics of the positive pedagogue, illustrating to the students the importance of choice, agency, trust, purpose and risk-taking in the language classroom.

> Before we explore the theory and research evidence for cross-curricular and creative approaches to language learning within the connecting curriculum, take a moment to consider your own autobiography and how your experiences, values and beliefs connect with the way you relate to the curriculum. What are your strengths and most important positive life experiences? To what extent do you draw on these in your own teaching? What are the aspects you consider your weaknesses or things you do not like? How do these impact on your planning and teaching?

Content and language integrated learning

By now you will have a strong sense of our holistic take on language learning, for instance in the connections between learning another language and its interrelated cultures and understanding our own language, identity and place in the world. Despite having heard many English teachers at primary languages training sessions state that they are non-linguists, we agree with Hood's (2018, p. 1) suggestion that 'all teachers are teachers of languages'. Also, all language subject specialists – who may be timetabled only for the subject lessons – need to see themselves as teaching across the wider curriculum, in the sense that language is taught through topics in addition to the close ties with personal, social and health education.

An example of conscious language, subject and social/emotional integrated teaching is the way teachers might support pupils with English as an additional language to participate in group presentations (for instance in the science lesson) through the provision of speaking prompts, such as 'We predicted that. . ./First we. . ./Then we. . ./We found that. . .'. This is also an example of Content and Language Integrated Learning (CLIL), a term first coined by David Marsh in 1994 under the auspices of the European Commission and which is described as 'a dual-focused educational approach in which an additional language is used for the learning and teaching of both content and language' (Mehisto, Marsh, and Frigols, 2008, p. 9). CLIL teaching is often used to describe bilingual contexts where subject content is taught through an additional language, but where, in reality, there may be little integration of content and language actually taking place (Morton and Linares, 2017). Here, however, we refer to the term with a focus on language integration in common with recent CLIL researchers (Linares, Morton, and Whittaker, 2012; Baten, Van Hiel, and De Cuypere, 2020). By this we mean that language awareness is at the heart of effective CLIL teaching and that development in the target language is supported through meaningful contexts which lead to conscious learning of the meaning of words and phrases.

Coyle, Hood, and Marsh (2010) suggest that there are numerous drivers behind a CLIL approach, which can be either reactive or proactive responses to perceived challenges or problems. We explore two examples of drivers and responses in the following text.

Example of a reactive response:

- An official language is adopted as the medium for part/all of schooling in countries where the language of instruction is foreign to the majority of learners, for instance some countries in sub-Saharan Africa.

The following case study provides an example of this.

Mozambique

- 'Vanu vohevohe vaidile n'chilambo valendene. Vanijaliwa ulimala vene. Pavele vanu pave na ulongo' – Article 1 of the Universal Declaration of Human Rights translated in Makonde, a Bantu language spoken by people in Northern Mozambique along the river Ruvuma (source omniglot.com).

Mozambique (formerly Portuguese East Africa – *África Oriental Portuguesa*) is a multilingual country which adopted Portuguese as an official language. Languages of the World- www.ethnologue.com – cites 43 languages including numerous Bantu languages spoken across the country, and most Mozambique people are fluent in more than one language. Eighty percent of residents in urban Mozambique speak Portuguese, and with Portuguese used as the main medium for learning in primary education, it is the more-educated Mozambiquan people who are fluent in the language.

However, 90 percent of children arrive at school without knowing the Portuguese language, and in 1993 Mozambique introduced a pilot bilingual education project. 'Bilingual education' refers in this context to the simultaneous teaching of Portuguese and one of initially two Bantu languages, Cinyanja and Xichangana, increasing to 16 indigenous languages by 2009. Henrikson (2010, p. 2) describes this approach as a 'Transitional Model of Bilingual Education' whereby the key objective is to develop pupils' initial literacy in their mother tongue (L1) at the same time as building oracy in the L2 (Portuguese), so that at a later stage, pupils can transfer the skills developed in the L1 to L2. The Mozambique Ministry of Education and Human Development cites the main benefits of bilingual education as increased commitment and engagement amongst learners, a feeling of being respected and a reduction in communication challenges when both L1 and L2 are used to support understanding of the topic (UNESCO, 2020).

Despite these benefits, Henrikson highlights a few challenges to the extension of the programme, which in its current form is limited to rural areas. These include high linguistic diversity of urban areas and persisting negative perceptions of the value of mother tongue education in African languages. Henrikson links these perceptions to what Kamwangamalu (2008) refers to as 'the ideology of development', an ideology which considers literacy is better achieved through the ex-colonial languages, such as English and Portuguese, in the contentious belief that African languages lack 'the complexity to be used in higher domains such as education' (Henrikson, 2010, p. 2).

Think about the foreign language(s) taught in your setting. What is the rationale for the choice of language(s)? How is this choice explained to the children/parents? Are there any arguments for selecting one or more different languages?

Example of a proactive response

- CLIL is introduced as a solution to enhance language learning or some other aspect of educational, social or personal development.

The following case study describes this type of response.

When I (Wendy) first started working as a local authority languages advisor, I was also employed part-time as a leading teacher at a local primary school where my roles included covering a Newly Qualified Teacher's (NQT) mixed-aged Year 3/4 class for two afternoons a week during the NQT's weekly planning and preparation time. Prior to me joining the class, the NQT had taught the class some basic French words but was not confident in developing language learning further at that time. I agreed to participate in a CLIL trial – a partnership initiative between Canterbury Christ Church University, and Kent and Medway local authorities – to investigate the benefits of the approach to enhance language learning in the primary and secondary context. Prior to commencing the trial, I spent a few afternoons during the first half of the spring term with the Year 3/4 class, developing their confidence in French. I agreed with the NQT to deliver the second half-term science unit on conductors and insulators through the medium of French, while the class teacher taught the complementary design technology unit 'Torches' in English.

I carried out a SWOT analysis (Strengths, Weaknesses, Opportunities and Threats) to review the potential benefits and challenges of the curriculum intervention (see Table 6.1).

Table 6.1 SWOT analysis

Strengths	Weaknesses
• Wendy was experienced in developing and teaching cross-curricular learning opportunities and embedding language learning with her previous classes. • Wendy's language skills enabled her to search for examples of French primary-school learning activities within the topic. • Wendy had the support and trust of the head teacher. • Some science content could be duplicated in English in the design technology lessons.	• Class had minimal knowledge of basic French. • Language was not high-profile in the school. • No existing resources or schemes were available for teaching the English science curriculum topic through French. • This was the first time Wendy had taught the science unit in either English or French. • No additional adults were available to support the CLIL sessions.
Opportunities	*Threats*
• Time allocation for French could be increased. • Outcome of the trial had potential to support a rationale for integrating language learning. • Purposeful use of French could support motivation and progression in language learning.	• The class may not have invested in lessons delivered by a cover teacher. • The class were used to a curriculum largely delivered as discrete subjects. • The dual focus might lead to cognitive overload. • The class were a mixed age group at different science and language starting points. • The class were involved in an end-of-term production which impacted on timetable planning.

My starting points for planning included identifying the following:

- Science subject objectives;
- Key vocabulary and language structures;
- Knowledge about language (KAL);
- Language-learning strategies.

I also had to consider the balance between L1 and L2 during teaching input, agree with the pupils' rules for L1 and L2 use in the science lesson and explain to parents the rationale for the CLIL trial.

Language learning strategies included:

- Repetition of key words and phrases;
- Visual and aural cues;
- Use of drama (for instance a human circuit circle game);
- Linking to prior learning (e.g. through gesture, rhyme and song);
- Involving the children in the learning intentions through a familiar start to the lesson - e.g. explaining the objectives using the target language through careful use of words and phrases and with visual and aural cues;
- Use of writing frames;
- Use of activities to clarify key concepts e.g. completing tables, matching activities;
- Displays labelled in L1 and the target language.

The Department for Children, Schools and Families' Leading Teacher Programme from 2008-2011 encouraged teachers to write case reports in the 'What Works Well' format, sharing real examples of how learning and practice had improved through lesson study (DfE, 2011). The outcomes of the CLIL intervention described in this case study were published as part of this initiative on the National Strategies 'What Works Well' website in a study titled 'Bright Sparks - Primary Languages through Science (CLIL Trial)' (Cobb, 2008).

The study outcomes included:

- Increased time allocated to the target language;
- Progression in the target language (for instance children guessed negative structures that they needed to describe electrical circuits which prompted future learning);
- Increased writing outcomes (for instance a Year 3 reluctant writer in English enthusiastically produced extended sentences in French);
- Motivation for language learning: 'I prefer learning French and science together. I really enjoy the games and activities that help me remember things';
- Maintained attainment in science and cognitive challenge: 'I understood the science just as well, but it made my brain work harder'.

Although the 'What Works Well' lesson study reports were subject to peer review prior to publishing, they were not intended as examples of rigorous research. Instead, they were aimed at collaborative sharing of effective practice in schools and providing suggestions of things teachers might consider if they were planning to introduce similar interventions, such as how to involve parent and pupil voice.

> Consider this case study on a relational and emotional level. What pro-social interventions would need to happen within and outside of the class context to elicit the positive language and science outcomes?
>
> Have you been motivated to volunteer your personal time to plan/support a new initiative? What were your personal drivers?

CLIL national guidelines

In response to the growing national and international interest in CLIL approaches, in 2007 the then DfES set up an Advisory Group for CLIL with a brief to provide guidance and strategic advice on developments in Content and Language Integrated Learning in England (Coyle, Holmes, and King, 2009a). In addition to membership from the languages community, the Advisory Group also included representation from the Geographical Association, other curriculum specialists, the British Council and SSAT (the Schools, Students and Teachers Network). A key outcome of their discussions was the publication of 'Towards an integrated curriculum - CLIL National Statement and Guidelines' (ibid). In developing the guidelines, the group drew on Coyle's (2005) '4C's Curriculum' to help teachers identify the benefits to teachers and learners in relation to four specific dimensions (see Table 6.2).

Table 6.2 4C's Curriculum

Content	Integrating content from across the curriculum through high-quality language interaction
Cognition	Engaging learners through creativity, higher-order thinking and knowledge processing
Communication	Using language to learn and mediate ideas, thoughts and values
Culture	Interpreting and understanding the significance of content and language and their contribution to identity and citizenship

Source: (Coyle, 2005 in Coyle, Holmes, and King, 2009b, p. 12)

In Chapter 3 we explored discussions around culture, identity and the communication of ideas, thoughts and values. If we now consider the Content aspect of the 4C's framework, the authors argue that CLIL:

- Provides learning contexts which are relevant to the needs and interests of learners;
- Supports the integration of language into the broader curriculum;
- Can be explicitly linked to literacy, forming conceptual and linguistic bridges across the curriculum (this should involve first- and second-language learning and EAL).

(p. 13)

Appropriate content allows the learner to discover new knowledge, developing different or existing skills and deepening understanding. It requires relevant contexts providing meaningful interactions and opportunities for personalised learning. If we consider the traditional languages curriculum that is built around a linear or cyclic progression through discrete language topics, we are likely to identify various gaps when mapping the learning opportunities against the 4C's framework (see for instance the gaps Toby and Lina identified in the case study in Chapter 4).

So how does the theoretical rationale for CLIL relate to the questions we raised earlier in the chapter?

What works best, discrete or embedded language teaching?

The number one strategy for language learning is repetition, repetition, repetition. We could quote a theorist or research study to support that statement, but we think you will trust us on that one! We are constantly exposed to our L1, and the more we use it, the more confident we become with manipulating it. Similarly, the more exposure we can have to L2, the more likely we are to become confident in the new language, and the easiest way to increase exposure in the classroom is to embed language teaching across the curriculum. So, practice is clearly important, but cognitive science tells us that not all practice is equal. Exposure alone does not lead to mastery; expert performance requires deliberate practice (Ericsson, Krampe, and Tesch-Römer, 1993). Deans for Impact (2015, no page) outlines three practical classroom implications drawn from cognitive science (Cepeda et al., 2006; Agarwal, Bain, and Chamberlain, 2012; Pashler et al., 2007) around the role of practice and the learning of new facts:

- Teachers can spread practice over time, with content being reviewed across weeks or months, to help students remember that content over the long term;
- Teachers can explain to students that trying to remember something makes memory more long-lasting than other forms of studying. Teachers can use low-/no-stakes quizzes in class to do this, and students can use self-tests (we revisit this principle in Chapter 8);
- Teachers can interleave (i.e., alternate) practice of different types of content. For example, if students are learning four mathematical operations, it is more effective to interleave practice of different problem types, rather than practice just one type of problem, then another type of problem, and so on.

We can look at these principles in terms of a CLIL approach to language learning as defined in the CLIL National Statement and Guidelines which we referred to earlier. The guidelines suggest that Primary CLIL can link with one or more subjects of the curriculum and can take the form of a theme or a project. The following case study provides an example of this.

> *AMLA scheme of work*
>
> In the introduction we explained the aims of the Croydon Schools Associated Modern Language Acquisition (AMLA) project and outlined the three key aspects of the team's theoretical approach:
>
> - Language as communication: interpreting, creating, and exchanging 'meanings that matter';
> - Language as culture: recognising the interrelationship between language, culture and learning;
> - Language as identity: reflection and evaluation – understanding self as communicator/self as learner.
>
> These core aspects, together with the cross-cutting theme of language awareness, were integrated into an example scheme of work which was disseminated to project schools. In writing the scheme of work, the project team took into account the different school and teacher starting points and the currently available resources, for example the existing use of language topic-structured published schemes. The project team designed the example programme to provide a structure which allows teachers to draw on existing resources in a progressive and creative way by clarifying expectations at each of four stages. Example units were provided through subject contexts and/or projects, and suggestions were provided for adapting the plans to other aspects of the primary curriculum. The six themes, language topics and examples of other subject links are outlined in Table 6.3.

Table 6.3 AMLA scheme overview

Theme	Language topics	Other curriculum links
All about me	families, friends, home, clothes	PSHE, history, RE
Health	food, drink, parts of the body	science, design technology
Journeys	countries, transport, weather	geography, history, PSHE, science, PE
Pastimes	sports, school	
Creative arts	colours, school, parts of the body	art, music
Natural world	animals, landscape	science, geography

Table 6.4 Jacques a dit instruction words and actions

French	English	Action
Levez-vous!	Stand up!	Hands gesture to whole group to rise/children stand up
Asseyez-vous	Sit down!	Hands gesture to whole group to sit down/children sit down
Ecoutez!	Listen!	Hands to ears
Répétez!	Repeat!	Rolling hands
Regardez!	Look!	One hand over eyes/make eye goggles with hands
Levez la main/ le doigt!	Put your hand up!	Hand/finger raised

All stages include suggestions for links to the primary English and mathematics curricula and for embedding language learning across the day. For instance, the first unit in the 'All about me' theme prompts teachers to use simple instructions at transition points introducing the language by playing *Jacques a dit* ('Jacques said' – the French equivalent of the English game Simon Says) with the children copying the actions only when Jack says so (see Table 6.4).

Once pupils have practised and become familiar with the instruction phrases, they can be used across the day at transition points in any subject lesson, the actions operating as memory prompts. New instructions can be introduced and adapted each week, for instance *mettez-vous en ligne/cercle* (line up/get into a circle), *posez les stylos* (pens down), *attendez* (wait) and pupil responses rewarded through use of praise words, for example *fantastique* (fantastic), *parfait* (perfect), *excellent* (excellent), *formidable* (brilliant).

We will revisit the AMLA overview in Chapter 7, with examples of progressive planning, but we introduce it here to demonstrate how core content can be revisited and consolidated across year groups within the same themes and within year groups across themes. The AMLA focus is not on learning a limited set of words or mastering a language skill within a block but returning to and extending the knowledge and skills over time. Learners can then practise concepts in different ways and in different contexts and are also provided with purposes and creative possibilities that enable them to direct and drive their own learning.

> What are you already doing to embed language learning across the day? What other routines could be adopted to provide language practice opportunities? Consider the existing resources and current topics in your learning setting. Are there any natural language links?

What are the cognitive and wellbeing impacts of multi-tasking in the bilingual classroom?

We started this chapter with a quote that reminds us of a common question we are presented with when we suggest integrating subject content and language learning or promoting bilingualism: 'But what about cognitive overload?' To respond to this question, we look first at learner engagement in the bilingual classroom and consider bilingualism as a model for multi-tasking (Poarch and Bialystok, 2014). You might also want to return to Chapter 2, which has a focus on the advantages of a bilingual approach.

Aamad

During a primary languages teaching seminar on a postgraduate school-based teacher training programme, discussions around CLIL approaches to language teaching lead to a few monolinguist trainees raising concerns about the impact on children of cognitive overload. Trainees are particularly worried about the cognitive impact of CLIL on children with additional needs and children with English as an additional language.

- 'They are already struggling with English or coping with learning a new language; how can they manage to focus on a foreign language and subject content?'

There are a few trainees in the group who have had personal experience of bilingual education, and the tutor asks them for their perspectives. As a group the bilinguals are universally positive about the perceived benefits of bilingualism and content-and language-integrated learning, although they also describe some of the challenges they face, particularly their experiences of total-immersion classrooms and the impact of this approach on their interactions with peers and their personal self-esteem.

Aamad is a trainee whose L1 is Urdu and who also speaks Hindi, Arabic and some German. He engages enthusiastically with group discussions but switches to intent focus on the tutor during any teaching input. Aamad explains the strategies that he has developed to enable him to manage learning in a language other than his mother tongue. He describes how he listens intently during sessions, identifies the key concepts that are being explored and focuses his attention on these. Unlike many of his monolingual peers, he takes copious notes during the lessons, organising ideas within themes and underlining key new language, which he revisits after sessions and follows up with further reading. Aamad explains how he shares his own language-learning strategies with EAL learners in his classroom. What Aamad is describing here is the executive control and self-regulation skills that he has developed that enable fluent language processing.

Poarch and Bialystok (2014) suggest that to some degree both languages in bilinguals are constantly active, even if only one language is supported by the environment, and that the cognitive mechanism that controls attention to the two language systems selects correctly for the context. This mechanism is generally attributed to executive function or executive control (see for example Costa and Sebastián Gallés, 2014; Buchweitz and Prat, 2014). Poarch and Bialystok (ibid) propose that bilinguals function in a constant state of linguistic multi-tasking, and this in turn appears to support bilingual advantages in controlling attention. For instance, research has found that bilinguals outperform monolinguals in tasks that involve conflict induced by task-irrelevant information such as during the Stroop task (Bialystok, Craig, and Luk, 2008; Blumenfeld and Marian, 2011) (see activity later in the chapter).

Executive functions – working memory, mental flexibility and self-control – are critical to learning and self-regulation. They are also linked to various facets of wellbeing including relationships, emotional and physical health and academic achievement. Executive function skills are not present at birth, but children are born with the potential to develop them, and children are more likely to develop strong executive functioning skills where they are supported in positive environments, both in the home and in other learning settings.

Wendy: Virginia, I often hear about children with EAL or additional needs missing out on foreign language lessons by well-intentioned schools that are worried about cognitive overload and/or think it is more important that they use that time to focus on core skills in English. What advice do you have for schools that have these kinds of concerns?

Virginia: You are right, Wendy – I also hear this a great deal. I think the key to unravelling this is to promote several concepts. Firstly, the benefits and power of cross-linguistic transfer. By this, we mean the ability to use what we know about one language to help understand another. Jim Cummins (a key writer in this field) believes that children will use their knowledge of L1 to help them understand L2/3/4, even if this is not actively encouraged. If they *are* encouraged, they would realise that their existing proficiency in L1 is something to be celebrated. Cummins (2005) suggests three particular ways by which to promote cross-linguistic transfer:

- 'Systematic attention to cognate relationships across languages' (p. 588);
- Children creating dual-language texts, with the first language being translated into English;
- Collaboration between children from different language backgrounds in projects.

Following these ideas, it certainly makes sense to keep EAL learners in foreign language lessons, and they have much to contribute.

My second argument would be that children with EAL are likely to feel a sense of empowerment during foreign language lessons, for two reasons. One, because of the likelihood of some cross-linguistic transfer, they may be 'first to the post' in terms of making contributions during the lesson. Two, rather than being the learner who is not

> yet fluent in English, the EAL learner is in the same position as all the other children in the class, learning a new language.
>
> My third argument (I have many more, but will leave it at three!) is that the social benefits of remaining in the classroom with peers – sharing, communicating, collaborating, making mistakes, learning, having fun – must surely outweigh an occasional time out of the classroom, focusing on core skills in English. I am certainly not against interventions per se, but I do feel we need to think very carefully about losses versus gains in these situations.

We hope you are beginning to be convinced that children's capacity for language learning, if presented in ways that engage and support this development, is considerable. However, any activities which further enhance their executive functions are always to be grasped and enjoyed. The Stroop Colour and Word Test is one such example. The Stroop test is a psychological experiment named after John Ridley Stroop which demonstrates that it is difficult to name the ink colour of a colour word if there is a mismatch between the ink colour and the word. It is a fun activity which can be used to practise colour words in the target language while also supporting the development of executive functioning skills, and you will find several examples of the task on the web.

Depending on the age and stage of the children, you might introduce the task first in English, for instance asking children to say out loud the English colour they *see*, not what they read. To begin, colour words can be presented in their correct colour (*red* written in red ink) and then in a different presentation (*red* written in blue ink). You could then ask the children to have another go with the colour words written in the target language, following the same presentation order.

The Stroop test can be adapted in many ways to support children to develop executive functioning skills. It is important though to analyse with the children the strategies that help them to achieve the task and how they can apply these skills to other learning situations. We suggest that you also explain to the children that some of them may have different degrees of colour blindness and that this will impact on how easy or hard they find the task. This discussion would be a good place to remind everyone of the unique world that we all live in. How exciting it would be if we could see other people's worlds with their eyes! What new understandings might we discover?

You might also want to try out variations of the Stroop test:

- Turn the words upside down;
- Use non-colour words, such as names of animals, in the target language;
- Use emotion words (see Chapter 4);
- Colour only half the word or the first or last letter.

Colour words in French are useful for identifying key sounds when children begin learning the language, so we have included in Table 6.5 suggested gestures to support children to identify and remember some colour words. For example the gesture for *vert* (point over there) connects both with the sound 'ert' and the French language pattern that six consonants are

Table 6.5 French colour words and suggested gestures

green	vert	Point 'over there'.
yellow	jaune	Yawn.
white	blanc	Point to the table.
blue	bleu	Stick out tongue.
red	rouge	Make monkey actions.
grey	gris	Grin.
black	noir	Stroke an imaginary black pet on your lap – focus on the 'ar' sound.

usually silent at the end of a word – *d, p, s, t, x, z*. Two examples that break the 'rule' which children can learn as exceptions are the numbers *huit* (eight – pronounced 'weet') and *six* (six – pronounced 'seece').

> Think of other transition games, warmups and cognitive challenges that you already use. Could any of these be adapted to incorporate the target language?

How can the language teacher make connections with the wider curriculum?

We mentioned earlier that the AMLA exemplar plans include links with the mathematics curriculum, and Lister and Palmer (2018) provide plenty of interesting examples of CLIL activities in their chapter 'Teaching Languages Creatively Through the Context of Mathematics'. They describe restricting the amount of language required as a fundamental aim of their practical suggestions and argue that this focus on repetition of language and approach ensures that CLIL activities can be delivered effectively with minimal or no linguistic expertise required. Here is a simple activity we share with non-specialist trainees which demonstrates how language practice activities (which could be maths lesson-starters) can also be cognitively challenging and support conceptual understanding within the subject:

Snip lotto

This repetitive activity helps children practise hearing, recalling and writing the numbers 1 to 12. Pupils are given a lotto sheet (see Table 6.6) and asked to write a number word in each of the boxes. Before children choose the numbers to write in each box, ask them to listen carefully to the game instructions to help them choose their numbers. Explain that you will be throwing two dice and calculating the sum (addition total) of the two numbers. The game involves snipping/tearing off one box from one of the ends of the lotto sheet if the total called out matches the number in the end box. Pupils can write any combination of numbers in the boxes (see the completed example) but will only be able to snip/tear off one box even if the same number appears at both ends (for example the lotto sheet shown has *deux* [2] at both ends). Numbers are only torn off from one end at a time, but players can tear off either end whenever they hear an end number called. We suggest you begin by modelling and calculating the first few sums, for example 2 + 3 = 5 (deux plus trois égale cinq), and then encourage the class to call out subsequent answers. When any of the pupils are left with just one

Table 6.6 Snip lotto sheet

deux	trois	onze	dix	dix	trois	quatre	sept	deux

Table 6.7 Probability table when rolling two dice

	1	2	3	4	5	6
1	(1, 1)	(1, 2)	(1, 3)	(1, 4)	(1, 5)	(1, 6)
2	(2, 1)	(2, 2)	(2, 3)	(2, 4)	(2, 5)	(2, 6)
3	(3, 1)	(3, 2)	(3, 3)	(3, 4)	(3, 5)	(3, 6)
4	(4, 1)	(4, 2)	(4, 3)	(4, 4)	(4, 5)	(4, 6)
5	(5, 1)	(5, 2)	(5, 3)	(5, 4)	(5, 5)	(5, 6)
6	(6, 1)	(6, 2)	(6, 3)	(6, 4)	(6, 5)	(6, 6)

number, they wait until they hear that number and only win the game when they are the first to place the final number down on the table.

If we consider this activity in terms of language and content-integrated learning, there are opportunities to discuss conceptual learning points in both the subject (maths) and the language (French). *Maths discussion prompts* might include:

- Which numbers did the winning pupil select and why?
- Are there any numbers from 1 to 12 that are more likely to be called out/will never be called out?

These initial questions can lead to a probability investigation during which the class work out the possible combinations of rolling two dice. Table 6.7 shows that there are 36 possible combinations.

From this the children can work out that the probability of the sum of two rolled dice being 2 is 1/36, and the probability of the sum 12 is also 1/36. There are six possible outcomes where the sum of the two dice is 7. The number of total possible outcomes remains 36. So, the probability of the sum of the two dice being equal to 7 is 6/36 or 1/6. The probability of the sum being 1 is of course zero, although there is usually someone who includes the target language word for 1 on their strip when we explain the rules of the activity for the first time, even with adults!

Such investigations can be developed in many ways with repeated opportunities to practice the target language, for instance looking at the probability of winning different choosing games/changing the game rules/changing the maths calculation (multiplications, divisions, subtractions).

Language discussion prompts might include the following:

1   **Plus**

We noted earlier that in the French language, six consonants are *usually* silent at the end of a word – d, p, s, t, x, z.

Plus (directly translated as 'more') is an exception (sometimes!) for instance when it has a positive meaning. So, in the addition statement 'Deux plus trois égale cinq', the French pronounce the final s in *plus* but not *trois*. Knowing when to pronounce the s in *plus* is a little tricky, but generally it is pronounced when the word has a positive meaning, whereas when *plus* is used to represent a negative meaning, the s is silent. For example:

- Il n'y en a plus. (There aren't any more.)

Of course it is not quite as simple as that (language rules are there to be broken!). For instance, the s is also silent in the positive expression 'A plus tard' (See you later).

So, word pronunciation in French is a question of learning by exposure, repetition and deliberate practice and taking a best-bet approach. We suggest celebrating sensible guesses, 'having a go' and modelling dictionary use and other self-checking strategies such as online pronunciation guides.

2   *Égale* (We recommend non-linguists take a deep breath before reading this section!)

The French maths sentence 'Deux plus trois égale cinq' is a matter of intense grammatical debate. An online search will bring up various blog discussions between French students and their teachers about whether to use *égale* or *égalent*. The arguments focus around whether *égale* is a verb or instead an adjective and therefore a redaction of 'est égale à' (is equal to). For instance, if the word has the function of a verb, the argument would be that surely it should be conjugated in the plural form *égalent*. Interestingly, although I (Wendy) first learned the phrase with the plural verb form *égalent*, most online debates appear to settle on *égale*. It is comforting to know that even French teachers and students grapple with French grammar rules, which should take the stress off both the specialist and non-specialist languages teacher getting the grammar 'right' (see also our later discussion on 'mistake obsession' in Chapter 8). Comparing the French sentence with the English translation provides an opportunity to unpick the function of each word in the sentence in English.

- Two plus three equals five.

If *two* and *three* are the subjects (referents) of the verb *equals*, presumably we could replace them with the plural pronoun *they*:

- They equals five.

Hang on a minute! That does not sound right! Surely it should be 'They equal five'! Or is the word *they* here not a pronoun but a singular proper noun and always capitalised? Perhaps what the sentence really means is 'The sum of two plus three equals five'. So, perhaps the subject (referent) of the verb is actually 'the sum'.

Have we confused you? We are rather confused ourselves and are certainly not suggesting that even confident linguists plan to include this second discussion in their primary classroom. However, in the language-aware classroom, these discussions often arise, and we suggest that you welcome them when they do (see the following case study).

> ### *Supercalifragilisticexpialidocious*
>
> Wendy recalls that during an undergraduate poetry seminar which included initial discussions on word functions, she was checking in with one group about progress with a poetry activity when at the other side of the room another group of students started laughing and singing along to music coming out of one student's mobile phone. When Wendy went across to investigate (making the positive assumption that they were purposefully engaged in some relevant activity) she found that they were singing along to the Mary Poppins song 'Supercalifragilisticexpialidocious'. The students explained that they had gotten distracted during their poetry-writing activity and were trying to work out whether the function of the word in the song was a noun or an adjective. Pleased that the teaching input had unexpectedly triggered their grammar investigation, Wendy opened the discussion to the wider seminar group. They decided that although the ending of the word, *Supercalifragilisticexpialidocious* sounds like it is an adjective, in the context of the song it takes the function of a noun, but you could listen to the song words with your class and make up your own minds.

Whilst we hope we have given you some ideas and food for thought in this section and throughout the chapter, making language connections with the wider curriculum is explored further in Chapter 7.

Summary

- Since the millennium, there has been a flowering of research studies investigating the importance of positive psychology on language teaching and acquisition including concepts of hope, courage, wellbeing, creativity, flourishing and possibilities;
- We all inhabit our own unique worlds;
- All teachers are teachers of languages;
- Content and Language Integrated Learning is a dual-focused educational approach in which an additional language is used for the learning and teaching of both content and language;
- The CLIL National Statement and Guidelines draws on the 4C's Curriculum: Content, Cognition, Communication and Culture;
- Repetition, repetition, repetition. Practice is important, but not all practice is equal. Expert performance requires deliberate and spaced practice;
- The target language can be easily embedded across the school day, for instance using the language of instruction and praise words;
- Bilinguals function in a constant state of linguistic multi-tasking, and this in turn appears to support bilingual advantages in controlling attention;
- Executive functions – working memory, mental flexibility and self-control – are critical to learning, self-regulation and facets of wellbeing;

- Non-linguists with minimal knowledge of the target language can effectively deliver cross-curricular language practice activities (such as maths lesson starters) that are cognitively challenging and support conceptual understanding within the subject;
- Grammar debates will often arise in the language-aware classroom and should be encouraged;
- Choice, agency, trust, purpose and risk-taking can be key motivators for learning in the language classroom.

References

Agarwal, P. K. Bain, P. M. & Chamberlain, R. W. (2012) 'The value of applied research: Retrieval practice improves classroom learning and recommendations from a teacher, a principal, and a scientist', *Educational Psychology Review*, 24, 3, pp. 437–448.

Barnes, J. (2018) *Applying Cross-Curricular Approaches Creatively*, Oxon: Routledge.

Baten, K. Van Hiel, S. & De Cuypere, L. (2020) 'Vocabulary development in a CLIL context: A comparison between French and English L2', *Studies in Second Language Learning and Teaching*, 10, 2, pp. 307–336.

Bialystok, E. Craig, F. I. M. & Luk, G. (2008) 'Lexical access in bilinguals: Effects of vocabulary size and executive control', *Journal of Neurolinguistics*, 21, 6, pp. 522–538.

Blumenfeld, H. K. & Marian, V. (2011) 'Bilingualism influences inhibitory control in auditory comprehension', *International Journal of Cognitive Science*, 118, 2, pp. 245–257.

Buchweitz, A. & Prat, C. (2014) 'The bilingual brain: Flexibility and control in the human cortex', *Physics of Life Reviews*, 10, 4, pp. 428–443.

Cepeda, N. J. Pashler, H. Vul, E. Wixted, J. T. & Rohrer, D. (2006) 'Distributed practice in verbal recall tasks: A review and qualitative synthesis', *Psychological Bulletin*, 132, 3, pp. 354–380.

Cobb, W. (2008) 'Bright sparks – primary languages through science (CLIL Trial)', in *What National Strategies Works Well Case Studies*, Department for Education, Available at https://webarchive.nationalarchives.gov.uk/20101225123718/http://nationalstrategies.standards.dcsf.gov.uk/search/case-studies/results/facets:24263?page=13 (Accessed 23.02.2021).

Costa, A. & Sebastián Gallés, N. (2014) 'How does the bilingual experience sculpt the brain?' *Nat Rev Neurosci*, 15, 5, pp. 336–345.

Coyle, D. (2005) *Developing CLIL: Towards a Theory of Practice*, APAC Monograph 6, Barcelona: APAC.

Coyle, D. Holmes, B. & King, L. (2009a) *Towards an Integrated Curriculum – CLIL National Statement and Guidelines*, The Languages Company, Available at www.rachelhawkes.com/PandT/CLIL/CLILnationalstatementandguidelines.pdf (Accessed 25.08.2020).

Coyle, D. Holmes, B. & King, L. (2009b) *Towards an Integrated Curriculum – CLIL National Statement and Guidelines*, The Languages Company, Available at www.rachelhawkes.com/PandT/CLIL/CLILnationalstatementandguidelines.pdf (Accessed 23.02.2021).

Coyle, D. Hood, P. & Marsh, D. (2010) *CLIL Content and Language Integrated Learning*, Cambridge: Cambridge University Press.

Crenshaw, D. (2008) *The Myth of Multitasking: How "Doing It All" Gets Nothing Done*, San Francisco: John Wiley & Sons.

Csikszentmihalyi, M. (1988) 'The flow experience and its significance for human psychology', in Csikszentmihalyi, M. & Csikszentmihalyi, I. S. (eds.), *Optimal Experience: Psychological Studies of Flow in Consciousness* (pp. 15-35), Cambridge: Cambridge University Press.

Cummins, J. (2005) 'A proposal for action: Strategies for recognising heritage language competence as a learning resource with the mainstream classroom', *The Modern Language Journal*, 89, 4, pp. 585–592.

Deans for Impact (2015) *The Science of Learning*, Austin, TX: Deans for Impact. Dewaele, Available at https://deansforimpact.org/wpcontent/uploads/2016/12/The_Science_of_Learning.pdf (Accessed 23.02.2021).

Dewaele, J., Chen, M., Padilla, X. M. & Lake, A. M. (2019) 'The flowering of positive psychology in foreign language teaching and acquisition', *Research Frontiers in Psychology*, 10, 212, p. 2128, DOI: 10.3389/fpsyg.2019.02128.

DfE (2011) 'What works well: Sharing practice to improve learning', Available at https://webarchive.nationalarchives.gov.uk/20110202094154/http://nationalstrategies.standards.dcsf.gov.uk/casestudies (Accessed 23.02.2021).

Didau, D. (2012) 'Are worksheets a waste of time?' Available at https://learningspy.co.uk/learning/are-worksheets-a-waste-of-time/ (Accessed 23.02.2021).

Ericsson, K. A. Krampe, R. T. & Tesch-Römer, C. (1993) 'The role of deliberate practice in the acquisition of expert performance', *Psychological Review*, 100, 3, pp. 363–406.

Henrikson, S. M. (2010) 'Reflections on the language education issue in Mozambique', Conference Paper, 3rd European Conference on African Studies, Available at file:///C:/Users/End%20User/Downloads/Leipzig_June_4-7_2009.pdf (Accessed 24.08.2020).

Hood, P. (ed.) (2018) *Teaching Languages Creatively*, Oxon: Routledge.

Kamwangamalu, N. (2008) 'Reflections on language policy balance sheet in Africa', Paper presented at the 15th World Congress of Applied Linguistics (AILA), Essen, Germany, August 24-29.

Linares, A. Morton, T. & Whittaker, R. (2012) *The Roles of Language in CLIL*, Cambridge: Cambridge University Press.

Lister, S. & Palmer, P. (2018) 'Teaching languages creatively through the context of mathematics', in Hood, P. (ed.), *Teaching Languages Creatively*, Oxon: Routledge.

MacKay, J. (2019) 'Evidence from neuroscience suggests that we cannot multi-task; Instead we switch tasks quickly', *Rescue Time: Blog*, Available at https://blog.rescuetime.com/multitasking/#:~:text=As%20multiple%20studies%20have%20confirmed,t%20actually%20getting%20more%20done (Accessed 18.08.2020).

Mehisto, P. Marsh, D. & Frigols, M. J. (2008) *Uncovering CLIL.: Content and Language Integrated Learning in Bilingual and Multilingual Education*, Oxford: McMillan.

Morton, T. & Linares, A. (eds.) (2017) 'Applied linguistics perspectives on CLIL', Available at www.vleebooks.com/Vleweb/Product/Index/927564?page=0 (Accessed 11.08.2020).

Pashler, H. Bain, P. M. Bottge, B. A. Graesser, A. Koedinger, K. & McDaniel, M. (2007) *Organizing Instruction and Study to Improve Student Learning*, U.S. Department of Education, Washington, DC: National Center for Education Research, Institute of Education Sciences.

Poarch, G. J. & Bialystok, E. (2014) 'Bilingualism as a model for multitasking', *Developmental Review*, 35, pp. 113–124.

Swain, M. (2013) 'The inseparability of cognition and emotion in second language learning', *Language Teaching*, 46, pp. 195–207.

Toren, M. (2017) 'Why multitasking is a myth that's breaking your brain and wasting your time', *Entrepeneur Europe*, Available at www.entrepreneur.com/article/299029 (Accessed 18.08.2020).

UNESCO (2020) 'Breaking educational language barriers in Mozambique', Available at https://en.unesco.org/news/breaking-educational-language-barriers-mozambique (Accessed 24.08.2020).

Yang, D. (2019) 'The myth of multitasking', *BrainWorld*, Available at https://brainworldmagazine.com/the-myth-of-multitasking/ (Accessed 18.08.2020).

7 Progression in language learning

K-k-k-karfter me!

Translation: 'Please look after me!'
  (spoken with a soft, pleading tone by young child to parent)

Introduction

We all make language errors from time to time, such as those embarrassing 'slips of the tongue' when we want to say one word but actually say something completely different; or we say a word or phrase with a dual meaning that could be misinterpreted by someone unfamiliar with the sociocultural context. Usually, if we are with friends, we just laugh at those moments or we apologise and hope our error will be quickly forgotten. Young children naturally make errors all the time – for instance assigning lexical status to a phrase whereby 'the cat' becomes 'thecat' – and some of their endearing early mistakes become accepted as special words and sayings which are loved and understood only by the immediate family, such as the opening quote by Wendy's youngest son.

Initial language acquisition is an intuitive process, through which young children fearlessly experiment with sounds and structures unaware of the grammatical conventions or syntactic structure of the language(s) they are learning. The learning of an additional language on the other hand is often a conscious (sometimes painful) and explicitly sequenced process of accumulating knowledge of linguistic features, typically taking place in a classroom setting (Castello, 2015). Of course, this will be a different experience again for EAL learners, as they will usually be learning English predominantly through immersion and then potentially a further foreign language in curriculum-based lessons.

In this chapter we consider expectations for progression in *language learning*, with a focus on progression in foreign language teaching in the language-aware classroom. We begin the chapter by looking at some general expectations around the core content of language schemes of work in the primary years. We then provide some specific examples relating to grammatical features, communicative competence and developing a metalanguage. The chapter then moves on to examine planning for progression, drawing on examples from each element of the Accelerated Modern Languages Acquisition (AMLA) project resources (see details of this project in the introduction to this book) with a focus on embedded language

DOI: 10.4324/9781003129738-8

learning and Content and Language Integrated Learning (CLIL). There is then a more specific focus on how progression in language learning can be promoted by a curriculum area – in this case creative arts. The final section explores how 'big questions' can be investigated to the advantage of both language progression and a curriculum area.

It is important to emphasise here that examples are being shared which work well in contexts we and other teachers have experienced and that apply cognitive principles which, on average, research suggests work well. There are many other schemes of work and supporting resources available, and although examples are useful as a starting point for planning, you will need to make your own professional judgement about what might work best in your context and with your students. We hope that the examples we share will give you an idea of what is possible in the holistic, language-aware classroom.

Establishing core content for a scheme of work in the primary years

Progressive schemes of work usually list core content for each teaching unit in an overview document. This content, which is often presented in a staged progression, may be organised in different ways and use some of the following headings:

- Vocabulary (this may be organised into transferable/core language and topic-based/non-transferable language);
- Grammar/Language structures;
- Knowledge about language (KAL);
- Language learning strategies;
- Phonics/Phonology;
- Texts – Stories/Rhymes/Songs;
- Dictionary skills;
- Culture/Intercultural understanding.

To illustrate how to identify core content to support progression in language learning, we have combined elements from these bullet points to provide two themes of our own, within which we present ideas for practice. Our intention here is that the examples will provide ideas for some of the other elements in the initial list, as you plan for progression in language learning. Our themes are:

- Grammatical features and communicative competence;
- Developing a metalanguage.

Grammatical features and communicative competence

We have chosen this as a theme because, regardless of the scheme you/the school decide to use, there will be some core grammatical features which children are likely to need to access to allow them to express their intended meanings in a competent and confident way. It is also an acknowledgment that knowing theoretical grammar does not, on its own, lead to this confidence and competence. When teachers create motivational and purposeful contexts for learning, children might well want to leap ahead in order to express their own thoughts and meanings and to answer their own questions, and therefore they may need to use structures that teachers had not intended to introduce in that lesson. It is helpful for teachers who are not language specialists to have an awareness of expected core content across units so that they can support children with the structures they need to enable them to express their ideas when they want to go beyond the language learning objectives for the lesson. The AMLA scheme of work recognised this, and it provided support and examples illustrating core grammar and linguistic structures, such as those illustrated with French language examples in Table 7.1.

Table 7.1 Grammatical forms with examples in the French language

Word form	Associated features	French language examples
Nouns	• grammatical gender • articles • singular/plural • irregular plural endings	• le chien (dog), la souris (mouse) • le, la, l', les, un, une, des • un château, des châteaux (castle/s) • l'oeil/les yeux (eye/eyes)
Adjectives	• agreement • position • demonstrative • possessive	• vert/verte (green) • un livre vert (a green book) • ce, cet, cette, ces (this/these) • mon, ma, mes/ton, ta, tes/son, sa, ses (my/your/his/hers)
Pronouns	• personal • reflexive	• je, tu, il, elle, on, moi, toi (I, you, he, she, we, me/one, you) • me, te, se, nous, vous – je m'appelle (my name is)
Prepositions		• dans (in), en haut de (above), devant (in front of), derrière (behind), avec (with)
Verbs	• present tense, range of regular • conjugation of common irregular verbs • interrogative form • negative form • impersonal constructions • imperatives • infinitive	• manger (to eat), partir (to leave), • vendre (to buy) • être – je suis, tu es, il/elle est, nous sommes (I am, you are. . .) • avoir – j'ai, tu as, il/elle as (I have, you have. . .) • Comment t'appelles-tu? (What is your name?) • Quel âge as-tu? (How old are you?) • Où habites-tu? (Where do you live?) • Aimes-tu. . . ? (Do you like. . . ?) • As-tu. . . ? (Do you have. . . ?) • Est-ce que je? (Can I. . . ?) • Qu'est-ce que c'est? (What is that?) • Où-est. . . ? (Where is. . . ?) • Il y a combien de. . . ? (How many . . . are there?) • Je n'aime pas (I don't like) • Il y a (There are) • Levez vous! (Stand up!) Asseyez-vous! (Sit down !) • J'aime aller (I like to go)
Adverbs	• place • time, • manner, e.g. *bien, mal, bon, mauvais*	• ici (here), loin (far), près (near) • le vendredi (on Friday) • bien (good), mal (wrong), bon (well), mauvais (bad)
Qualifiers		• trop (too), très (very), beaucoup (a lot), assez (quite)
Conjunctions		• et (and), parce que (because), donc (so), ou (or), mais (but)
Question words		• Où? (Where?) • Comment? (How?) • Combien? (How many?) • Qui? (Who?) • Pourquoi? (Why?)

A more detailed list of suggested grammar points to be covered at Key Stage 2 with suggestions in French, Spanish and German is presented in the Key Stage 2 Language Coordinator's Handbook (ALL Connect, no date), one of a number of support tools freely available to download in the Primary area of the Association for Language Learning website, which can be accessed at: www.all-languages.org.uk.

Once a systematic approach to teaching grammatical features is established, it is possible to focus more on *communicative competence*. This is a term coined by Hymes in 1966 (cited in Tarvin, 2015, p. 2) in reaction to Chomsky's abstract notion of competence – 'the speaker-hearer's knowledge of his language' – and its distinction from performance – 'the actual use of language in concrete situations'. Furthering Hymes' claim that knowing how to form grammatically accurate sentences is not enough to have communicative competence (CC), Canale and Swain (1980) argued that CC involves four sub-competences:

- Grammatical (knowledge of phonology, morphology, syntax, semantics and lexis);
- Sociolinguistic (the ability to produce sociolinguistically appropriate expressions);
- Discourse (the ability to produce coherent and cohesive expressions);
- Strategic (knowledge of verbal and non-verbal strategies to solve communication problems as they arise).

Helping learners to develop communicative competence therefore requires much more than a focus on correct knowledge and use of grammatical form; it demands a holistic curriculum which enables learners to be able to respond spontaneously, empathically and using appropriate sociocultural norms in a range of language transaction contexts. For example, children should understand that non-verbal communication is inseparable from verbal communication. How and where we stand or sit to speak, our tone of voice and our facial expressions can often convey messages more convincingly than the words we say.

Examples of aspects of communicative competence that learners in the primary school context need to develop include:

- Taking part in simple conversations;
- Giving information;
- Asking and answering questions;
- Describing (colour, size, location, possession, appearance);
- Asking for and giving opinions;
- Giving reasons;
- Following/Giving instructions;
- Expressing ability;
- Using numbers and expressing quantity.

Common question-and-answer responses that children are likely to need are provided in Table 7.2, with examples again in the French language.

In addition to the suggested question-and-answer phrases in Table 7.2, we have previously established the importance of teaching, practising and role modelling the language of

Table 7.2 Question-and-answer phrases in the French language

Question	Translation	Example answer
Ça va?	How are you?	Ça va bien/mal, comme çi comme ça
Comment tu t'appelles?	What's your name?	Je m'appelle...
As-tu?	Do you have?	J'ai... Je n'ai pas
Quel âge as-tu?	How old are you?	J'ai dix ans.
Qu'est-ce que c'est...?	What is...?	C'est...
C'est combien?	How much/many?	C'est...
Quelle est la date aujourd'hui?	What is the date today?	C'est le premier mars.
Tu aimes...?	Do you like...?	J'aime, je n'aime pas, j'adore, je deteste, je préfère...
C'est de quelle couleur?	What colour is it?	C'est...
Quel temps fait-il?	What's the weather like?	Aujourd'hui il fait...
Où habites-tu?	Where do you live?	J'habite...
Où est...?	Where is...?	C'est dans/derrière/devant/en haut de/près de
Qu'est-ce que tu aimes faire?	What do you like doing?	J'aime jouer au tennis.
Qu'est-ce que tu fais le weekend?	What do you do at the weekend?	Le samedi je joue au tennis.
Qu'est-ce que tu portes?	What are you wearing?	Je porte....
Est-ce qu'il y a...?	Are there any...?	Oui/Non, il y a... il n'y a pas de...
Pourquoi?	Why?	Parce que c'est amusant/c'est marrant...

clarification and polite requests (see language structures in Chapter 5, Table 5.1). In Chapter 6, we also suggested teaching and using the language of instruction throughout the day. Many teachers find it helpful to display these core structures as prompts around the room. Providing resources for children to access core language structures through the use of displays, word banks and speaking/listening/writing prompts enables them to make significant progress in their learning whilst at the same time providing much-needed scaffolds for teachers and support staff who may not be language specialists.

In relation to communicative competence, and as part of children's progression in language learning, you might also want to consider the use of gesture and how this might be brought into some of the elements on the earlier bullet-pointed list, for example how gestures might be utilised when giving instructions or asking questions. The following case study provides an example of how successful this practice has the potential to be.

Using gesture to support language learning

Bilbrough is an English teacher and researcher who has been working in schools and academies in Spain for over 25 years. In 1998 he developed a set of gestures for teaching every word of each sentence (including objects, verbs, adjectives, pronouns and prepositions) and compiled them into a dictionary. He began using gestures to accompany his spoken utterances and encouraged the students to do the same. He found that these gestures helped the students to quickly understand the English expressions, and he was therefore able to introduce a wider range of interesting texts into his classroom, such as stories, jokes, poetry and songs, which he describes as a 'wealth of linguistic richness [he] had not been able to achieve before' (Bilbrough, 2019, no page). Bilbrough's research (2017) suggests that gestures allow for a more accelerated input of oral language due to the enhanced comprehension they provide, which, in turn, allows for a more rapid recycling of high-frequency language at the full-sentence, communicative level.

How does your own use of gesture during teaching support the students' language comprehension? How do you support the students in reflecting on the benefits of the use of gesture as a language learning and communicative strategy? How might more systematic use of gesture support all learners (and particularly EAL learners) across all subjects?

Developing a metalanguage

Our second chosen theme is that of developing a metalanguage. Progression in language learning can be supported by promoting the use of metalanguage, by which we mean the language we use to talk about language. We may feel that a sentence written in our native language sounds awkward but may not be able to explain why. Metalanguage discussions enable student and teacher to discuss the function of words and phrases in a sentence and decide what changes are needed to deliver the intended meaning or express the meaning in a more impactful way. Common examples of classroom metalanguage are words such as *verb, adjective, noun* and *pronoun*. French examples of metalanguage include:

- Nom (n.) – noun;
- Adjectif (a.) – adjective;
- Verbe (v., v.t., v.i.) – verb;
- Pronom (pron.) – pronoun;
- Adverbe (adv.) – adverb.

The letters in brackets in these examples refer to the abbreviations used in dictionaries to identify word forms. Verbs may be distinguished by the letter *v* or may be classed as either transitive (v.t.) or intransitive (v.i.). Transitive verbs have either a direct or indirect object and need to 'transfer' their action to something or someone. The object is the thing or person that is involved in the action but does not carry it out and is the answer to either a 'What?' or 'Whom?' question. See for instance the following example using the verb *manger* (to eat).

- Je mange un croissant. (I am eating a croissant)
- What am I eating? I am eating a croissant.

Intransitive verbs do not have an object.

- J'arrive. (I arrive.)

Some verbs can be both transitive and intransitive depending on how the verb is used in the sentence:

- I walk. (intransitive)
- I walk the dog. (transitive)

Children should be able to identify the subject, verb and object in a sentence by the end of primary school, although they do not need to know the difference between transitive and intransitive verbs. They may, however, come across the verb symbols in bilingual dictionaries and may wonder what they stand for. As teachers, we should not feel we need to know the answers to all the questions children ask and could instead set a challenge for the child, group or class to investigate the answer and teach the rest of the class. A useful website to direct children to for their grammar investigations is www.grammar-monster.com. The more we can encourage students to ask questions and to look out for patterns or irregularities or surprises in their own and in the target language, the more language-aware they will become, supporting their progression in language learning.

Given that there are no markers in the English language to distinguish between transitive and intransitive verbs, and that there is no expectation for primary children to learn about them, you may wonder why we mentioned them (other than to help children identify the words in a dictionary). The reason is, our own understanding of these grammatical points can help us to support children with their developing oral and written language, in both English and other languages. Consider the following sentence which contains a common error that children might make:

- The teacher discussed **about** the importance of learning languages.

To check whether the verb *discussed* is transitive or intransitive (you do not need to use these terms with the children), you could ask, 'What or whom did the teacher discuss?' The answer is, 'the importance of learning languages'. So, the answer as a full sentence would read:

- The teacher discussed the importance of learning languages.

> Think about some common errors that children make in their writing in any subject. What are the current opportunities for language-aware discussions in the classroom? What strategies could you introduce to help children uncover errors in their writing? For example, you could investigate strategies suggested on www.grammar-monster.com.

To encourage children to start thinking and talking about language, dictionary activities work well. To be able to use bilingual dictionaries, children first need to learn the alphabet in the target language. They can do this through listening to and singing alphabet songs and chants, such as the military style 'call and response' marching song as illustrated here:

	Teacher (call)	Class (response)
-	A B C D E F G	*A B C D E F G*
-	H I J K L M N	*H I J K L M N*
-	O P Q R S T U	*O P Q R S T U*
-	V W X Y Z	*V W X Y Z*

This example uses the French alphabet, which at first glance looks the same as the English alphabet, although the letter names sound quite different with a number of surprises that children can listen out for and discuss, such as *G* ('jeh') which sounds more like English *J* and *J* ('jee') which sounds like English *G*. The letters *K*, pronounced 'kah' and *W*, pronounced 'doobler veh' (double *V* rather than the English double *U*) are only used in words loaned from other languages. The French language has six vowels – *a, e, i, o, u, y* – whereas we generally refer to five vowels in English – *a, e, i, o, u* – although a vowel is not so much a letter as the sound represented by more than one letter. So, in English, *y* can be either a consonant, for instance when it starts a word or syllable (*yard, lawyer*) or a vowel when it forms a dipthong (a sound formed by the combination of two vowels in a single syllable), for instance in the words *toy* and *say*. Likewise, there are more than six vowel sounds in French, including nasal vowels which are pronounced by passing air through the mouth and nose – '*an*', '*in*', '*on*', '*un*'.

The similarities and differences between writing systems are fascinating, and children will enjoy comparing alphabets in their home and target languages. There are six main alphabets in current use (Armenian, Cyrillic, Georgian, Greek, Korean, Latin/Roman, N'Ko and Tifinagh), and these can be explored on the Omniglot website – https://omniglot.com.

The Association of Language Learning Transition Toolkit (ALL Connect, no date, p. 37) has suggestions for practising and developing dictionary skills, such as 'Quick Draw Spanish', a game in which the pupils compete to draw their 'weapon' (dictionary) and 'shoot' (find a word) as quickly as possible. Another suggested activity is 'Syllable Score'. This game involves pupils taking turns rolling two or three dice to come up with a two- or three-digit number, which becomes a page number. For example, after rolling three dice (a time limit could be given for this) the first student may have the digits 1, 3 and 5 which stand for the number 135. The student turns to page 135 in the dictionary and finds the word with the most syllables. The number of syllables is the number of points the student wins.

Planning for progression in language learning

In this section, we start by exploring some general ideas which support planning for progression in language learning and include what we hope are some useful exemplars. We then move on to examine what this might look like when related to a specific curriculum area – creative arts – and provide six examples of activities that might support language learning within this area.

Although most language schemes include similar content in terms of grammatical structures, other taught vocabulary – particularly nouns – will depend on the topics or themes covered in each unit, and there are some common topics typically used in published language schemes. As we discussed previously, the AMLA team took a pragmatic approach when designing the Key Stage 2 scheme of work overview; we aimed to make links with the resources that were likely to be available in many schools, which are often built around these familiar core topics. The team created a thematic overview with topics that could be recycled each year and linked them to other subjects of the primary curriculum. We have added 'big questions' to the scheme overview in line with our discussions about leading questioning classrooms in Chapter 9, and we share examples of planning for learning around 'big questions' in Table 7.3. These big questions will be discussed in more depth later in the chapter.

The repeated theme approach reflects one of the key principles in planning for progression, which is to build on prior knowledge. For instance, what do children already know in the target language, in their home language, in other languages and more broadly within the theme? By repeating themes and linking with other subjects, known language can be recycled, reinforced and extended.

An example guide to progression in primary languages is the Key Stage 2 Languages Progression and Assessment document which emerged from the Ensemble Languages Project (2015). This collaborative project, which involved seven schools led by staff from the Leicester Teaching School, began in the summer of 2014 and was aimed at supporting teachers with elements of the new languages curriculum in England that they might find challenging. The progression exemplars outlined expectations in terms of progression at the end of each stage. For instance, the Year 3 languages progression overview lists a set of skills, knowledge and understanding that children 'arriving in Year 4' should be able to evidence. One example states that by the end of Year 3, children should be able to 'ask and answer questions on a limited range of topics such as age, where they live, and the date of their birthday, which they have practised regularly'.

Table 7.3 AMLA thematic scheme overview

Theme	Big questions	Language topics	Example curriculum links
All about me	Who am I? Where do I belong?	families, friends, home, clothes	PSHE, history
Health	What keeps my body, mind and spirit healthy?	food, drink, parts of the body	science, design technology
Journeys	Where am I going? Where do I want to go? How can I get there?	countries, transport, weather	geography, history
Pastimes	What makes me who I am? What connects me to others?	sports, school	PSHE, science
Creative arts	What can I learn from the creativity of others? How can I express my ideas and feelings in creative ways?	colours, school, parts of the body	art, music
Natural world	What can I do with others to look after our world?	animals, landscape	science, geography

Table 7.4 'Can do' statements for speaking

Speaking	
Grade 1	I can say and repeat single words and short simple phrases.
Grade 2	I can answer simple questions and give basic information.
Grade 3	I can ask and answer simple questions and talk about my interests.
Grade 4	I can take part in a simple conversation, and I can express my opinions.

Source: Language Ladder Steps to Success (DCSF, 2007)

Not all progression guides are as easily accessible for the non-specialist language teacher as the overviews in the Ensemble Languages Project progression guidance, which was designed specifically with such teachers in mind. This is particularly the case where progression statements are either vaguely expressed or where the guides are overwhelmingly detailed. In Table 7.4, you will find an example from the Language Ladder Steps to Success (DCSF, 2007), showing 'can do' statements for speaking. Consider how useful you would find these, when assessing progression.

> Review the 'can do' statements for speaking at Grades 1 to 4 in the Language Ladder Steps to Success overview (DCSF, 2007) in Table 7.4. What linguistic evidence would you need to differentiate between Grade 2 'giving basic information' and Grade 3 'talking about my interests'?

If you found the question in the last reflection difficult to answer, you may find the following language exemplars useful. Teachers have told us in training sessions that the exemplars are also helpful as a guide to what to focus on in their teaching. For example, within the theme of 'pastimes', progression in speaking and listening can be modelled through questions and answers around what children do at the weekend.

In response to the teacher's prompt, 'Que fais tu le weekend?', examples of progression are illustrated in the following possible answers:

Stage A

- Je joue au tennis.

An example of a child's response at Stage A is a simple statement such as, 'I play tennis'.

Stage B

- **Le samedi** je joue au tennis **et le dimanche** je joue au football.

In this example at Stage B, the child includes time adverbs and a conjunction to join two ideas together: '*On Saturday* I play tennis *and on Sunday* I play football'.

Stage C

- Le samedi je joue au tennis. **J'aime** le tennis. . . **c'est cool mais je déteste** le football.

The child's likes and dislikes are shared in an extended response at Stage C: 'On Saturday I play tennis. *I like* tennis. . . *it's cool, but I hate* football.'

Stage D

- Le samedi je joue au tennis **avec** mon frère. J'adore le tennis **parce que** c'est **très** amusant mais je déteste le football. **A mon avis** c'est **trop** dangereux!

At Stage D the child's response is further developed through the addition of prepositions (e.g. *avec*) and justifications for opinions using qualifiers (e.g. *très* and *trop*). 'On Saturday I play tennis *with* my brother. I love tennis *because* it is *great* fun, but I hate football. *In my opinion* it is *too* dangerous!'

Exemplars like these sentences are useful because they help to identify the focus for teaching for progression in terms of the grammatical structures that support meaningful communication and which can be revisited across topics. Of course, there are dangers in providing any form of progression exemplar; one such danger is that planning and teaching may focus on a linear progression through key content, leading to an assessment against expected knowledge within a limited set of contexts. This in turn could mistake memorised language structures for authentic and spontaneous communicative competence and could also discourage the creative leaps and bounds that might see children making progress well outside of the planned content both linguistically and holistically. It is important therefore, when planning for progression, to keep in mind the 4C's Curriculum (cited in Coyle, Holmes, and King, 2009) discussed in Chapter 6 – Content, Cognition, Communication, Culture – with its focus on high-quality language interactions, creativity, higher-order thinking and enabling learners to mediate their own ideas, thoughts and values through the language.

Progression through creative arts

As CLIL proponents Coyle, Hood, and Marsh (2010, p. 53) express, successful content or thematic learning and related acquisition of new knowledge, skills and understanding lies at the heart of the learning process. In this section we explore examples of activities that support progression through the creative arts theme, not least because we believe that learning through and about the arts can have a powerful impact on children's wellbeing and lifelong prospects. Geisler (2021), reflecting on the devastating impact of reduced exposure to the arts during the COVID-19 pandemic, cites Director of the Arts Education Partnership Jamie Kasper's summary of more than 300 research studies whose findings show that engagement with the arts 'accelerated all development' including emotional and social development, critical thinking, problem solving, independence, resilience, risk-taking and more.

We begin here with some straightforward ideas for using language within a creative arts theme before moving on to consider project-based ideas for addressing 'big questions' relating to the theme.

Within a creative arts theme, at a basic level we might be posing simple questions using colours vocabulary such as:

- C'est de quelle couleur?   (What colour is it?)
- C'est blanc ou vert?   (Is it white or green?)

We might consolidate colours vocabulary through a range of activities, such as holding up colours that match words in a colours song, sung to the tune of 'Frères Jacques', and then getting children to create their own versions of the song by manipulating coloured cards:

Vert, bleu, blanc
Vert, bleu, blanc
Rouge et jaune
Rouge et jaune
Vert, bleu, blanc
Vert, bleu, blanc
Rouge et jaune
Rouge et jaune

Language reinforcement activities that are also cognitively challenging can be introduced at transition points and lesson starters. Here are six examples which link language and creative arts:

Example 1 – odd one out

Provide children with a list of colours and ask them to think of an odd one out and a reason, and another and another. For instance, consider the following list. Which colour is the odd one out?

jaune, vert, rouge, violet

The answers children suggest might include references to secondary/primary colours, phonics, syllables, alphabetical order, favourite colours, colours of the flag of French Guiana, happy/sad colours etc. Any example a child gives should be welcomed if it is supported by a clear rationale. This activity helps children to think about words in different ways, whilst at the same time offering lots of opportunity for pronunciation practice.

Example 2 – extending patterns

This activity can be linked to maths (patterns and sequences) and music (rhythms). The challenge here is to work out the next set of colour words in each of the sequences in Figure 7.1. As in the previous example, challenge children to try to come up with more than one answer.

bleu	blanc	rouge	rouge	blanc	bleu		
vert	orange	noir	orange	vert	orange		
rouge	jaune	orange	bleu	jaune	vert	blanc	noir

Figure 7.1 Extending patterns

Possible responses for the first sequence (assuming this is one part only of a longer sequence) could include the following:

A   bleu, blanc, rouge, rouge, blanc, bleu, bleu, blanc, rouge, rouge, blanc, bleu . . .
B   bleu, blanc, rouge, rouge, blanc, bleu, rouge, rouge, bleu, blanc, rouge, rouge. . .

Possible responses to the second sequence could include:

C   vert, orange, noir, orange, vert, orange, noir, orange, vert, orange, noir, orange, vert. . .
D   vert, orange, noir, orange, vert, orange, noir, vert, orange, noir, orange, vert, orange, noir . . .

Ask children to clap out the rhythm to the different patterns and feel the different emphasis the changed order of words makes. For instance, see the possible responses to the first sequence with possible **strong beats** and *rests* indicated:

A(i)   **bleu**, blanc, rouge, *rest,* **rouge**, blanc, bleu, *rest,* **bleu**, blanc, rouge, *rest* . . . (4 beats/bar)
A(ii) **bleu**, blanc, rouge, **rouge**, blanc, bleu, **bleu**, blanc, rouge. . . (3 beats/bar)
B   **bleu**, blanc, rouge, rouge, **blanc**, bleu, rouge, rouge, **bleu**, blanc, rouge, rouge (4 beats/bar)

We think there is just one solution to the third sequence of colours, although you may have a good reason to suggest another, and any reasoned response should be welcomed from students. This is our solution:

Rouge **plus** jaune **égale** orange, bleu **plus** jaune **égale** vert, blanc **plus** noir **égale** gris.
Red + yellow = orange, blue + yellow = green, white + black = grey.

This last sequence illustrates the importance of focusing on the core structures that support meaning across topics and subject areas and challenging learners to think about language in different ways, which in turn helps to consolidate the learning in the long-term memory. That 'ah!' moment when children make connections between primary and secondary colours and the mathematical equation is the moment when you know that the children have really engaged with the learning (see also the discussion in Chapter 6 about the use of *égale* in these constructions). The children are also more likely to be actively looking out in future lessons for an activity designed to make them think outside the box.

Example 3 – language awareness through colours

In this activity in the first box (see Table 7.5), the translations of the English colour words are correctly listed under each language, but the words in each column are mixed up. Children are asked to sort the names of the colours in each language and put them correctly in the second box so that they match the English word. Children can usually complete most of the table by recognising patterns and linking with their general awareness of the other languages. When we use this activity with non-specialist teachers, we often find that they are left with just two Portuguese words – *preto* and *vermelho* – and are not sure whether they match with either the English colour word *black* or *red*. Often, they incorrectly select *preto* as red because the two words sound the closest when spoken aloud. However, the clue we give is that one of the two remaining choices is similar to an English colour synonym.

When we do this activity with adults, the painters in the group usually guess correctly that the clue word is *vermilion*, a naturally occurring orangish red pigment which has been used since ancient times and today mostly comes from China. So *vermelho* is Portuguese for *red*. When using this activity with children, they could be given a synonym dictionary or word bank to find out the matching colour word.

Table 7.5 Language awareness through colours

English	Italian	Spanish	French	German	Portuguese
yellow	blu	rojo	vert	schwarz	preto
green	verde	verde	jaune	grün	azul
black	nero	azul	noir	weiß	verde
white	bianco	negro	bleu	gelb	vermelho
red	giallo	blanco	rouge	rot	amarelo
blue	rosso	amarillo	blanc	blau	branco

English	Italian	Spanish	French	German	Portuguese
yellow					
green					
black					
white					
red					
blue					

Example 4 - artist study

A cross-curricular art and language study unit on Picasso (see the artist's biography later in this section) could involve creating and describing self-portraits in the style of the artist using the following example language structures:

Est-ce qu'il a les yeux bleus? (*Does he have* blue eyes?)
Est-ce qu'il a un nez noir **ou** bleu? (*Does he have* a black *or* blue nose?)
Est-ce que tu aimes la peinture? (*Do you like* the painting?)
Pour quoi? (*Why?*)
Parce que . . . (*Because* . . .)

Example 5 - running dictation

This activity is a group barrier game designed to practise speaking and listening skills and to reinforce vocabulary. Barrier games are a specific form of an information-gap activity where child A (or the teacher) has information that child B (or the group) needs. These games provide opportunities for reinforcing newly acquired language in real contexts (Bell Foundation, 2021). Running dictation involves the children taking it in turns to come to the teacher, who reads out one sentence from the following description of a face (which could be a picture in the style of Picasso):

- Il a deux yeux bleus. Il a une bouche jaune. Il a un nez noir. Il a une tête verte. Il a deux oreilles rouges.

The first child goes back and repeats the sentence from memory to the group, who then draw that part of the picture. Another child from the group then runs to the front to hear the teacher say the next part of the description and so on. This activity can be extended over time by providing each child with art materials and giving increasingly more complex instructions in the target language. The children can then compare their pictures and discuss how they interpreted the instructions:

- Draw a large circle in the middle of the page;
- Draw three eyes in the circle;
- Draw two noses above the eyes;
- Draw a square below the circle;
- Draw two ears on top of the circle;
- Draw a mouth under the eyes;
- Colour the eyes yellow;
- Colour the mouth blue;
- Colour the ears red.

This activity can also be completed in pairs with children sitting back-to-back and taking it in turns to draw and describe a picture for their partner to copy.

Wendy:	Virginia, I regularly used to play barrier games in English with my class like the drawing activity described earlier, before I thought about doing them in the target language. I found that they were useful in helping children to tune their ear to the teacher and to each other and required them to express their ideas clearly. The games were also very useful for creating calm classrooms with otherwise challenging groups. I know that barrier games are often suggested as activities to support English as Additional Language learners too. Are there other games or activities that you would recommend teachers use to support language development and executive functioning skills?
Virginia:	One of my favourite games was one that I invented called the 'verb-adverb' game. In this game, you create small cards – one blue pile and one red. All the blue cards have verbs written on them – *run, laugh, sneeze, cry, smile* – and all the red cards have adverbs written on them – *lazily, fast, sadly, wildly, suspiciously*. A volunteer chooses one card from each pile, so they might end up with 'laugh wildly'. They then act this out to the class who try to guess the verb and the adverb. I always played this in English, reinforcing these particular aspects of grammar in a fun, no-pressure, inclusive environment. However, looking back, I wish I had extended this to my foreign language lessons, as it would work extremely well when supporting language progression. You could also ask your EAL learners what the verb/adverb is in their language and create a wonderful multilingual working wall.

Example 6 – Mantle of the Expert – the class curators

Studies of artists can also provide an opportunity to practise the target language within imaginary scenarios. Mantle of the Expert (Heathcote, 2002) is an education approach that uses imaginary contexts to generate purposeful and engaging activities for learning. In this pedagogical approach, the teacher plans a fictional context where the students take on the responsibility of the expert team. The children are then commissioned by a client to work on an assignment which involves tasks requiring them to develop skills across the curriculum. For example, the children could be commissioned by an art gallery as curators for a special exhibition to be held at the school, which parents and other guests including target-language speakers (e.g. language students from the local college) will be invited to attend. Children could be tasked to research information about selected artists and create artefacts and artwork adopting a particular style they have studied. They could record trailers for the exhibition to be uploaded to the school website or shown in whole-school assembly and prepare descriptions of the artwork in the target language to share with visitors.

Describing pictures is an opportunity to reinforce adjectival agreement and prepositions as well as to express opinions and feelings using structures such as these examples:

- Cette peinture est magnifique!
- (This painting is beautiful!)
- Dans la peinture il y a . . . au centre/en haut/en bas/à droite/à gauche.
- (In the painting there is . . . in the centre/at the top/at the bottom/on the right/on the left.)
- Qu'est-ce que ce vous voyez dans la peinture? (What do you see in the painting?)
- Je vois. . . (I see)
- A mon avis. . . (In my opinion)
- J'adore! (I love it!)

Addressing big questions to support progression in language learning

Earlier in the chapter we mentioned using 'big questions' to support progression in language learning (you might want to return to Table 7.3 as a reminder), and we return to this again in Chapter 9 as we consider the leadership of languages and taking a whole-school approach to language learning. Exploring questions and undertaking investigations are central to making progress in language learning since they promote authentic communicative interactions (Stoddart et al., 2002). In this section we examine these pedagogies, continuing the theme of creative arts from the previous discussion and using three big questions as starting points:

- What can I learn from the creativity of others?
- How can I express my ideas and feelings in creative ways?
- What/who determines artistic genius?

This exploration could begin with a supplementary question: 'If sadness were a colour, what colour would it be?' An introduction to the activity could involve a discussion around the word *blues*, which is a noun, as opposed to the word *blue*, which usually takes the form of an adjective in sentences (for example, 'the blue dress/the sea is blue'). Definitions could be explored: ' . . . feelings of melancholy, sadness, or depression . . . also used for melancholic music of black American folk origin, typically in a twelve-bar sequence' (Oxford Languages, 2021).

Children could be asked to match up colours vocabulary with emotions words before listening to extracts of music (which might be songs from different cultures or periods) using colours vocabulary. They could then use the words, known structures and patterns of agreement and extend these to describe the music:

- C'est de quelle couleur?
- Je pense que c'est bleu parce que la musique est triste/calme.

We all see colours in different ways, and so teachers need to be mindful not to make assumptions about what colour a child will associate with an emotion. Barchard, Grob, and Roe

(2017) explain that psychological tests sometimes use examples of figurative language such as 'I feel blue', and that this can be problematic because figurative language may not mean the same thing cross-culturally. For example, in their study in the USA, only 65.9% of participants associated blue with sadness. This reader's response to Cherry's (2017, no page) article about the psychology of the colour blue reveals this rather well:

> Blue is the [colour] of sky, ocean, sleep, and twilight. It is a [colour] that makes me feel so good. When I see it, I almost feel like I am in heaven. For me, blue is the [colour] of sincerity, inspiration, and spirituality. It makes me feel like I am good enough.

These different impressions can be used to begin addressing the first two 'big questions' identified earlier:

- What can I learn from the creativity of others?
- How can I express my ideas and feelings in creative ways?

The expression of ideas and feelings can be further explored through children sharing their colour associations using list poems with the following language structures:

Blau wie. . .   (German: Blue like. . .)
Rosso come. . .   (Italian: Red like. . .)
Jaune comme. . .   (French: Yellow like. . .)
Marrón como. . .   (Spanish: Brown like. . .)

These expressions can be completed at a simple level using a word bank or bilingual dictionary to search for common examples:

Jaune comme une banane.
Jaune comme une banane **et** le soleil.
Jaune comme une banane **et** le soleil **en haut.** (Yellow like a banana and the sun on high.)

Children can use these structures to share their colour associations in creative ways:

Bleu comme une mer calme et un vent doux.
(Blue like a calm sea and a gentle breeze.)

Sharing likes, dislikes and feelings through list poems provides an opportunity to share ideas whilst practising adjectival agreement:

J'aime. . .
la fleur rouge
le soleil jaune
le chat noir
et la pomme verte

Je n'aime pas...
la fleur noire
le soleil rouge
le chat violet
et la pomme marron

Je déteste...
la fleur grise
le soleil noir
le chat rose
et la pomme blanche

Children can be challenged to share their colour associations through an *Elfchen* (which means 'little elf' or 'little eleven'), which is a poem that is similar to a Haiku in that it has a set form. However, an Elfchen is unique in that it has 11 words, the lines having 1-2-3-4-1 words, respectively. Children can write Elfchen poems describing pictures that conjure up different feelings for them, starting with a colour word:

blau
der Himmel
das ruhige Meer
die Dämmerung und Schlaf
glücklich

blue
the sky
the calm sea
the twilight and sleep
happy

So far, we have focused on the first two 'big questions', suggesting ways that languages, investigations, creative arts and so much more can be interwoven to support progress in language learning, not to mention social skills, collaboration, reading and writing. Now we will examine the third question: What/who determines artistic genius? This question might be tackled through a Self-Organised Learning Environment (SOLE) project (these centre around 'big questions' - see more discussion in Chapter 9). O'Malley (2017) suggests that SOLE projects work best where the big question is related to the topic and linked to an intended outcome. The question 'What/who determines artistic genius?' can be introduced to the class to prompt an investigation into role models from different cultures, which in turn can lead to the children sharing and learning new artistic skills and modes of expression for their personal thoughts and feelings. This question could be integrated into a creative arts transition unit with students from Key Stage 2 and Key Stage 3 sharing outcomes. A starting point for class discussions might involve comparing the biographies and works of Picasso and Blanchard, two artists who were both born in Spain and who later lived and worked in France. Here are the details you might want to use:

Picasso

Often described as a genius because of his constant breaking of artistic boundaries and his huge influence on 20th century art, Picasso was born in Malaga, the son of an art teacher. Picasso's full name, which was derived from a list of saints and relatives, was Pablo Diego José Francisco de Paula Juan Nepomuceno Crispín Crispiniano María Remedios de la Santísima Trinidad Ruiz. He moved with his family from Malaga to Barcelona and then went to Madrid to study at the Real Academia de Bellas Artes de San Fernando. Picasso first visited Paris in 1900, returning in 1901 to exhibit at the Gallerie Vollard and remained in Paris through the German occupation, later living mainly in the South of France. Picasso and Georges Braque are both credited for creating Cubism, an artistic movement employing geometric shapes in human and other forms.

María Blanchard

María Blanchard can also be considered a genius – a category in art from which women have traditionally been largely excluded – when measuring her achievements 'against the social and artistic conventions available to Spanish women at that time' (Xon De Ros, 2018, p. 393). María was born with severe skeletal disabilities as a result of an accident her mother had during her pregnancy and was encouraged to sit and paint because she found movement so painful. María was teased at school and turned to painting to express her emotions. In 1903 she moved to Madrid, where she studied at the same academy Picasso attended. After winning third prize at a National Exhibition of Fine Arts, she received funding to study in Paris, where she discovered Cubism and remained there teaching, painting and exhibiting until she died in 1932.

Despite some similarities between Blanchard and Picasso, such as their country of origin, their journeys to Paris and their involvement in the cubism community, it is not easy to uncover much information written about Blanchard or see her art outside of Spain. There are many ideas posted online for using the art of Picasso for classroom activities but little evidence of Blanchard's work being used in schools. The poet Kendig noticed the relative invisibility of Blanchard while searching for inspiration from her works. Kendig describes coming across a picture of Blanchard in an online biography 'standing in the shadows giving an art lesson to a female student who is herself seated in wheelchair' (Kendig, no date, no page). Kendig suggests that Blanchard is giving a second lesson through the picture itself: 'a lesson in getting the work done, despite disability and pain, despite poverty, despite gender and the lack of critical acclaim'.

> Review the planning for arts teaching in your setting. To what extent do the works and people studied represent the diversity of the students? How might your art curriculum support students with their progression in language learning and cultural understanding?

Final thoughts on contexts for progression

Structuring this book has been a challenge, and we might argue that our penultimate chapter (Chapter 9 – Leadership of languages) should come before planning for progression since we can only plan effectively when we know what our goals are. In that chapter we consider the National Curriculum aims for target language learning, including 'foster[ing] children's curiosity', 'deepen[ing] their understanding of the world' and 'learn[ing] new ways of thinking' (DfE, 2013). These are big, bold aims that can only be achieved within creative critical-thinking contexts such as the examples we have shared earlier and which (as we discuss in Chapter 4) encourage risk-taking with the language within a context-rich, collaborative working environment. We simply hope that we have shown some useful ways to structure progression in the primary school and that these activities can be delivered by teachers without specialist linguistic knowledge. In the next chapter we tackle the more challenging issue of how and what to assess!

Summary

- Initial language acquisition is an intuitive and experimental process; language learning is a conscious sequenced process of acquiring knowledge which can be painful and lead to anxiety about 'getting it wrong';
- Metalanguage is the language we use to talk about language;
- In language-aware classrooms, students need to be encouraged to ask questions and to look out for patterns and surprises in their own and the target language;
- Cognitively challenging reinforcement activities require children to think about language in different ways;
- Mantle of the Expert (Heathcote, 2002) is an education approach that uses imaginary contexts to generate purposeful and engaging activities for learning;
- It is important, when planning for progression, to keep in mind the 4C's: Content, Cognition, Communication, Culture;
- Developing students' communicative competence demands a holistic curriculum which enables learners to be able to respond spontaneously, empathically and using appropriate sociocultural norms in a range of language transaction contexts;
- Communicative competence can be developed through activities such as barrier games, which also support development of executive functioning skills;
- A context-rich and collaborative working environment has the potential to increase a willingness to take risks with language use.

References

ALL Connect (no date) 'KS2 language coordinator's handbook', Available at https://allconnectblog.wordpress.com/category/ks2-coordinators-handbook/ (Accessed 10.01.2021).

ALL Connect (no date) 'Transition toolkit', Available at www.all-languages.org.uk/wp-content/uploads/2016/04/Transition-Toolkit.pdf (Accessed 27.01.2021).

AQA (2016) French (8658) 'Scheme of assessment', Available at www.aqa.org.uk/subjects/languages/gcse/french-8658/scheme-of-assessment (Accessed 17.02.2021).

Barchard, K. A. Grob, K. E. & Roe, M. J. (2017) 'Is sadness blue? The problem of using figurative language for emotions on psychological tests', *Behaviour Research Methods*, 49, pp. 443–456.

Bell Foundation (2021) 'Great idea: Barrier games', Available at www.bell-foundation.org.uk/eal-programme/guidance/effective-teaching-of-eal-learners/great-ideas/barrier-games/ (Accessed 29.01.2021).

Bilbrough, M. A. (2017) *A Gesture-Based Approach to Teaching English as a Foreign Language*, Department of English Philology, University of Seville, Available at https://dialnet.unirioja.es/servlet/tesis?codigo=145162 (Accessed 10.02.2021).

Bilbrough, M. A. (2019) 'English classes with gesture', Available at www.gestureway.com/press.htm (Accessed 10.02.2021).

Canale, M. & Swain, M. (1980) 'Theoretical bases of communicative approaches to second language teaching and testing', *Applied Linguistics*, 1, 1, pp. 1–47.

Castello, D. (2015) 'First language acquisition and classroom language learning: Similarities and differences', Available at www.birmingham.ac.uk/Documents/college-artslaw/cels/essays/secondlanguage/First-Language-Acquisition-and-Classroom-Language-Learning-Similarities-and-Differences.pdf (Accessed 29.01.2021).

Cherry, K. (2017) 'The color psychology of blue, very well mind', Available at www.verywellmind.com/the-color-psychology-of-blue-2795815 (Accessed 13.01.2021).

Coyle, D. Holmes, B. & King, L. (2009) *Towards an Integrated Curriculum – CLIL National Statement and Guidelines*, The Languages Company, Available at www.rachelhawkes.com/PandT/CLIL/CLILnational-statementandguidelines.pdf (Accessed 25.08.2020).

Coyle, D. Hood, P. & Marsh, D. (2010) *CLIL Content and Language Integrated Learning*, Cambridge: Cambridge University Press.

Department for Children, Schools and Families (2007) 'Language ladder steps to success', Available at https://allconnectblog.files.wordpress.com/2015/01/ks2-progression-module-languages-ladder-dcsf-00811-2007.pdf (Accessed 10.01.2021).

DfE (2013) 'The national curriculum in England key stages 1 and 2 framework', Available at www.gov.uk/government/publications/national-curriculum-in-england-primary-curriculum (Accessed 02.10.2020).

Ensemble Languages Project (2015) 'KS2 languages progression and assessment overview', Available at www.ensemble-mfl.co.uk/ (Accessed 13.01.2021).

Geisler, J. (2021) 'Pandemic takes a swipe at fine arts education, but might just prove how much it's worth', *ERIE Times News*, Available at https://eu.goerie.com/story/news/2020/10/18/pandemic-takes-swipe-fine-arts-but-might-just-prove-its-worth/5871193002/ (Accessed 10.02.2021).

Heathcote, D. (2002) 'Contexts for active learning – four models to forge links between schooling and society', Available at www.mantleoftheexpert.com/wp-content/uploads/2018/01/dh-contexts-for-active-learning.pdf (Accessed 27.01.2021).

Kendig, D. (no date) 'Speaking of María Blanchard wordgathering: A journal of disability poetry and literature', Available at https://wordgathering.syr.edu/past_issues/issue15/essays/kendig2.html (Accessed 20.01.2021).

Lamb, P. & King, G. (2020) 'Another platform and a changed context: Student experiences of developing spontaneous speaking in French through physical education', *European Physical Education Review*, 26, 2, pp. 515–534.

O'Malley (2017) 'Getting started with self-organized learning environments', Available at www.edutopia.org/blog/getting-started-self-organized-learning-environments-jacquelyn-omalley (Accessed 20.01.2021).

Omniglot (no date) Available at https://omniglot.com/ (Accessed 14.02.2021).

Oxford Languages (2021) Available at https://languages.oup.com/google-dictionary-en/ (Accessed 13.01.2021).

Stoddart, T. Pinal, A. Latzke, M. & Canaday, D. (2002) 'Integrating inquiry science and language development for English language learners', *Journal of Research in Science Teaching*, 39, 8, pp. 664–687.

Tarvin, L. D. (2015) 'Communicative competence: Its definition, connection to teaching, and relationship with interactional competence', *Research Gate*, DOI: 10.13140/RG.2.1.3214.2807.

Xon De Ros (2018) 'María Blanchard and the ideology of primitivism', *Bulletin of Spanish Studies*, 95, 5, pp. 393–410.

8 Assessing progress in language learning

Think of the tools in a tool-box: there is a hammer, pliers, a saw, a screwdriver, a rule, a gluepot, nails and screws. – The function of words are as diverse as the functions of these objects.
(Ludwig Wittgenstein)

Introduction

The Expert Subject Advisory Group Modern Foreign Languages (2015) produced guidance materials to support assessment of the 2014 KS2 Languages Curriculum which suggested a set of principles that should underpin the assessment of language learning. The first three principles outline that assessment should:

- Foster motivation, enjoyment and progress in learners;
- Support learners to feel confident and successful and help build resilience, enthusiasm and persistence in continuing to learn languages;
- Be embedded in the language-learning process, respecting that language development includes making mistakes, whilst also establishing high expectations for individuals.

(ibid., p. 1)

We have used these principles to build the structure for this chapter, suggesting ways to assess children's progress in language learning, which include and go beyond the more traditional methods of formative and summative assessment. Some of the suggestions are opportunistic rather than planned, and this may raise questions in terms of how these opportunities might be recognised and how, if they occur, we can make the most of them. We hope that some of the examples provided will give you confidence in your ability to do this.

There are clearly significant differences in terms of assessing EAL learners' progression in English and assessing all the pupils (including EAL learners) in terms of their progress with the target foreign language. EAL learners are immersed in English all day, every day and therefore opportunities for assessment in terms of teacher observations are ongoing. In contrast, assessment for the foreign language must be specifically built into weekly and termly plans. However, despite these differences, we would argue that there are many crossovers, and often planned opportunities for the whole class will also provide you with a wealth of information relating to your EAL learners' progress in English and the other target language.

We ask you, therefore, to keep an open mind with the suggestions made in the following sections and to consider how useful they might be for *all* the learners in your class and their individual needs.

Assessment opportunities to promote motivation, enjoyment and progress

With language learning, motivation and enjoyment are paramount if children are to make progress. Approaches to teaching and learning which are underpinned by this idea tend to provide rich opportunities for assessment, but we need to be open to these and perhaps think outside the more traditional approaches to assessing progress. We have therefore, decided on three key areas to discuss, which we hope will provide a wealth of ideas and practical strategies which enable you to monitor your pupils' progression:

- Using creative pedagogies and practices;
- Promoting and assessing intercultural understanding;
- Making the most of unplanned opportunities.

Using creative pedagogies and practices

We find that non-specialist language teachers are often concerned about how they can embed formative assessment into their lessons, yet when we talk through with them ideas for planning, we usually identify pedagogies and practices that they have already built into the learning sequence where assessment can take place. Sometimes it is just a matter of recognising moments where there is the potential to really provoke enjoyment and motivation alongside providing ideal opportunities for assessment; at other times it requires a little more thinking to ensure the most creative approaches.

Powerful pedagogies and practices include the use of role play, presentations, retelling of stories and events, and performances of songs. An example of role play might be through the use of a TV quiz show format. Children could be challenged to work in groups to revise what they have learnt so far on a particular topic in the target language – colours for example. They could then be given time to undertake further research around that topic and collate and share this information.

The class can then be set up as a quiz show in which each group member is asked to create their own preferred identity as panel member. The pupils can introduce themselves in role, giving information about hobbies, imaginary family members and favourite subjects. Performing in role in this way will support learner resilience as they are able to deflect 'mistakes' on to the imaginary character they are portraying. It is important, however, to remember to 'de-role' children afterwards if they are 'performing' as a different character. This action of casting off the attributes of the created persona enables children to separate the character from themselves (this may be particularly important for some vulnerable children) and can easily be achieved by asking the children to turn to a partner and share a personal fact, such as their favourite snack, or by prompting them to literally 'shake the character off'.

The TV quiz role play becomes both a motivating 'test', with mixed attainment groups working together to answer questions, and also an opportunity to gather evidence of real time communicative competence. Potentially, quiz questions can be cleverly devised and differentiated to assess reading and writing skills too. These carefully constructed experiences can be enjoyable and motivating whilst also supporting executive functioning skills including self-regulation, attention, focus and cognitive flexibility within a supportive classroom ethos.

Other pedagogies and practices might include end-of-unit performances of songs, stories and other presentations created during the topic focus, which provide an opportunity to assess accurate pronunciation as well as evidence of success at communicating ideas in the target language. The following case study provides an example.

The AMLA Stage C French unit within the 'All about me' theme concludes with a short project investigating the scouting movement in France and French-speaking countries, such as Senegal, and exploring the African Region of the World Association of Girl Guides and Girl Scouts (WAGGS) – https://www.wagggs.org/en/. Member organisations aim to develop girls' and young women's leadership potential through direct project work focused around literacy, peace-building, nutrition, HIV and AIDS prevention, environmental issues, the prevention of violence against women and children and women's rights.

Brownies in France are called 'Jeannettes', and the Senegalese Brownie Law (Loi de la Jeannette) is:

- Une Jeannette est toujours propre.
- Une Jeannette dit toujours vrai.
- Une Jeannette est toujours gaie.
- Une Jeannette est toujours active.
- Une Jeannette pense d'abord aux autres.

Inspired by the work of the WAGGS Africa Region, the children work in groups to translate the 'Loi de les Jeannettes' before creating their own club. After deciding on their club name – the name of an African animal – the children work together to create their law and gesture(s) together with a clapping rhyme which they perform and teach to the rest of the class. This activity provides opportunities for assessing speaking, listening, reading and writing, including understanding and applying adjectival agreement, not to mention aspects of intercultural understanding.

The activities mentioned in this section have been very much centred on children working in groups, giving them the opportunities to collaborate, share and discuss (see Chapter 2 for further discussion on the importance of promoting authentic opportunities for oral interaction). This enables the teacher to stand back and observe, a chance to gather invaluable assessment evidence. These group activities are essential for children with EAL, who may not yet have the confidence or language skills to present information independently or contribute to the more traditional teacher-led question-and-answer sessions.

The two questions I (Virginia) am always asked when working with students and teachers who are focusing on supporting children with EAL are: 'How do you assess children when they cannot speak English and when you do not speak or understand their first language?' and 'If children cannot speak, read or write English, what is to be assessed?' In answer to these questions, observing children in unpressured settings – playground, role-play corner, during games and drama – and when they are working in small groups can provide a considerable amount of information relating to their understanding and ability to participate, interact and use language. You might see a gradual increase in verbal contributions, or you may be able to assess their understanding of a topic by how they participate in a role-play activity. Group activities promote collaborative dialogue, where children are involved in problem solving and the building of knowledge and understanding together. Rogoff (1990, p. 39) equates this to an apprenticeship model where problem solving takes place 'with an active learner participating in culturally organised activity with a more skilled partner' and where collaborative talk can 'mediate cognition' (Swain, Kinnear, and Steinman, 2011, p. 43). This is essential for EAL learners.

Within this collaborative dialogue, there are opportunities to engage in ongoing assessment. Lantolf and Poehner (2008) refer to this as 'dynamic assessment' (DA). With DA, assessment and instruction go hand in hand as the learner develops and the mediator becomes more aware of the learner's abilities and responds to these. This could happen between child and child or between child and teacher, and it links closely with Vygotsky's (1962) theories on the Zone of Proximal Development (ZPD) and support from the 'more able other'. Lantolf and Poehner refer to two types of DA, the most relevant here being 'interactionist' which is about responding immediately to specific needs in ways that are considered the most appropriate at that moment in time, sensitive to learners' 'maturing abilities' (ibid., p. 34). Interactionist DA accepts that development is neither linear nor predictable, and therefore the ZPD is in constant flux, and mediation and assessment has to occur within 'flexible dialogue' (ibid., p. 39). Assessment can occur within this dialogue; it is a holistic view of assessment where you are seizing and recording moments which reveal a growing understanding – whether that be reading comprehension, use of particular words, using more complex written or oral sentences or any other aspect of the curriculum.

Promoting and assessing intercultural understanding

Motivation, enjoyment and progress are all more likely if children feel that they belong to a supportive community, where all cultures, languages, backgrounds and experiences are identified, nurtured and celebrated. Throughout this book we have emphasised the importance of integrating cultural understanding and language learning (see particularly Chapter 3), and therefore the assessment of progress in this area is as important as the assessment of language progression. Interestingly, the word *assessment* derives from the Latin *assidere* ('to sit beside'), which is extremely apt given that the concept of intercultural understanding is tied up with notions of 'self', 'other', 'neighbour' and 'stranger' (McAndless et al., 2020). It might be argued however, that measuring intercultural understanding as an aspect of communicative competence is a more challenging goal and cannot so easily be implemented through activities and the use of resources.

We would suggest that, firstly, we need to clarify that intercultural understanding involves knowledge and understanding about our own and other cultures and the similarities and differences between them. However, as Williams-Gualandi (2015, p. 7) suggests, knowledge alone is not enough. Intercultural understanding also involves critical reflection, problem solving, questioning, open-mindedness, respect and empathy and is 'a developmental, experiential process that involves both engagement with other cultures, and engagement with an understanding of self' (ibid., p. 10). Complicated, therefore, and challenging to assess!

As teachers we cannot begin to assess intercultural understanding in our classes with any confidence, without pausing to reflect on what this means for us as educators and individuals. We also need to think more generally about how assessment is carried out in our class, given that assessments 'are one of the most powerful determinants of practice in the classroom' (Kozma and Roth, 2012 cited in McAndless et al., 2020, p. 4). In this book we have sought to promote a holistic approach to language learning, and therefore we suggest we need to be honest about the purpose and importance of the assessments we use, particularly given the pressures of high-stakes accountability contexts.

McAndless et al. (2020) propose a schema aimed at understanding the underlying intent of intercultural-understanding assessment levels across all educational phases. Borrowing from Haraway's (1992) semiotic square, with its four quadrants representing four different attitudes to the cultural other, they consider the following four notions:

- Strangers we learn cultural facts about;
- Neighbours we learn cultural facts about;
- Strangers involved in transformative action;
- Neighbours involved in transformative action.

We have borrowed these four notions to suggest 'big questions' as end-of-unit reflection prompts for learners (teacher and pupil), and you can see these in Table 8.1.

Table 8.1 Prompts for learners, to enable teacher assessment of intercultural understanding

Strangers we learn cultural facts about For example, finding out about the German resistance through a reading of Rose Blanche (McEwan, 2004)	What have I learned about the perspectives, beliefs and values of people past and present? What will I do with this knowledge? What actions should I take? Will this knowledge and understanding change my perspectives, beliefs and values?
Neighbours we learn cultural facts about For example, finding out about the different games we play	What have I learned about my class peers and neighbours? How are we the same/different? What makes them and me special? What role models from different cultures inspire me?
Strangers involved in transformative action For example, discussing environmental issues	What have I learned about the needs of others? What could I do to help? What help do I need? Who can I ask to support me?
Neighbours involved in transformative action For example, collective action to respond to a social justice issue	What have I learned from working with others to support change? What have I learned from working collaboratively to challenge stereotypes? How are we connected? What makes us 'one'?

> What is your own definition of intercultural understanding? How do you feel about your own confidence in this area? Are there aspects that you feel would benefit from further investigation? How might you go about assessing children's intercultural understanding?

Making the most of unplanned opportunities

Opportunities for formative assessment often occur without our planning, and these are to be grasped with grateful hands! These are usually moments when children take over the lesson in some way - perhaps because they are familiar with the theme you are introducing, or perhaps something you share or show connects with a previous experience they have had in school or in a different context. Unfortunately, because of the pressure of fulfilling curriculum objectives, meeting targets and 'getting through' the content, these moments are sometimes missed or ignored, and powerful opportunities go to waste.

One of the challenges of teaching is knowing when to abandon the intended pathway through the lesson and go with the ideas of the children. Sometimes this can feel risky, particularly when we are working in a culture of surveillance and accountability and feel that much of what we do as teachers is judged and scrutinised (Ball, 2004). However, what we have to keep in the front of our minds is that every teacher and every child will be different, and all will react to different stimuli, environments, questions, resources etc. in diverse ways. So control is an illusion! Alexander talks about the idea that when teachers and children work with a curriculum, it undergoes 'a series of translations, transpositions and transformations' (2009, p. 8), and this is a wonderful way of acknowledging the impact of those working with a curriculum. The following example, focusing on an EAL learner, illustrates how this type of situation might arise and the opportunities it affords.

> Many years ago, I (Virginia) was teaching a Year 6 class a geography lesson focusing on countries, continents and oceans. On the interactive whiteboard I was showing a world map, and children were coming up and marking the names of any countries and continents that they knew. We then moved onto oceans, and before I could ask for any volunteers, my one Bulgarian boy in the class shot to his feet, grabbed the pen and wrote all the oceans in the correct places within seconds. He then turned and beamed at the class, before turning back to the board and pointing out his home country and the area of his home town. At that stage, Pieter had very little English, but he made his ideas very clear, and the remainder of the class were captivated!
>
> This small incident, where purely because of the unfolding events I was a bystander and temporarily 'out of a job' (!), provided me with a wealth of assessment evidence in a very short time. I became more aware of Pieter's cognition, his knowledge and understanding, use of language and his levels of confidence.

This example describes the role that an EAL learner played in this lesson and how an unplanned activity benefitted all the children in the class. But more relevant to this chapter, this unplanned incident enabled me to stand back and observe this particular child and also the reactions and interactions of all the class. Very often we are so involved with the lesson and supporting children, preparing resources and undertaking classroom management, that we do not have time and space to take that step away which gives us a chance to see the children's progress with fresh eyes. So, if the children decide to 'hijack' your lesson, make the most of it!

Assessment that builds confidence, enthusiasm, resilience and persistence

Effective assessment of language learning requires a careful balance of activities whereby children can identify their own progress and enjoy both the challenge and rewards of learning a new language, whilst realizing that a certain degree of resilience and persistence is required. This section of the chapter examines three ways that these four characteristics can be supported, so that children enjoy the process and we as teachers can assess their progress without triggering any of the stresses often associated with assessment. These three ways are:

- Testing;
- Portfolios;
- Virtual technologies.

Effective use of testing

Being tested on what we have been learning boosts long-term memory (Toppino and Cohen, 2009), and evidence suggests that students who test *themselves* remember information better than students who spend the same amount of time trying to learn the same material.

However, by our use of the word *test* here we are not referring to the kind of high-stakes testing that can lead to considerable anxiety for both teacher and student and lead to debates about unfairness (for instance questions that disadvantage particular student groups) and which involve measurements against externally agreed norms. Norm-referenced tests are measures that compare a student's knowledge or skills to the knowledge or skills of the 'norm group', which could be class peers, or in the case of high-stakes testing a nationally or internationally agreed norm. Norm-referenced test results rank a student's performance in comparison to the performance of students in the norm group; however the ranking itself does not indicate whether or not they meet or exceed a specific standard or criterion.

Class teachers typically set criterion-referenced tests, which are measured against a standard or set of criteria and are designed to assess the knowledge and skills the students are most likely to have learned in order to check how close the student is to mastering a specific standard. As such, these tests will not measure the learning that a student may have made outside of the 'most likely' set of knowledge and skills and are therefore, arguably, limited and limiting. In order to set these tests, assessment scales might be used, and these are widely available for foreign-language assessment and also scales to support assessment for EAL learners. You may want to visit the NALDIC website (https://naldic.org.uk) or the Bell Foundation (www.bell-foundation.org.uk/) for examples.

The third type of assessment testing is self-referential or ipsative assessment, which compares existing performance with previous accomplishment (Hughes, 2014), for example a personal best time for running three laps round the local park. Hughes argues that although ipsative assessment regularly takes place informally in schools, for instance through the giving out of special awards for personal academic or other progress at assembly time, it is rarely used as a formal approach to assessment. Since ipsative assessment rewards *progress* rather than achievement, it has the potential to motivate all learners (Hughes, 2017) and Ventista (2018) suggests that this type of testing may be particularly beneficial for learners consistently performing at the lower end of their student group. This is because instead of feeling that they are not performing well enough when measured against a particular standard and constantly comparing themselves to their peers, they can feel rewarded when their personal progress is recognised; thus 'ipsative assessment encourages them to be better than their previous selves' (ibid, no page).

The word *ipsative* comes from the Latin *ipse* meaning 'of the self'. Our holistic approach to language learning throughout this book has centred on the child's developing sense of self, and you will not be surprised therefore that we agree with Armstrong's (2020) suggestion that ipsative assessments are potentially more important and useful than criterion-referenced tests or norm-based standardised assessments. Ipsative assessments might take the form of repeated and self-selected vocabulary or grammar knowledge tests, student-selected examples of work outcomes indicating progress over time, or video/audio recordings of language tasks/performances at the start/end of the year, supported by pupil/teacher/parent conferences.

> Review your current planning. Are there activities that can be easily adapted to support teacher and pupil assessment? Could you include further opportunities to 'test' children's language progression in non-threatening and motivating ways?

Portfolio approaches to assessment

While tests are clearly useful for information retrieval, they do not give teachers a full picture of real foreign language usage. Portfolio assessment has this advantage, as it refers to the creation by the student of a record of class activity. Arroway (2021) suggests that there are three key benefits to using portfolios to support student assessments:

- They track and record classroom activity in a creative and easy way;
- They can help make the teacher's final assessment more accurate;
- Students are involved in recognising their own progress.

Given that we previously argued that ipsative assessment might be more valuable than the teacher's formative and summative assessments (here we are referring to the importance of learner goal-setting and monitoring progress against their previous best), the third benefit of portfolio approaches suggests a strong rationale for using portfolios in the language-learning classroom.

An example of this can be seen in the European Language Portfolio (ELP). The ELP was developed by the Language Policy Programme of the Council of Europe with the following purposes in mind:

- 'To support the development of learner autonomy, plurilingualism and intercultural awareness and competence;
- To allow users to record their language learning achievements and their experience of learning and using languages'.

(Council of Europe, 2020, no page)

The ELP was designed to motivate learners 'by acknowledging their efforts to extend and diversify their language skills at all levels' and 'to provide a record of the linguistic and cultural skills they have acquired' (ibid., no page). The ELP was also intended to be something that they could refer to when they were moving to a higher level of study or when they sought employment at home or abroad.

The Council of Europe created a 'Junior' version of the ELP as an initiative linked to the European Day of Languages in 2001. It was intended to be an open-ended record of a pupil's achievements in languages which could be kept by the teacher on behalf of the pupil and also provide valuable information to transfer to the next class/school. Scotland's National Centre for Languages (SCILT, 2014) provides an adapted version of the ELP on its website (https://scilt.org.uk/) aimed at allowing learners to transfer their knowledge across languages and celebrate wider achievement and learning experiences that take place in and out of the classroom. This case study shows how Wendy utilised a language portfolio approach in her teaching.

Languages Portfolio

I (Wendy) introduced an adapted version of the Languages Portfolio in my first school, adhering to the ELP developer guide slogan, 'Adapt to the curriculum but value out-of-school learning!' (Schneider and Lenz, 2001, p. 19). The first section of the portfolio is a biography where children share information about the languages they speak and their wider language and intercultural experiences. I learned so much about the children through the discussions we had around their language experiences (I found out that one Romanian child in my class spoke seven languages!). Other children who thought they spoke just English realised that they knew lots of words and phrases in different languages and understood aspects of a range of cultures from the holidays they had experienced and from the films, television programmes and online media they had engaged with. Children who spoke languages other than English were able to track their progress with their home languages in addition to their progress in speaking, listening, reading and writing in the target language. The children could also map their progress against simple 'can do' statements and could set targets for future goals.

If you decide to develop your own version of the Junior European Languages Portfolio, you might want to link pupil 'can do' targets to the progression steps in the KS2 Languages Progression and Assessment, which emerged out of the Ensemble Languages Project (2015) and which we discussed in Chapter 7. You could also plan reflection points at the end of each lesson/unit, as in the AMLA project plans, so that children can link the target language and intercultural understanding learning with their own language and culture.

Virtual technologies for assessment

The use of virtual technologies can motivate children and build their confidence, as for many these online environments are familiar. They can also provide opportunities for self-assessment and teacher assessment. If you have ever tried to learn a language through an online application (app) you may have experienced some of the benefits and limitations of learning through virtual technologies. One key benefit is the opportunity for independent learning and the option to study at your own pace in your own time. Most apps provide visual support which can help with consolidating memorisation of the new language and, where speaking tasks are also incorporated, this is clearly better than trying to speak the language on your own. On the other hand, apps are quite impersonal compared to face-to-face learning and rarely mimic genuine communicative transactions. They can also limit the learner's creative responses to the topic being studied. Therefore, the best use of online apps is to practice and test language knowledge; apps may also provide a motivating stimulus for language learning particularly where they replicate the gaming experiences that children experience outside of the classroom.

Next, we share case studies of two examples of virtual tools designed to provide non-threatening and motivating assessment opportunities.

The Language Magician

Ten partners from four European countries, led by the Goethe-Institut London, built a strategic partnership to support foreign-language teaching and learning at primary school. One main aim of the European Languages Project was to develop a computer game called 'The Language Magician' that could be used by teachers to assess their pupils' language abilities using 'non-threatening testing methods', recognising the challenge of finding assessment methods that 'protect rather than diminish motivation' whilst also providing 'valid and reliable measurements of learners' attainment' (Courtney and Graham, 2019, p. 6).

Versions of the game, which was based on extensive research, together with training manuals for teachers are available in English, French, German, Spanish and Italian. The game was tested in 40 schools with over 6,000 pupils in four countries, and the outcomes were evaluated in research projects by university partners. Findings by Courtney and Graham (ibid.) showed that learners responded positively towards the game irrespective of their levels of attainment, suggesting the potential for digital game-based assessment to support early language-learning progression. Access to the game and support materials are free for schools and can be downloaded from the Language Magician website (www.thelanguagemagician.net/).

Assessing progress in language learning 151

> What can you see as the advantages of using virtual technologies to support learning and assessment? What might be the challenges?

Circumstances often result in new strategies and approaches and, as teachers, we are responsible for being open to new ideas and ways of teaching and learning. The following case study describes how the COVID-19 pandemic led to the use of new online tools for language assessment.

Video tools for language assessment

School closures during the COVID-19 pandemic forced teachers to find new ways of teaching and assessing during distance learning. The abundance of language-learning apps and teacher sharing through social media meant that there were many tools to experiment with, and this enabled language teachers to develop new skills in challenging times. One such app is Flipgrid -https://info.flipgrid.com/ - a free tool designed to foster short video-based discussions on classroom topics and enable educators, learners and families to stay connected. Teachers can post prompts (such as questions, images or videos), and students can then record a video response. Videos can be set up to be shared just with the teacher or to support peer-to-peer interactions. During school closures, some students who previously suffered from social anxiety and performance-related worries in school environments enjoyed the opportunity to privately record their responses in the home environment and to connect one-to-one with their class teacher.

> Can you think of ways that you might incorporate the use of video to support children's motivation and to provide you with a creative way to assess progress in language learning?

Using mistakes when assessing progress in language learning

If we go back to the principles identified in the chapter introduction, taken from the Expert Subject Advisory Group Modern Foreign Languages (2015), the third of these includes the recommendation of 'respecting that language development includes making mistakes, whilst also establishing high expectations for individuals'. In this section, we explore the idea that making mistakes can be a positive, powerful way to develop learning and to support assessment of progress but that this needs to be approached carefully and in a way that is mindful of children's mental wellbeing.

We began Chapter 7 by reflecting on the natural errors children make during the initial language-acquisition stages as they experiment with language and how we often find these error expressions endearing. However, in the language-learning classroom, an emphasis on these mistakes can be detrimental to motivation, self-esteem and progress. Bartram and Walton (1991, p. 2) talk about a 'mistake obsession' not generally found outside the world of language teaching and learning and suggest that those who are less confident about their own language proficiency worry about it more than others because of their anxiety about 'correcting the rightness/wrongness of their students' English'.

Languages are constantly changing, and rule usage shifts over time; what was unacceptable in the past may gradually become an accepted norm. Even confident English speakers will ask questions about which words need hyphenating or whether to add an s after an apostrophe to show possession for a single noun that ends in s; for example, whether we should write *James's* or *James'* (both are now acceptable, although the latter is more common). Bartam and Walton (ibid.) remind us that our knowledge of our own language is only very partial; what is a 'normal' expression in London may be unheard of in Liverpool. However, although languages are constantly changing and adapting, this does not mean that anything goes at any time. Bradshaw (2013, no page) argues that 'the better the grammar, the clearer the message [and therefore] the more likelihood of understanding the message's intent and meaning'. If we are unsure about grammar rules in English or the target language, it is perfectly acceptable to say, 'I don't know'; in fact, it is good to say, 'I am not sure. Let's find out what the experts say' and then do some research with the students through checking dictionaries and grammar texts. Discussing grammar and punctuation rules in this way will help learners to both understand and learn them.

> Do you worry about your own language mistakes? How do you respond when they are pointed out to you? How do you respond to the children when they make mistakes? What is the impact of your response if you correct mistakes? How might different approaches to language mistakes support progression in language learning? How might these mistakes contribute to effective assessment?

As we discussed in Chapter 7, knowledge of grammar rules is only one aspect of communicative competence. Therefore, when we are assessing children as language learners, we should focus on all four elements – grammatical, sociolinguistic, discourse, strategic – and the comprehensibility of the linguistic interactions, rather than an excessive focus on accuracy of form. If we initially consider how successfully and strategically children have communicated *their ideas* in a variety of ways, we might praise these achievements more and focus less on highlighting errors in grammatical features other than to prompt students to correct the specific elements that we have been focusing on for that lesson. This focus on strengths rather than weaknesses may have a positive impact on both our own and the students' confidence with communicating through the language.

At the same time, we should not be afraid of mistakes, since research evidence suggests that they can help us learn faster. For instance, a study by Kornell, Hays, and Bjork (2009, p. 989) aimed to examine whether unsuccessful retrieval attempts impede future learning or enhance it. Their research involved using materials that ensured that retrieval attempts would be unsuccessful. For instance, participants in the 'test' group were presented with fictional general knowledge questions which they attempted to answer before being shown the answer. Participants in the 'read only' group were presented with the question and answer together. The researchers found that unsuccessful retrieval attempts involving the different types of materials used in the study enhanced learning and concluded that unsuccessful tests are helpful not hurtful (although they stipulate that providing feedback is critical). When children are supported to develop self-regulatory and control functions through engaging in metacognitive discussions around the emotional feelings involved in error making (Lucangeli et al., 2019), they are more likely to become resilient learners aware of their own strengths and areas for improvement.

Budden (2008, no page) suggests that there is a delicate balance to be had between an avoidance of over-correction (students may lose motivation and the lesson/activity may be disrupted if every mistake is corrected) and overlooking all errors in order to 'let the conversation flow'. He suggests talking to students to find out how they like to be corrected, for instance by using a traffic light system:

- Red = Don't correct me at all. (They may have had a rough day or be tired!)
- Orange = Correct things which are really important or things I should know.
- Green = Correct as much as you can, please.

Armstrong (2020) suggests that many 'mistakes' may be simple slips (we made many of these in our first drafts of this book), and a simple gesture such as a hand signal can indicate the type of error - for instance an angled finger to prompt the writer to add an accent to a spelling. In collaborative classrooms, students can also supportively correct each other, and Armstrong also suggests setting regular 'timeout' slots to look at mistakes as a group. Other approaches include pupil self-correction as the first 'port of call'.

Wendy: I make mistakes in my writing all the time. My mind is often racing and thinking about lots of things at once, and it is very common for me to write things back-to-front or write the completely wrong word without realising that I have made a mistake. For instance, at the beginning of a school day I would be so busy thinking about the first lesson that I would rarely write the correct date on the board; usually I would write either the wrong day of the week or the wrong month or the wrong year (sometimes it would be February before I started writing the correct year!). I would challenge the children to spot my 'deliberate' mistakes, and they always did! I also *deliberately* - note the italics for intent - planned mistakes for lessons; for instance, I would give some wrong answers when children were self-marking tests and encourage the children to challenge the answers, explaining why they were wrong. I think this helped to consolidate the concepts we were learning.

Virginia, how do you suggest we should respond to the mistakes made by children with English as an additional language?

Virginia: A great question, Wendy! Firstly, I want to emphasise the fact that the errors made by EAL learners are some of our most valuable pieces of assessment evidence. From these, we begin to learn what specific support a child needs at any particular time. The errors might involve using incorrect nouns, for example saying 'sky' instead of 'sea' when talking about a seaside environment. This immediately provides us with information regarding a particular lexical set of words. Lexical sets are connected words relating to a subject. Table 8.2 is an example of a lexical set relating to the seaside.

So, our child has said 'sky' instead of 'sea'. We could now do a small intervention, going through the lexical set needed for this subject, and this could be with the whole class (if they are very young children, this intervention would be useful for all) or with the individual/a small group. Lexical sets are even more powerful when translations can be made so that the resource shows English and the child's language (see Portuguese example Table 8.3).

A different error might involve word order and, again, this provides useful assessment evidence and indicates the next type of support that might be useful. In this case, providing jumbled-up sentences that the child is required to put into the correct order is a useful exercise and one that, in my experience, all children love to do! These should not be abstract, de-contextualised sentences using downloadable worksheets - instead they need to be related perhaps to a topic under study or something that the child is interested in. If this exercise is completed within topic work, all children can be involved, even though you are specifically aiming at those who will benefit most from word order support.

Another useful strategy in response to mistakes is 'recasting'. This is where you repeat what the child has said, but with the error corrected. For example, the child might say, 'I love to swim in the sky', to which you would respond, 'Ah, you love to swim in the *sea*'. Too often I hear children corrected in a less positive way, for example, 'No, not sky - it is sea'. Just by changing our use of language and thinking of *recasting* as opposed to correcting, we can support children's self-esteem rather than making them feel they are wrong and potentially less likely to try in the future.

Table 8.2 Lexical set - at the seaside

sand
sandcastle
windbreak
pebbles
sea
waves
crab
rock pool
cliffs
sunshade
sun cream
ice cream

Table 8.3 Lexical set – at the seaside – in two languages

sand	a areia
sandcastle	o castelo de areia
windbreak	o quebra-vento
pebbles	os seixos
sea	o mar
waves	as ondas
crab	o caranguejo
rock pool	o grupo de rock
cliffs	os penhascos
sunshade	o guarda-sol
sun cream	o creme solar
ice cream	o sorvete

Bartram and Walton (1991) propose a set of questions teachers should ask themselves before responding to children's mistakes. We have adapted their questions in the following bullet points. Which do you think are the most important? How will your answers influence your responses to the language mistakes children make?

- Does the mistake affect communication?
- Is the current focus of the lesson on accuracy of form?
- Is this really an error or my imagination?
- Why did the student make the mistake?
- If this is a spoken error, does the student often speak?
- What student behaviour might my correction provoke?
- Are other students making the same mistake?
- Is this something the students have already encountered?
- What day/time is it?
- What's the weather like today?

Summary

- Language assessment should foster motivation, enjoyment and progress;
- To ensure progress, language learners need to feel confident and successful;
- As teachers, we need to help build resilience, enthusiasm and persistence in continuing to learn languages;
- Assessment needs to be embedded in the language-learning process;
- Creative pedagogies, practices and resources should be utilised to support language learning;
- Planned and unplanned activities can provide invaluable assessment evidence;
- Assessment of intercultural understanding is challenging but essential in a language-focused classroom;
- Making the most of mistakes and addressing them in a positive way supports language learning.

References

Alexander, R. (2009) 'Towards a comparative pedagogy', in Cowen, R. & Kasamias, A. M. (eds.) *International Handbook of Comparative Education* (pp. 911–929), New York: Springer.

Armstrong, T. (2020) *10 Things Educators Should Know About Ipsative Assessments*, American Institute for Learning and Human Development, Available at www.institute4learning.com/2020/03/05/10-things-educators-should-know-about-ipsative-assessments/ (Accessed 19.02.2021).

Arroway, R. (2021) *The Guide to Using Portfolio Assessment in Language Teaching: 6 Tips for Success*, Fluent U Enux Education, Available at www.fluentu.com/blog/educator/assessment-in-language-teaching-2/ (Accessed 17.02.2021).

Ball, S. J. (ed.) (2004) *The Routledge Falmer Reader in Sociology of Education*, London and New York: Routledge Falmer.

Bartram, M. & Walton, W. (1991) *Correction: A Positive Approach to Language Mistakes*, Cengage Learning.

Bradshaw, W. B. (2013) 'Why grammar is important', *HuffPost*, Available at www.huffpost.com/entry/why-grammar-is-important_b_4128521 (Accessed 19.02.2021).

Budden, J. (2008) 'Error correction', in *Teaching English*, British Council, Available at www.teachingenglish.org.uk/article/error-correction (Accessed 19.02.2021).

Council of Europe (2020) 'The European languages portfolio', Available at www.coe.int/en/web/portfolio (Accessed 19.02.2021).

Courtney, L. & Graham, S. (2019) '"It's like having a test but in a fun way": Young learners' perceptions of a digital game based assessment of early language learning', *Language Teaching for Young Learners*, 1, 2, pp. 161–186.

Ensemble Languages Project (2015) 'KS2 languages progression and assessment overview', Available at www.ensemble-mfl.co.uk/ (Accessed 13.01.2021).

Expert Subject Advisory Group Modern Foreign Languages (2015) 'Assessment in modern foreign languages in the primary school', Available at www.all-languages.org.uk/wp-content/uploads/2016/01/ESAGMFLGroupAssessmentStatement.pdf (Accessed 19.02.2021).

Haraway, D. (1992) 'The promises of monsters: A regenerative politics of inappropriate/d others', in Grossberg, L. Nelson, C & Treichler, P. A. (eds.), *Cultural Studies* (pp. 295–336), London: Routledge.

Hughes, G. (2014) *Ipsative Assessment: Motivation Through Marking Progress*, Basingstoke: Palgrave Macmillan.

Hughes, G. (2017) *Ipsative Assessment and Personal Learning Gain: Exploring International Case Studies*, London: Palgrave Macmillan.

Kornell, N. Hays, M. J. & Bjork, R. A. (2009) 'Unsuccessful retrieval attempts enhance subsequent learning', *Journal of Experimental Psychology: Learning, Memory, and Cognition*, 35, pp. 989–998.

Kozma, R. B. & Roth, M. (2012) 'Forward', in Griffin, P. McGaw, B. & Care, E. (eds.), *Assessment and Teaching of 21st Century Skills* (pp. v–viii), New York: Springer.

Lantolf, P. J. & Poehner, M. E. (2008) *Sociocultural Theory and the Teaching of Second Languages*, London: Equinox.

Lucangeli, D. Fastame, M. C. Pedron, M. Porru, A. Duca, V. Hitchcott, P. K. & Penna, M. P. (2019) 'Metacognition and errors: The impact of self-regulatory trainings in children with specific learning disabilities', *ZDM Mathematics Education*, 51, pp. 577–585.

McAndless, T. Fox, B. Moss, J. & Chandir, H. (2020) 'Assessing intercultural understanding: The facts about strangers', *Educational Review*, DOI: 10.1080/00131911.2020.1825336.

McEwan, I. (2004) *Rose Blanche*, Devon: Red Fox.

Rogoff, B. (1990) *Apprenticeship in Thinking*, New York: Open University Press.

Schneider, G. & Lenz, P. (2001) 'European language portfolio: Guide for developers', Available at https://rm.coe.int/1680459fa3 (Accessed 19.02.2021).

SCILT (2014) 'Junior European language portfolio', Available at https://scilt.org.uk/News/NewsView/tabid/1311/articleType/ArticleView/articleId/3436/SCILTs-Junior-European-Language-Portfolio-available-for-download-now.aspx (Accessed 19.02.2021).

Swain, M. Kinnear, P. & Steinman, L. (2011) *Sociocultural Theory in Second Language Education an Introduction Through Narratives*, Bristol: Multilingual Matters.

Toppino, T. C. & Cohen, M. S. (2009) 'The testing effect and the retention interval: Questions and answers', *Experimental Psychology*, 56, 4, pp. 252–257.

Ventista, O. (2018) 'Can you become better than yourself?' *Evidenced Based Education*, Available at https://evidencebased.education/ipsative-assessment/ (Accessed 19.02.2021).

Vygotsky, L. S. (1962) *Thought and Language*, Cambridge, MA: The MIT Press.

Williams-Gualandi, D. (2015) 'Intercultural understanding: What are we looking for and how do we assess what we find?' *International and Global Issues for Research*, Working Papers Series No. 7, Available at www.bath.ac.uk/publications/department-of-education-working-papers/attachments/intercultural-understanding-what-are-we-looking-for.pdf (Accessed 19.02.2021).

9 Leadership of languages – a whole-school approach to planning and implementing a language-focused curriculum

How does language evolve? How did we get from Shakespeare to here?
(School in the Cloud, 2020 Location: Goa, India)

The School in the Cloud platform was inspired by Sugata Mitra's 1999 pioneering 'Hole in the Wall' experiments into self-directed learning or what Mitra terms as 'Minimally Invasive Education (MIE)' (Mitra, 2012), in which groups of children taught themselves to become sophisticated computer-users on a machine sunk into the wall of a New Delhi slum. The School in the Cloud initiative continues Mitra's research by enabling educators to run their own Self-Organised Learning Environment (SOLE), within which an educator poses a 'big question', such as these examples from India, and students form small groups to find an answer.

'Big questions' are so called because, as in the questions that start this chapter, taken from School in the Cloud, they do not have an easy answer. They may be open, difficult, uncomfortable. They may even be unanswerable.

You will be aware through the previous chapters that we believe there are many 'big questions' that language-aware classrooms and schools need to consider, such as 'How gender-inclusive are the practices in our school?' and, 'To what extent are all children provided with the linguistic support necessary to access the curriculum and fulfil their potential?' These questions have led us to long conversations, some of which we have shared with you, and although we have not always presented easy answers, we hope that you have found examples throughout each chapter of pragmatic ways to begin to put into place an effective and inclusive language-focused curriculum.

It seemed only right therefore, to continue the theme of 'big questions' as we near the end of this book and to link these questions to key aspects we believe leaders need to consider when developing an effective whole-school language approach. The chapter starts with an introduction to our five 'big questions' and then goes on to address each in turn with examples from practice and case studies to illustrate key points. We finish in a different way to the previous chapters with, rather than a summary, a look at some of the potential language-leadership challenges and how we might approach these to ensure leadership for change.

We believe that we are *all* language teachers and that leadership can take place at *all* levels. As teachers we are always tackling complex issues, but adopting a values- and evidence-based approach allows us to establish some straightforward principles and practices that will help us to nurture and manage the inclusive classrooms to which we all aspire. Whether you are reading this chapter as a school leader, subject leader, class teacher or student teacher, we hope that you find the ideas useful in helping to identify the role you can play as a leader of a language-focused curriculum.

Our big questions

1. What are the aims of the wider school curriculum?
    - Establishing the aims of the wider school curriculum
2. Where should we position English/L1, ancient/modern languages, language awareness and English as an additional language within school policy?
    - Establishing the purpose (intent) of the curriculum
3. Who should lead on language-focused curriculum development, and how can language leadership promote democratic citizenship?
    - Creating and leading a whole-school languages curriculum – the role of student and parental voice, choice and global citizenship
4. How can we engage children with 'big questions' through the language curriculum?
    - Implementing the curriculum (understanding the art and science of language learning)
5. How can we know whether the curriculum is meeting the stated aims?
    - Understanding the role of language in structural inequalities based on race, social class, gender and other differences;
    - Evaluating the curriculum (audit tool).

> We have stated our 'big questions'. What are your 'big questions'?
> These might be questions that have emerged through your reading of previous chapters and/or questions that relate to your teaching context. For example, what are the 'big questions' prompted by your school mission and values statement?

Big question 1: What are the aims of the wider school curriculum?

As we have discussed in previous chapters, the teaching of languages cannot stand alone and, therefore, to establish the purpose of the languages curriculum we need first to understand the aims and purpose of the *whole* curriculum. For instance, in England every state-funded school must offer a curriculum which is balanced and broadly based and which:

- Promotes the spiritual, moral, cultural, mental and physical development of pupils at the school and of society;
- Prepares pupils at the school for the opportunities, responsibilities and experiences of later life.

(DfE, 2013)

These two statements link to the English School Inspection Framework (Ofsted, 2019), which, in its quality-of-education judgement, refers to the extent to which schools equip pupils with the knowledge and 'cultural capital they need to succeed in life'. The term 'cultural capital' was originally coined in the 1970s by the sociologist Pierre Bourdieu to explain how power in society was transferred and social classes maintained. Bourdieu identified three types of capital – economic, cultural and social – and suggested every individual has a portfolio made up of different volumes of each type. Bourdieu argued that children from 'culturally wealthy' families inherit that wealth and because they speak the same cultural language – for instance in the books they read and the places they have visited – they are perceived to be 'brighter' and more articulate by their teachers than children who do not share the same knowledge or experiences (Grenfell, 2014). The Ofsted understanding of 'knowledge and cultural capital' is derived from the National Curriculum definition of cultural capital as: 'the essential knowledge that pupils need to be educated citizens, introducing them to the best that has been thought and said and helping to engender an appreciation of human creativity and achievement' (DfE, 2013).

What this definition does not make clear is who decides what is 'the best that has been thought and said' within any culture nor what value should be placed on what has been thought, said and created within the multicultural contexts of our diverse school communities. To illustrate, if we search online for a list of 'the best writers of all time' we are likely to be presented with a predominance of (mostly male) English-language writers such as Shakespeare, Brontë, Chaucer, Conrad and Dickens. However, these lists are perhaps not so much about what *writing* (or language) is the best than what *texts* (and which languages) have been the most influential.

The origin of the phrase 'the best that has been thought and said' is the preface to Matthew Arnold's enormously influential and controversial series of essays, 'Culture and Anarchy'. For Arnold (1822–1888) – inspector of schools and professor of poetry at Oxford University – culture is rooted in a pursuit to lead a good life through the study of perfection, and this involves drawing on the best that has been known, thought and created in the world. There is, however, a real danger of a biased or exclusive perspective on what constitutes the cultural capital needed for a successful life in the development of any national or school curriculum which could potentially lead to limiting practices in the classroom, which exclude groups or individuals (see our discussions on artist studies in Chapter 7). It is critical, therefore, that schools consider how they can draw on the diverse voices of their school communities when creating curriculum policies.

Reading Arnold now may lead us, as Garnett (2006, p. xxviii) suggests, to a deep appreciation of the 'foreignness' of the Victorian era within which he wrote (Garnett, 2006, p. xxviii), and yet despite the huge gulf between this period of colonial history and the constantly changing globalised world in which we now live, it is interesting to note that many of Arnold's outlined principles of critical engagement can still be found paraphrased in values statements on various school websites today, both in England and internationally. For instance, see our interpretation (in brackets) of some of Arnold's principles:

- The embracing of disciplined curiosity   (asking questions);
- The commitment to transformation rather than affirmation   (growth and open mindsets);
- The development of a 'sensibility for perfection'   (pursuit of excellence);
- The setting of a purpose and being obstinate in its pursuit (goal orientation).

Earlier references to 'a study of perfection' and 'the pursuit of excellence' are rather daunting and may make us forget that all children bring cultural capital to the classroom in their unique beliefs, interests, cultural and family heritage and traditions. We believe that developing cultural capital from the early years is about valuing the diverse cultural wealth that the children bring with them as well as opening their minds to the 'awe and wonder of the world in which they live' (Ofsted, 2019a, p. 13), which leads us on to an examination of spiritual development within the curriculum.

> What does 'cultural capital' mean to you?
> What do you consider to be the best that has been thought and said?

Like culture, spirituality has been variously defined. It can be interpreted in a religious sense as the individual's relationship with a deity or faith system. It can also be described as a list of characteristics in a person such as beliefs, a sense of awe and wonder, mystery, a search for meaning and purpose, gratitude, hope, love, courage, self-knowledge, feelings and emotions (Geisenberg, 2000). The Ofsted Inspection Framework (2019b) includes judgements on the extent to which children demonstrate the following aspects of spiritual development:

- An ability to be reflective about their own beliefs (religious or otherwise) and perspective on life;
- Knowledge of, and respect for, different people's faiths, feelings and values;
- A sense of enjoyment and fascination in learning about themselves, others and the world around them.

Exploring the spiritual dimension inevitably leads to the asking of 'big questions' such as 'Who am I?' and 'Where do I belong?', questions that can be explored in the classroom by celebrating and sharing aspects of the uniqueness and similarities of children's identities through language-focused teaching (see examples in previous chapters and also in the case studies later in this chapter).

Just from these few examples, it is evident that an authentic commitment to an effective language-focused curriculum needs to be underpinned by wider aims which reflect the fact that our spiritual, cultural and linguistic lives are bound up with history and politics, with the local and the global, the personal and the professional. A flexible approach to the prescribed curriculum objectives is often needed to ensure that our aims for the wider school curriculum take into consideration the diversity within our setting and put the children at the heart of these aims. This then allows for a language focus to underpin our approach to planning, teaching and assessment across all subjects.

Big question 2: Where should we position English/L1, ancient/modern languages, language awareness and English as an additional language within school policy?

In answering this question, we would like to argue the case for an overarching language policy. In the previous section, we considered the holistic aims of the wider curriculum and noted the explicit promotion of the spiritual, moral, cultural and mental development of children in the National Curriculum of England. We can see references to these holistic aspects outlined in the Languages Programme Purpose of Study (DfE, 2013) (note the words in bold), which we interpret later in this section:

> Learning a foreign language is a **liberation from insularity** and provides **an opening to other cultures**. A high-quality languages education should **foster pupils' curiosity and deepen their understanding of the world.** The teaching should enable pupils **to express their ideas and thoughts** in another language and to understand and respond to its speakers, both in speech and in writing. It should also provide opportunities for them to **communicate for practical purposes, learn new ways of thinking** and **read great literature in the original language.**
>
> Language teaching should provide the **foundation for learning further languages, equipping pupils to study and work in other countries.**

It is worth noting that the broad aims as outlined in the purpose of study, with their emphasis on intercultural understanding, curiosity and open mindsets, present something of a contrast with the list of subject objectives to be taught. These guideline objectives omit any explicit mention of culture or personal development, and they focus primarily on the technical aspects of learning a language. This primary focus on technical objectives within the curriculum content also contrasts with the earlier guidance document, the Key Stage 2 Framework for languages (DfES, 2005), which gave equal weighting to the three core strands of oracy (speaking and listening), literacy (reading and writing) and intercultural understanding.

We can compare the holistic aims stated in the Languages Purpose of Study with the English Programme of Study listed here, again with our highlights:

> The overarching aim for English in the National Curriculum is to promote **high standards** of language and literacy by equipping pupils with a strong command of the spoken and written language, and **to develop their love of literature** through **widespread reading for enjoyment**. The National Curriculum of England aims to ensure that all pupils:
>
> - **Read** easily, fluently and with **good understanding**;
> - Develop the habit of **reading widely and often, for both pleasure and information**;
> - Acquire a wide vocabulary, **an understanding of grammar and knowledge of linguistic conventions for reading, writing and spoken language**;
> - Appreciate **our rich and varied literary heritage**;
> - Write clearly, **accurately** and coherently, **adapting their language and style in and for a range of contexts, purposes and audiences**;

- **Use discussion in order to learn;** they should be able to **elaborate and explain clearly their understanding and ideas;**
- Are competent in the **arts of speaking and listening,** making **formal presentations,** demonstrating to others and participating in debate.

Although the English curriculum appears much more explicitly linked to a standards agenda, with the emphasis on accuracy, coherence and formal presentations, there are clear crossovers with the more learner-centred and holistic aims of the languages curriculum. See our interpretations in Table 9.1.

Table 9.1 Links between the English curriculum and the languages curriculum

Stated purpose of the languages curriculum	Interpreting the purpose	Links to the English curriculum
Liberation from insularity and an opening to other cultures	Encouraging open mindsets Welcoming classrooms Acknowledging and confounding biases and stereotypes Providing accessibility to new ideas Exploring individual and group identities	Appreciate our rich and varied literary heritage
Foster pupils' curiosity and deepen their understanding of the world	Asking and encouraging 'big questions' Sharing and identifying with a variety of cultural perspectives through diverse story contexts	Read widely and often, for both pleasure and information
Express their ideas and thoughts	Providing a range of opportunities for self-expression through the language, for instance through storytelling, art, music, drama, poetry and digital media	Elaborate and explain clearly their understanding and ideas
Communicate for practical purposes	Establishing a real purpose for language learning linked to children's interests, their current and possible lives Making connections with real world issues	Adapt their language and style in and for a range of contexts, purposes and audiences
Learn new ways of thinking	Encouraging creative problem solving and critical thinking Stepping into others' shoes Seeing ideas with different cultural lenses	Use discussion in order to learn
Read great literature in the original language	Comparing different cultural interpretations of traditional tales Exploring the origins of familiar songs and rhymes	Develop their love of literature through widespread reading for enjoyment Read with good understanding

(Continued)

Table 9.1 (Continued)

Stated purpose of the languages curriculum	Interpreting the purpose	Links to the English curriculum
Build foundation for learning further languages	Being language-aware Looking for patterns in sounds and symbols within and across languages Making connections between languages	Understand grammar and know linguistic conventions for reading, writing and spoken language
Equip pupils to study and work in other countries	Making links with international study partners for instance through collaborative projects with partner schools Exploring career opportunities for bilingual and multilingual language speakers	Are competent in the arts of speaking and listening

> Review our interpretation of the Languages Purpose of Study. How many of the examples listed are routinely happening in your classroom/school?

The study of foreign languages is usually considered a 'foundation' subject within English education policy at both primary and secondary phases. The study of English is identified as a core subject. Oxford Languages (2020) defines the foundation subjects as 'the subjects which form the basis of the National Curriculum, including (or loosely, those other than) the compulsory core subjects'. A definition which explains the combination of foundation subjects (including arts, humanities, physical education and modern languages) as the basis for learning is perhaps at odds with national and local policy and practice in England, which often prioritises 'core' at the expense of 'foundation'. For example, in England during the COVID-19 pandemic, national policy guidance allowed schools to deliver a slimmed-down curriculum focusing on maths and literacy in the 'catch-up' curriculum, despite narrow 'closing the gap' initiatives having failed the most vulnerable learners even before the national lockdown (Cobb and Stevenson, 2020).

Our interpretation of the word *foundation* as an 'underlying basis or principle' (Oxford Languages, 2020) leads us to argue that rather than seeing the teaching of modern languages as distinct from (and less of a priority than) the English curriculum, schools would be better placed to have one overarching language policy which includes both the teaching of English and other ancient or modern languages as well as the teaching of English as an additional language.

> *An example school language policy*
>
> You will find several schools following the International Baccalaureate (IB) curriculum who have published examples on their school websites of overarching language policies. You can find out more about the IB on the organisation's website, www.ibo.org/. One such example, is Kingsville Primary School in Victoria, Australia. The Kingsville vision statement is:
>
>> to build a purposeful community of active learners who can meet the challenges of a rapidly changing world and become responsible global citizens.
>
> English is the foundation of the school's language programme. Italian is taught as an additional language, and the children are immersed in Italian culture. Mother-tongue language use both at home and in the school environment is encouraged and supported. The language policy statement published on the school's website recognises how 'the richness of authentic language' supports both the child's full cognitive development and the maintenance of individual cultural identity. It begins with the following philosophy statement:
>
>> At Kingsville Primary School we believe that language forms the basis of all learning and is integral to the complete development of the student: physical, social, emotional, cultural and academic. Language allows the individual to think about, question, respond to, reflect upon, and make sense of the world. It is through language that we make connections and communicate with our fellow human beings. Language is therefore taught not only through literacy but also across all curriculum areas. We believe that all teachers are language teachers. Kingsville provides an authentic, stimulating learning environment which promotes the learning of language, about language, and through language.
>>
>> (Kingsville Primary School, 2020, no page)

Education in International Baccalaureate (IB) schools adopts an inquiry-based learning approach. The Kingsville Primary School language programme is built on this model, beginning with students' needs, experiences and interests and encouraging learners to ask 'big questions' based on six cross-curricular themes:

- Who we are;
- Where we are in place and time;
- How we express ourselves;
- How the world works;

- How we organise ourselves;
- How we share the planet.

A language policy which views all teachers as language teachers crosses traditional subject boundaries. Cross-curricular in nature, it enables the school to identify language strengths and priorities across the community and involves all staff (and the wider community) in addressing these. In contrast, separate policies for English, English as an additional language and modern languages can lead to a hierarchy where all staff see themselves as English teachers but may view the teaching of modern languages and English as an additional language as largely the remit of the language specialist. If you remember, in Chapter 7 we suggested an approach to building a languages curriculum around repeated themes with examples of progressive structures, core content and classroom language for immersive and creative teaching opportunities. If you have not yet read this chapter, it might be useful to go back to it now.

Wendy: Virginia, what do you see as the main hindrances to schools adopting an overarching language policy from your perspective as a researcher of English as an additional language?

Virginia: I think one of the key challenges, Wendy, is avoiding a 'deficit' approach to language, which considers those who are not yet fluent in the curriculum language, as 'lacking'. If children with EAL or native speakers who are working to develop their oral and written English are perceived as 'problems', this is likely to hinder the movement towards an overarching language policy, because they are regarded as 'separate' and 'different' – needing 'normalising'. A conceptual leap is required here, whereby all members of the school community see themselves (in the words of Kingsville Primary School) as learners *of* language, who are learning *about* and *through* language.

Wendy: Do you think perhaps there is a degree of dualism here too in that a teacher's well-intentioned desire to do good interprets difference as need, and therefore the child with EAL becomes a problem to be solved rather than a gift to the class with a set of strengths to be uncovered? At the same time, teachers may also see themselves as 'lacking' and deny their own linguistic strengths, often linked to a bad experience of language learning at school and memories of not getting it 'right'.

I have a few activities I use with teachers to uncover their language strengths, such as a Dutch reading comprehension activity adapted from the brilliant little language-awareness book *How Language Works* by Barry Jones (1984) which quickly sees 'monolinguist' teachers translating answers into English from the Dutch language based on their recognition of cognates and similarities in word structure, then writing answers in Dutch and finally creating their own unique responses to the text as newly discovered language 'experts'.

> Review the language policies in your own setting. Is there a perceived hierarchy? Do you or your staff prioritise one language above another? What would you want to achieve by introducing an overarching language policy?

If you decide to introduce a language policy, we suggest you keep it simple. Consider what you most want teachers, parents and children to remember. You may find the following prompts useful for section headings:

Intentions of the policy and values statement
- What are the school language philosophy and aims?

How the policy was developed
- Who was involved in developing the policy? Involving the wider school community, including parents and children, will ensure a greater 'buy in' (see discussion in the next section of the chapter).

Entitlement
- What can parents expect for their children and themselves?
- How will you ensure inclusive provision?
- How will home languages be recognised, valued and used to enhance learning in English?
- How will you meet additional needs?

Attitudes and competencies to be developed
- What characteristics are you promoting through the policy?
- What skills, knowledge and understanding will be developed?

Language across the curriculum
- How will the policy be interpreted across subjects?

Teaching approaches
- How is the curriculum organised?
- What evidence-based approaches will be used?
- What resources are used?
- Who is involved in teaching the curriculum? (You might explain how you draw on the language strengths across the teaching/non-teaching staff/parents/community/language specialist student teachers.)
- What additional support is available (for instance, speech, language and communication specialists, links with language specialist schools/university departments)?
- How can home learning support the taught curriculum?

Assessment
- How will you assess language development?

Evaluation
- How and when will you review how well the policy is working?
- Who is responsible for reviewing the policy?

Big question 3: Who should lead on language-focused curriculum development, and how can language leadership promote democratic citizenship?

Within the answer to this question, we would like to consider the creating and leading of a whole-school languages curriculum and the role of student and parental voice, choice and global citizenship within this. Establishing a whole-school approach to a language-focused curriculum requires involving and reflecting the interests of all stakeholders in the school. This is a good place to reflect on who the stakeholders are in your setting; your list might include the following:

- Children;
- Parents;
- Subject leaders;
- Classroom teachers;
- Teaching assistants;
- Governors;
- Administrators;
- Caretakers;
- Cleaners;
- Wider community (consider for instance faith groups, community hubs and language schools).

Being a lone subject leader can be challenging. We have often found that the role of leadership of modern languages or English as an additional language is given to teachers in the early stages of their careers. It can be difficult to secure staff and parental 'buy in' if you are a new and inexperienced teacher, and you may also feel that you are not confident yourself in these subjects. Having said this, we have known several non-specialist subject leaders who have effectively driven whole-school language policies through their enthusiasm for the subject and by actively seeking support from parents, the local authority and partner schools.

However, if you can establish a language policy team – which might include English, modern languages and English as an additional language leads, the Special Educational Needs Coordinator and the Early Years Foundation Stage Communication and Language Lead – you will be in a stronger position to get the agreement of all staff to support your whole-school approach. You will also need to work together with other policy leads to ensure that the language policy is explicitly linked to documents such as assessment and admissions.

Language leaders can emerge at unexpected times. Consider for instance transgender student, Meera, who we introduced to you in Chapter 4. Meera's sensitive discussion with the tutor about pronoun use and the potential for false assumptions about an individual's gender led the tutor to reflect on the use of gendered language in her teaching and assignment feedback and transformed her future transactions with her students. Our job is to be open to ideas that might transform the leadership of this area. The next case study provides an example of this.

> *The unexpected language leaders*
>
> > Language is a powerful tool. It does not just name our society. It shapes it.
> > (Sinéad Burke, 2020a, p. 104)
>
> Teacher and designer, Sinéad Burke has achondroplasia, the common form of dwarfism. At 3'5" tall, she is responsible for introducing the term for a little person, 'dune beag', to the Irish language. Sinéad may be a physically little person, but there is nothing little about her heart, her ambition, her courage or her leadership. She talks eloquently about her time as a classroom leader; how she encouraged the children to ask questions, to be curious about difference and what makes each of us unique:
>
> > Since my very first day in primary school, I understood the power of education and its value in being a catalyst to combat ignorance, to challenge the status quo and to give agency and opportunity to the most vulnerable.
> > (Burke, 2020b, no page)
>
> In her book **Break the mould: How to take your place in the world** (Burke, 2020a), Sinéad draws on her own experiences and encourages young readers to believe in themselves, have pride in who they are and use their voices to make the world a fairer, more inclusive place.
>
> The power of language features strongly in her book; for instance, the power of words to shape identities, to dream, to ask questions, to reframe (Child: 'Why are you so small?' Teacher: 'Why are you so big?'), to have a voice and to change the world. In the book, Burke shares some of her favourite words: *ameliorate, cantankerous, empathy, mélange* and *ineffable*. She says she likes 'the action of pronouncing them and learning the ways in which [her] face has to shift and change to say them correctly' (2020a, p. 102).

One way to discover potential allies in this leadership approach is to carry out an audit of the language strengths across the school community. You may be surprised at the breadth of language experience of the staff; you should include in your audit the caretaker, administrators, cleaners and volunteers. You may already have information about the home languages spoken by parents and carers, although we encourage you to carry out a full audit of the languages spoken by children and families; you may be surprised to find that many EAL learners speak several languages in addition to L1. You may discover that some children attend community language schools. Using a portfolio approach to language assessment could be an opportunity to gather this information (see for example the European Language Portfolio which we explore in Chapter 8). Your language audit may also uncover some international school connections you might use to establish partner school links.

Strong, effective leadership, with all stakeholders in mind, requires consideration of democratic citizenship and how this can be promoted through school partnerships. Both democracy and citizenship are difficult concepts to pin down. We may all profess to value them, but we interpret them differently. As Crick suggests, 'To give any definition [of democracy] for a class to learn would not be particularly democratic' (Crick, 2012, p. 13). We can trace back the origin of the word *democracy* in ancient Greek to the word *dēmokratia* from the root words *dēmos* ('common people') and *kratos* ('rule, strength'), and Plato's attack of the concept as the rule of the poor and ignorant over the educated and the knowledgeable. Crick suggests that the general interpretation of 'democracy' today is a combination of the idea of the power of the people and of legally guaranteed individual rights. However, he also argues that we should be careful about calling any system of government in which we live 'democratic' without pausing to reflect on what qualifies this judgement. Given that schools are required to operate under a governing body, you might pause here to consider to what extent your setting's governance could be termed a true democracy.

In England, citizenship is a statutory foundation subject in secondary schools and a non-statutory subject in primary schools. The National Curriculum aims include ensuring that children acquire a sound knowledge and understanding of how the United Kingdom is governed, its political system and how citizens participate actively in its democratic systems of government. For young children, citizenship education focuses on learning about themselves as individuals and members of their communities. As children move through the primary years, they learn about the wider world and the interdependence of communities within it. They also:

> develop their sense of social justice and moral responsibility and begin to understand that their own choices and behaviour can affect local, national or global issues and political and social institutions. They learn how to take part more fully in school and community activities.
>
> (DfE, 2015, p. 3)

Article 12 of the United Nations Convention on the Rights of the Child (UNICEF, 1989), ratified by over 100 nations, makes a strong general call for children's democratic participation:

> States Parties shall assure to the child who is capable of forming his or her own views the right to express those views freely in all matters affecting the child, the views of the child being given due weight in accordance with the age and maturity of the child.

Article 13 goes on to say:

> The child shall have the right to freedom of expression; this right shall include freedom to seek, receive and impart information and ideas of all kinds, regardless of frontiers, either orally, in writing or in print, in the form of art, or through any other media of the child's choice.
>
> (UNICEF, 1989, p. 5)

At a day-to-day level, these rights can be met in the classroom through giving children choice to express their thoughts and lead the way with their ideas. At a governance level, the rights can be met through children taking part in the school's decision-making processes, for instance, through developing a shared set of class rules, participating in school councils and voting for choices such as what might be the 'language of the month' for the whole school to study or how displays across the school might reflect the diversity of the school population.

At a global community level, e-Twinning fosters the participation of teachers, students, parents and the local community by giving them the opportunity to participate in and potentially lead projects, campaigns and professional development opportunities with partner schools across 44 different countries (Licht, Pateraki, and Scimeca, 2019). Each year, projects are organised under themes, and current and past examples are available on the e-Twinning portal – www.etwinning.net/en/pub/get-inspired/projects.cfm.

In 2019 the e-Twinning theme was Democratic Participation, and in 2020 the theme was 'Classrooms in Action: Tackling Climate Change'. The e-Twinning portal provides ready-made project kits and step-by-step guides to successful projects such as 'Culture in a Box' (ages 4-18), 'Cultural Heritage' (12-15), 'How did we get here? Stories of Migration' (11-15) and 'Living in Harmony' (10-15). In the next case study, Wendy has an amusing anecdote of her first experience of partnering with a school in another country.

German pen pals

In my (Wendy's) first teaching school (a three-form entry junior school), my head teacher and I decided that we would aim for the school to achieve a 'gold' award through a local authority scheme aimed at rewarding schools for subject leadership in the run up to the statutory entitlement in England for languages teaching originally planned for 2010. In addition to being the languages subject lead, I was also the music coordinator, and I led twice-weekly assemblies where we sang songs in French and other languages and enjoyed multicultural music. French language was becoming embedded across the school day, delivered mainly by class teachers who we supported through regular language development opportunities at the start of staff meetings. We had developed close connections with the local language specialist secondary school. Weekly language clubs took place in our school, led by six form students, and we were also supported by the secondary languages lead with other special events such as a French puppet show, participation in language-focused projects alongside other local primary schools and an opportunity for the junior children to experience a secondary school language laboratory lesson. In addition, we arranged regular multicultural immersive experiences including projects that enabled children to work with community artists from the organisation Music for Change (www.musicforchange.org/). We were ticking every box on the gold award criteria except for the one involving a direct link with a partner school abroad.

My head teacher announced that she had a link with a teacher in a German school and gave me the details so that I could connect my class with hers. This was fantastic, except that I did not speak any German! I quickly upskilled in the language by reading my teenage son's German school textbook and delivered a couple of German language lessons to my Year 5 class. The second of these involved the children making cards for the partner school children introducing themselves in German using structures such as:

> Ich heiße. (My name is . . .)
> Ich bin 10 Jahre alt. (I am 10 years old.)
> Ich habe einen Brüder. (I have one brother.)
> Ich habe keine Brüder oder Schwestern. (I do not have any brothers or sisters.)
> Mein Lieblingslied ist. . . (My favourite song is. . .)
> Ich mag Fußball (I like football.)

The children probably made many grammatical errors in describing themselves, but in our joint ignorance we proudly packaged up the cards and posted them off to Germany. A few weeks later a big package arrived addressed to my class. It contained a letter from the class teacher who thanked us for our lovely cards and said that as our skills in the German language were clearly superior to her children's knowledge of English, her class had written back to us in their native German! I duly handed out the reply letters to the children, and we had great fun translating the messages into English.

We later had an inspection visit from the local authority languages advisor to check whether we met the criteria for an award of either bronze, silver or gold. After a tour around the school and a final visit to my classroom where our German partner school pen pal letters were proudly displayed on the wall, the gold award was ours!

You can find more information about partnering with another school on the British Council website: www.britishcouncil.org/school-resources/partner.

> Consider who your potential allies are for promoting a language-focused whole-school policy, with leadership that considers the voices of the whole community. These might be among the school staff, the parents, the local authority, the local university (for instance, have you thought about requesting language specialist teacher trainees?), the secondary school/higher education college or language subject leaders in the school consortium/other schools.

Big question 4: How can we engage children with 'big questions' through the language curriculum?

In each previous chapter we have referred to language-learning research and theory to support our approach to a holistic, whole-school, language-focused approach. In this section, we look at research evidence that is currently informing curriculum planning more generally and apply this 'learning science' to the language curriculum. However, we urge you to be cautious in adopting a 'research-led' curriculum approach, mindful of the danger of underestimating the importance of pupil-teacher relationships and taking too abstract an approach. Instead, we suggest that you focus on 'research-informed' curriculum planning and maintain a tight focus on the curriculum's intended aims.

In addition to the science of learning, in this section we consider the artistry of language teaching and learning, and we conclude the section with practical examples of teaching that involve students engaging in 'big questions'.

'The science of learning' refers to a relatively recent field of learning sciences that draws on different disciplines to study how children learn and why some strategies work better than others. The Science of Learning is also the title of the Deans for Impact summary of cognitive science research which identifies six key questions about learning. The authors believe that every teacher educator should be able to grapple and answer these questions, 'guided and informed by the existing scientific consensus around basic cognitive principles' (Deans for Impact, 2015, no page).

The six questions are:

1. How do students understand new ideas?
2. How do students learn and retain new information?
3. How do students solve problems?
4. How does learning transfer to new situations in or outside the classroom?
5. What motivates children to learn?
6. What are common misconceptions about how children think and learn?

In Table 9.2, we provide practical examples of implementing some of the cognitive principles referred to in the Deans for Impact summary through a language-focused curriculum.

Table 9.2 Implementing cognitive principles

Cognitive principles	Practical examples
1 Students learn new ideas by reference to ideas they already know.	Activate prior knowledge by: • Showing and discussing a related video/photograph/playing music; • Making explicit links between the new language and L1; • Providing word mats with key language prompts.
2 Students should think about meaning when they encounter to-be-remembered material. Practice is essential to learning new facts, but not all practice is equivalent.	Provide cognitively challenging practice opportunities; for example, provide a list of words to be remembered and ask children to suggest the odd one out and the reason, and then another, and then another. Point out that all languages have exceptions to 'rules'; highlight and learn these. Space practice over time, revisiting and building language structures over weeks, months and years. Discuss language-learning strategies; for instance, explain that trying to remember something makes memory more long-lasting than other types of studying. Discuss how tricky words are sticky. Plan for low-stakes class quizzes, self-tests and micro-teaching opportunities and presentations to the class/an invited audience.

(Continued)

Table 9.2 Continued

Cognitive principles	Practical examples
3 Each subject area has some set of facts that, if committed to long-term memory, aids problem-solving by freeing working memory resources and illuminating contexts in which existing knowledge and skills can be applied.	Identify key grammar and linguistic structures, and vocabulary including polite classroom requests and responses and question-and-answer phrases to be introduced progressively. Build on these through the scheme of work and plan opportunities for practice across the curriculum.
4 The transfer of knowledge or skills to a novel problem requires both knowledge of the problem's context and a deep understanding of the problem's underlying structure.	Give equal weighting to intercultural understanding, literacy and oracy, including explicit discussions about the language within a cultural context. Embed language learning within whole-school curriculum contexts to make links with learning in other subjects. Sequence learning within repeated themes across year groups.
5 Self-determined motivation leads to better long-term outcomes than controlled motivation through the use of, for example, rewards and punishment. Students will be more motivated and successful in academic environments when they believe that they belong and are accepted in those environments.	Share with the students the long-term benefits of learning a language. Provide motivational and purposeful contexts for language learning. Establish an inclusive, welcoming classroom ethos which celebrates diversity and promotes intercultural understanding and a culture of belonging.
6 Cognitive development does not progress via a fixed progression of age-related stages.	Create motivational and purposeful contexts in which children will want to leap ahead in order to express their own thoughts and understanding and to answer their own questions. Provide resources to enable these leaps such as dictionaries, word banks and speaking/listening/writing prompts. Provide purposeful and challenging projects for bilingual children.

An understanding of key concepts in cognitive science, such as those highlighted in Table 9.2, is helpful in designing and implementing the language-focused curriculum. However, human language as a communication and thinking tool is hugely complex; language can be interpreted as an embodied process which cannot be separated from motor, sensory and emotional systems (Adams, 2016). Consider for instance the link between communication and gesture and how facial expressions can betray the emotions hidden behind spoken words.

We turn now therefore to the artistry of language learning. You will already have a sense of what we understand by the term 'teacher artistry' in the language-focused curriculum through our discussions in the previous chapters around pupil-teacher relationships, creativity, making connections and playful language learning. The artistry of language learning is about creatively and sensitively using evidence-based practices in contexts that are meaningful to the learners and that engender a sense of agency, curiosity, purpose, belonging and motivation. These aspects can be supported by recognising that language learning is shifting increasingly from formal to informal contexts (Chick,

2019), for example the use of applications such as Duolingo – a very popular, free, easily accessible language-learning online resource. The COVID-19 pandemic has resulted in more creative approaches to learning generally, and many teachers have seen the benefits of 'gamifying' the curriculum to encourage home learning (Favis, 2020). Effective leadership and strong curriculum planning allow for these creative, artistic approaches, and the sharing of ideas is to be actively encouraged to promote creative responses and divergent thinking. The following case study provides a creative approach which promotes the use of powerful questions.

Questions we didn't know we wanted to ask

Language teacher, Deborah Cummins (2020) suggests that questions where learners are expected to find just one answer – the 'right one' – are thankfully less prevalent now in classrooms. For Cummins, the teachers who stood out for her were always questioners – teachers whose feedback was not limited to grade marks or blunt comments but who instead asked questions prompting learners to go deeper and to see things from different perspectives.

In her own classroom, Cummins uses the poetry of Pablo Neruda to promote the kind of questioning that prompted her own growth both as a writer and as a person. In Neruda's *Book of Questions* (1991, translated from the Spanish by William O'Daly), the writer structures each poem as a set of questions, each question remaining unanswered. We have selected a few of our own questions in the style of Pablo Neruda that might provide ideas for leading a more artistic approach to language across the curriculum and could be translated in the target language:

> What do the trees say when they wave at each other in the breeze?
> Can I paint a rainbow with my heart?
> Does the wheat hear with its ear?
> How long is a truth true, before it becomes a lie?

Cummins explains that she prompts her Grade 5 class to think about why very young children ask so many questions and why children stop asking them when they get older. If you try this with your class, you might get answers such as, 'Young children don't know any better' and 'Older people know everything', or 'We're afraid to ask'. Some of the questions that emerged when Cummins discussed this with her class were:

- What's more important/more powerful: the answer or the question?
- Do all questions have answers?
- Do all questions have only one right answer?
- How do we make discoveries about the world?
- How do we find out about one another?

> Read the bullet-listed questions in the case study. How would you answer each question? How will your responses feed into your planning of a language-focused curriculum?

Big question 5: How can we know whether the curriculum is meeting the stated aims?

In order to evaluate the effectiveness of a curriculum in meeting its aims we need to consider the whole teaching and learning context including the interactions between the learners, between the teacher and learners, between the home and school and the engagement of individual learners themselves, as well as the wider ethos of the school. Examination of this wider context includes considering the role of language in structural inequalities based on race, social class, gender and other differences. If you have carried out or are planning a school-based research project you may recognise this reference to structural inequalities from your reading of the British Educational Research Association (BERA, 2019) research guidelines. By 'structural inequalities' we refer to the embedded biases within the policies and practices of the school/class which may advantage some members of the community and disadvantage others. As we have explored in previous chapters (see in particular Chapter 5), language can play a key role in perpetuating such inequalities, and you should be conscious of this potential both in your curriculum plan, your leadership of this plan and in your evaluation of its implementation against the stated aims. Establishing a set of guiding principles against which you can measure the extent to which the curriculum is meeting its aims is a good place to start, and these principles can be embedded into the school improvement framework.

> Has this book helped you to develop a set of guiding principles for language-aware curriculum planning? What are your key take outs from reading this book?

Although frameworks are not a solution to successful implementation, they can be useful for taking stock and establishing actions for change. The AMLA Language Awareness Programme (Cobb, 2014) provided an evaluation tool for leaders to audit a school's existing language policy and to support ongoing evaluation. We have updated the evaluation toolkit prompts to align with the discussions in this book, and this can be found in Appendix 1. School leaders may find this useful to reflect on the current status of language learning in the setting and set targets for the language-focused curriculum. Class teachers may want to consider how the prompts relate to teaching and learning within the classroom and engagement with families. We suggest that if this tool is used, a SWOT analysis (see Table 9.3) is also carried out so that you can identify Strengths and Weaknesses as well as Opportunities and Threats within your setting. A SWOT analysis is a useful tool which subject leaders may wish

Table 9.3 SWOT analysis

Strengths	Weaknesses
What are the language strengths of staff/children/parents/the wider community? What other resources are available? What links do you already have with partner schools/the local authority/university? What strengths are there across the curriculum? (For instance, subject options for content and language-integrated learning e.g. arts; science; physical education; personal, social and health education)	What are the language and other professional development needs of the staff? What other resource needs are there? (For instance, lack of time for modern languages)
Opportunities	Threats
What will we gain by adopting a language-focused approach? How might this focus support other school priorities? (For example, consider: inclusion/English language development/parental engagement/citizenship.) How might a content- and language-integrated approach free up space in the overcrowded timetable? What are the potential benefits for children? (For example: confidence, self-awareness, career options, agency, creativity, voice)	What opposition might you meet? (For instance, staff/parental attitudes/accountability judgements) What is the potential impact of budget and time restrictions?

to use before introducing any new language initiative. We have suggested some questions you might want to consider in the SWOT framework.

Potential language leadership challenges and solutions and leadership for change

Rather than a bullet-pointed summary, as in the other chapters, we have decided to draw this chapter towards its close with Burke's (2020, p. 202) steps to enabling change, which you might also find useful in your leadership of the language-focused curriculum:

1. What do I care about?
2. Why is this important to me?
3. What are the barriers?
4. How can these challenges be overcome?
5. What skills do I have to overcome these hurdles?
6. Who else is advocating for these issues?
7. How could we work together?
8. What does progress mean?
9. How am I bringing other people with me?
10. How do I inspire others to do the same?

178 *Leadership of languages*

Taking a whole-school approach to languages and a language-focused curriculum is challenging – in its leadership and its implementation – and we end the chapter here by identifying some of the potential challenges you might face and how they might be approached (see Table 9.4). We wish you every success with your language-focused curriculum and the leadership thereof.

Table 9.4 Challenges and responses

Challenges	Responses
English is and will remain a universal *lingua franca* (adopted as a common language by speakers whose native languages are different).	This is a partial myth. Although the English language is likely to continue to be the communication tool for much global commerce, knowledge of English does not guarantee competence in the language or understanding between different cultures. English is not a true *lingua franca*; the English language expresses a particular cultural perspective (or different English perspectives) and therefore can never be interpreted as a universally global language.
Learning languages leads to unnecessary cognitive overload.	While introducing entirely new information through a second language is likely to lead to cognitive overload, particularly for lower-level learners, there are many strategies to avoid this (for instance, by discussing information first in the home language or by linking the learning to other prior knowledge and experiences). Bilingual learning has many cognitive benefits. These include improved memory, problem-solving, critical-thinking and enhanced executive-functioning skills.
The subject leader is inexperienced, for instance the newly qualified teacher (NQT)/the bilingual teaching assistant (TA).	We are all language teachers. Language leadership is a team responsibility, and schools should not rely on any one individual. The enthusiastic and research-informed NQT and language specialist TA are key assets to the team.
The leader wears too many hats and has a limited budget (for instance in the one-form entry primary school).	A language-focused, whole-school approach is a good opportunity to make connections with the wider community and draw on the resources of parents and other community members to enhance the available resource provision. For example, some schools encourage volunteering as an excellent way of enhancing a community member's work experience and future job prospects. Working closely with a partner university to engage language specialists as teacher trainees can also be mutually beneficial.
There is no guarantee that the same language will be taught in the primary and secondary school, so learning may not be retained.	A language-focused, whole-school approach is a good opportunity to enhance transition arrangements with partner schools, for instance through consideration of the 5 transition bridges: 1 Managing pupil information (sharing data between schools); 2 Supporting personal and social needs; 3 Joining up the curriculum (for example engaging the children with cross-phase projects); 4 Sharing pedagogies (joint professional development and staff training); 5 Engaging pupils as agents (actively involving pupils in the process, encouraging pupil voice, sharing pupil passports which identify pupil strengths and preferences). Learning any language is a foundation for learning other languages.

References

Adams, A. (2016) 'How language is embodied in bilinguals and children with specific language impairment', *Frontiers in Psychology*, 7, pp. 1–13.
BERA (2019) *Ethical Guidelines for Educational Research* (4th ed.), Available at www.bera.ac.uk/publication/ethical-guidelines-for-educational-research-2018-online#guidelines (Accessed 08.12.2020).
Burke, S. (2020a) *Break the Mould; How to Take Your Place in the World*, London: Wren and Rook.
Burke, S. (2020b) 'Sinéad burke', Available at www.sinead-burke.com/ (Accessed 19.11.2020).
Chick, A. (2019) 'Motivation and informal language learning', in Dressman, M. & Sadler, R. W. (eds.), *The Handbook of Informal Language Learning*, Chichester: John Wiley & Sons.
Cobb, W. (ed.) (2014) *Language Awareness Programme*, Croydon: Accelerated Modern Language Acquisition.
Cobb, W. & Stevenson, B. (2020) 'Call for change: Looking forward to education post COVID-19', Available at https://blogs.canterbury.ac.uk/expertcomment/call-for-change-looking-forward-to-education-post-covid-19/ (Accessed 10.12.2020).
Crick, B. (2012) 'Democracy', in James, A. (ed.), *Sage Handbook of Education for Citizenship and Democracy*, London: Sage.
Cummins, D. (2020) 'Questions we didn't know we wanted to ask', *Poetry Foundation* Available at www.poetryfoundation.org/articles/90420/questions-we-didnt-know-we-wanted-to-ask (Accessed 08.12.2020).
Deans for Impact (2015) 'The science of learning', Available at https://deansforimpact.org/wp-content/uploads/2016/12/The_Science_of_Learning.pdf (Accessed 20.11.2020).
DfE (2013) 'The national curriculum in England key stages 1 and 2 framework', Available at www.gov.uk/government/publications/national-curriculum-in-england-primary-curriculum (Accessed 02.10.2020).
DfE (2015) 'Citizenship programmes of study: Key stages 1 and 2', Available at www.gov.uk/government/publications/citizenship-programmes-of-study-for-key-stages-1-and-2 (Accessed 15.11.2020).
DfES (2005) 'Key stage 2 framework for languages', Available at www.all-languages.org.uk/wp-content/uploads/2016/04/KS2-Framework-for-Languages-part-1.pdf (Accessed 10.11.2020).
Favis, E. (2020) 'With coronavirus closing schools, here's how video games are helping teachers', *The Washington Post*, Available at www.washingtonpost.com/video-games/2020/04/15/teachers-video-games-coronavirus-education-remote-learning/ (Accessed 08.12.2020).
Garnett, J. (ed.) (2006) *Matthew Arnold Culture and Anarchy*, Oxford: Oxford University Press.
Geisenberg, A. (2000) 'Spiritual development and young children', *European Early Childhood Education Research Journal*, 8, 2, pp. 23–37.
Grenfell, M. (ed.) (2014) *Pierre Bourdieu Key Concepts*, Oxon: Routledge.
Jones, B. (1984) *How Language Works*, Cambridge: Cambridge University Press.
Kingsville Primary School (2020) 'Kingsville primary school language policy', Available at www.kingsvilleps.vic.edu.au/page/200/School-Policies (Accessed 22.02.2021).
Licht, A. H. Pateraki, I. & Scimeca, S. (2019) 'If not in schools where? Learn and practice democracy with e-Twinning', Available at www.britishcouncil.org/sites/default/files/learn_and_practice_democracy_with_etwinning_en.pdf (Accessed 15.11.2020).
Mitra, S. (2012) 'The hole in the wall project and the power of self-organized learning, Edutopia', Available at https://www.edutopia.org/blog/self-organized-learning-sugata-mitra (Accessed 17.07.2021).
Neruda, P. (1991) *The Book of Questions*, Translated by O'Daly, W., Washington, DC: Copper, Canyon Press.
Ofsted (2019a) 'Early years inspection handbook for Ofsted registered provision', Available at https://assets.publishing.service.gov.uk/government/uploads/system/uploads/attachment_data/file/828465/Early_years_inspection_handbook.pdf (Accessed 01.02.2021).
Ofsted (2019b) 'The education inspection framework', Available at https://assets.publishing.service.gov.uk/government/uploads/system/uploads/attachment_data/file/801429/Education_inspection_framework.pdf (Accessed 22.02.2021).
Oxford Languages (2020) 'Oxford English dictionary', Available at https://languages.oup.com/dictionaries/ (Accessed 09.11.2020).
School in the Cloud (2020) Available at www.theschoolinthecloud.org/ (Accessed 04.11.2020).
UNICEF (1989) 'The United Nations convention on the rights of the child', Available at www.unicef.org.uk/what-we-do/un-convention-child-rights/ (Accessed 15.11.2020).

10 Concluding thoughts

To learn a language is to have one more window from which to look at the world.

(Chinese proverb)

Introduction

In earlier chapters, we referred to Zaidi's research into using dual-language texts in the classroom. In the article, Zaidi (2020, p. 273) writes that the aim was to explore how these texts might: 'enhance language awareness among students and educators while drawing connections to linguistic identities and ultimately fostering greater attention to and appreciation for linguistic and cultural diversity in the classroom.'

The focus here was on the texts, but we felt that this quote could effectively be used as an underpinning ideal behind everything we do in the classroom. If, within our planning, teaching, resourcing and assessments we can keep in mind the importance of our own linguistic identities and those of the students we teach and ensure that we keep linguistic and cultural diversity at the forefront of our minds so that it becomes simply an integrated aspect of everything we do, we will have a much better chance of providing an education that is relevant, useful, innovative and engaging.

This final chapter examines the importance of developing values and principles which provide us with a foundation on which to build our approach to a language-focused classroom. We then move on to examine the notion of teacher agency, as this is vital if we are to feel empowered to act by our values and principles, followed by a focus on professional learning and development – essential to becoming agents of change. Throughout the book, we hope we have been honest in acknowledging the challenges likely to be faced as we become more language-aware and as we develop our own and our pupils' intercultural understanding. A few more challenges are explored here in this final chapter, and we provide two very personal examples of mistakes we have made along the way. The chapter, and indeed the book, ends with us articulating our vision for the future, with a very final authors' dialogue.

Values and principles

Values are deeply held beliefs which influence the decisions we make and which, in the classroom will influence our pedagogies, practices and the resources we use. Often, when we are

DOI: 10.4324/9781003129738-11

unsure of a course of action, we will (implicitly or overtly) consult our values set – sometimes in conjunction with discussion with others – before taking action. Sometimes there is a tension between our values and the values of those around us or the place in which we work. Being able to articulate our values and analyse from where these have emerged empowers us to stand up for what we believe and defend our actions, should this be necessary. Barnes (2020, p. 16) refers to 'near-universal human values like kindness, humility, generosity, sustainability or social justice', and we would like to believe that these have underpinned many of the ideas in this book, as we think about language-aware classrooms that celebrate diversity.

> What values underpin your ideas about language learning and intercultural understanding? Where have these emerged from? What have been the key influences on your thinking?

Throughout my (Virginia) professional life (spanning different careers), I have sought to develop principles which reflect my values. I started my working life as a horse-riding instructor, and I remember that, when I was training, my own instructor said, 'Never say "don't" when teaching – for example, "Don't look down as you ride towards a jump"; instead, make it affirmative: "Always look up as you approach a jump"'. This has become a key principle for me throughout my working life, and I often talk to trainee teachers about maintaining this affirming approach with children in the classroom – for example, if a child asks, 'Is it ok if...?', where possible, always say yes. This might be qualified with 'And you might also like to try...' rather than saying, 'No, I think it would be better if...'. I am forever thankful to my instructor for instilling this particular principle, as it has become embedded into the foundations of my personal and professional life.

As I moved into more specific areas of education – teaching Primary English and supporting EAL learners – further sets of principles have emerged, underpinned by my values set. Here are six principles that provide a foundation for the approaches I take when working with children with EAL and trainee teachers:

- Children with EAL should be seen as having something 'extra' rather than the deficit model which views them as 'lacking';
- Children's existing knowledge about language and the world and their cultural practices should form the starting point for teaching and learning, thereby improving the educational experience of all children;
- Opportunities for genuine, dialogic interaction are key to oral and written language development;
- Use of a child's first language should be actively promoted;
- Planning, teaching and assessment need to reflect both content and language learning;
- Planning and teaching should be designed to cater for the needs of EAL learners and will be of benefit to all children in the class. Conversely, planning and teaching designed for monolingual native speakers of English will not sufficiently support children with EAL.

It does not matter whether you agree or disagree with the principles I have prioritised – what matters is that you feel you have the knowledge and understanding to develop sets of principles for all areas of your own teaching. This knowledge and understanding relies of course on a commitment to ongoing learning and reflection, and we will examine the importance of professional learning and development later in the chapter.

When you are considering the values that underpin your actions, and as you put together principles to guide you through this complex world that is education, it is worth keeping at the forefront of your mind what Powney and McPake (2001) refer to as 'the complicated reality of individuals' lives'. This allows us to avoid the dangers of stereotyping, marginalising and trying to make 'others' like us. Instead, our ideas and practices become underpinned by a genuine interest in the diversity we encounter in the people and places we are privileged to experience.

Teacher agency

In Chapter 1, we used the article 'Educational Landscapes' to discuss the role of the teacher in raising awareness about language. The author believes that, if an educational setting is to be successful in raising the profile of linguistic diversity, it is the teachers who need to lead the way. We would agree and would argue that teachers are the ones in a position to transform the curriculum and the lives of their charges (see Figure 10.1).

In order to do this, we need to be agents of change, either by grasping the autonomy afforded to us by the situation we are in or by creating that autonomy for ourselves. Let us explain this a little more.

Arguably, teachers in England have limited autonomy, working as they do within a prescribed curriculum and assessment system. Alexander (2004, p. 11) maintains that in England, pedagogy is 'subsidiary to curriculum' and that teachers have been forced to become 'technicians who implement the educational ideas and procedures of others, rather than professionals who think about these matters for themselves'. However, we would argue that if we have a firmly embedded values set and guiding principles - as discussed earlier in the chapter - then there is more chance that we can act on these and translate these into language-focused classroom practice which goes beyond a mere delivery of the prescribed curriculum. Barnes argues that 'values must be dynamic, promoting action, commitment and creativity' (Barnes, 2020, p. 30), and if our practice is values-led, we should indeed be empowered to be agents of change.

Frost maintains that agency involves pursuing 'self-determined goals through self-conscious strategic action' (Frost, 2006, p. 20), which implies that with or without permitted autonomy, an individual decides to take action. Biesta and Tedder (2007, p. 137), however, consider that agency 'results from the interplay of individual efforts, available resources and contextual or structural factors', and there can of course be tensions between these elements. Sometimes we are given relative freedom - autonomy - within the workplace, and this is often dependent on the leadership team within the setting. As teachers, we have to position and re-position ourselves according to directives (Dixon, 2016), sometimes making the

Figure 10.1 Teachers leading the way

most of freedoms offered – in terms of curriculum interpretation, use of resources etc. – and at other times having to create our own freedoms, knowing that the decisions we make are based on evidence, experience and embedded in our own values.

As teachers, educators and researchers, we cannot ignore the political climate in which we work, but we believe that it is possible to work creatively within it. This relies on professional judgement, challenging our own assumptions and attitudes and a realisation that commitment to our own continuing professional development is essential. Developing opportunities to share ideas and experiences, to use the narrative of our own lives, and to undertake research and enquiry which broaden and deepen our own knowledge and understanding might in some way help to combat the effects of centralised power. If we are to become agents of change, capable of transforming the curriculum and the classrooms in which we teach, in order to transform the lives of the children and families with whom we work, a focus on and commitment to our own professional learning and development is essential. The next section explores this.

The importance of professional learning and development

Developing a language-focused classroom, built on intercultural understanding and a creative approach to language teaching across the curriculum, requires constant evaluation and monitoring of our confidence, knowledge and understanding in these areas. Ofsted (2005, p. 2) found evidence to suggest that it is teachers who are the biggest factor in raising achievement, and yet teachers may feel constrained by working within 'education policy which encourages teachers and schools to celebrate children's linguistic diversity but which does not require or promote mainstream teachers' linguistic knowledge and training' (Safford and Drury, 2013, p. 73). Unfortunately, professional development to support the area of language may not be as forthcoming as other development opportunities perceived to be of a higher priority, and indeed, Fumoto, Hargreaves and Maxwell (2007) found that teachers had received very little training or further development in this area. Being proactive and creative with your approach to your own learning and development is essential.

Throughout our careers we have both taken up any available professional development opportunities and cannot over-emphasise the benefits of learning from and being inspired by like-minded and experienced colleagues. We have found the language-focused teaching community to be made up of passionate and enthusiastic individuals eager to collaborate and share ideas, such as those we have pointed you to throughout the book.

In Table 10.1 we have identified several language-focused associations and other organisations that you or your school might be interested in exploring. Most associations offer discounted or free membership for students, although you will find that many resources are freely accessible without full membership.

Many of the organisations identified in Table 10.1 facilitate collaborative networks, and we recommend joining (or facilitating) some kind of support network, particularly given the challenges subject leaders may face in promoting a language-aware, whole-school approach (see Chapter 9). However, not all professional development opportunities have equal value; we have ourselves at times been captivated by inspiring presentations at conferences and other events and, in our rush to embed a new approach into our teaching, we have sometimes forgotten that we need to be critical consumers of information and ideas. Cordingley et al. (2015,

Table 10.1 Professional development resources

Association and website	Focus	Example benefits
Association for Language Learning (ALL) www.all-languages.org.uk/	For those involved in the teaching of foreign languages at all levels	Weekly languages-focused news digest; Primary and Secondary Zone resources including subject leadership; CLIL Zone; Primary hubs and Secondary networks; The Language Learning Journal; events diary including ALL Conference
National Association for Language Development in the Curriculum (NALDIC) https://naldic.org.uk/	Professional forum for the teaching and learning of English as an additional language	Conferences and CPD events; professional networks; EAL Journal; assessment framework; journal blog
Association for Language Awareness (ALA) www.languageawareness.org/	Different fields of Language Awareness (e.g. mother-tongue learning, foreign-language learning, teacher education, language use in professional settings)	Member Forums; Language Awareness Journal; ALA Conference
International Association for Languages and Intercultural Communication (IALIC) http://ialic.international/	Languages and intercultural understanding	Conferences; IALIC Journal; research forum
United Kingdom Literacy Association (UKLA) https://ukla.org/	Literacy education	Networks (e.g. literacy and multiculturalism); International Ambassadors; diversity and inclusion resources; journals
Centre for Literacy in Primary Education (CLPE) https://clpe.org.uk/	Charity working with all those involved in teaching literacy in primary schools	Booklists (e.g. Black History, Refugee Experience); reading and writing scales; research and development projects; articles
British Council www.britishcouncil.org/	Building connections, understanding and trust between people in the UK and other countries through arts and culture, education and the English language	School and teacher resources (e.g culture around the world); study and work opportunities; Connecting Classrooms; newsletter; international school award; free global webinars
European Centre for Modern Languages www.ecml.at/	Language education including plurilingual and intercultural education	Resources (e.g. integrating students from migrant backgrounds, involving parents in plurilingual and intercultural education); webinars

p. 6) noted in their findings from international reviews into effective professional development that many development opportunities for teachers in England had hitherto been:

- Insufficiently evidence-based;
- Not focused on specific pupil needs;
- Inconsistent in quality.

They also noted that many opportunities in England were of poor quality compared to those experienced by colleagues internationally. We therefore suggest that you consider the following questions, which we have adapted from Cordingley et al.'s (ibid, p. 10) recommendations, when selecting professional development opportunities for yourselves or your school.

> Use these question prompts to evaluate any professional development opportunities your school currently offers:
>
> - Are opportunities spaced over time with an opportunity for follow up, consolidation and support activities?
> - Is the provision responsive and adapted to my particular development needs?
> - Is the programme underpinned by both subject knowledge and evidence-informed, subject-specific pedagogy?
> - Are there opportunities for me to experiment with what I am learning about in the classroom?
> - Are the activities closely linked to student outcomes?
> - Is peer support encouraged and facilitated?

Sometimes our professional learning needs to be led by a reflection on our own lives and how this influences our values, principles, actions and future plans. Johnson (2006, p. 243) suggests that, in order to develop our knowledge and understanding, we need to explore through our own stories and narratives, and indeed, we discussed using our autobiographical insights as educators in Chapter 4. This can be some of the most important professional development we undertake as we begin to see where our ideas 'fit' within the educational landscape and identify areas where further learning would enhance future practice.

Finding your way

In Chapter 8 we explored the importance of making errors in language learning and how, if approached sensitively and purposefully, these errors can be transformative in moving knowledge and understanding forward. This idea needs to expand into our own approach to building language-focused, inclusive, culturally aware classrooms as, assuredly, we will all make mistakes along the way! Think about the myriad strands we are trying to pull together here:

- Negotiating the curriculum;
- Negotiating top-down direction and surveillance;
- Pressure from parents/stakeholders for settings to reflect only the dominant language/culture;

- Identifying and celebrating the linguistic and cultural experiences of children and their families;
- Working within an ever-changing political and educational landscape.

These are just a few elements, and we are sure you could extend this list considerably! It is inconceivable, therefore, that we will not make mistakes along the way, and this must be accepted and these mistakes used to enable us to move forward. Here are two examples from our own experiences.

I (Wendy) took the lead on writing our chapter on Language and Gender (Chapter 5), and the 'Meera' case study is a fictionalised account of something that happened in my classroom early on in my practice as a teacher educator. That incident, when Meera explained to me the emotional consequences of using masculine and feminine pronouns without knowing an individual's pronoun preferences, brought home to me the power of language to impact on the way we feel about ourselves. It also made me question my previous pedantry with 'correcting' aspects of grammar. So, you might be surprised to know that just after I had written Chapter 5, I was asked to edit a report I had written (in haste) because the language I had used assumed the gender of an external examiner. Like 'Meera', the examiner's name sounded feminine to me (it also ended in a), so once again in my eagerness to complete the report I had simply assumed! My learning continued!

I never felt that Meera judged me, and I was glad that the relationship we had developed meant that the issue could be aired freely. We all make mistakes, and this is the 'elephant in the room' that we should discuss with our students when we first agree on our class rules. Whatever our goals are, at some time we will falter; often it is enough just to listen, to say 'sorry' and continue to learn from each other.

I (Virginia) was in a doctoral review meeting with my two supervisors and the chairperson. For me, these meetings were predictably stressful as I was called upon to explain my reasoning and developing ideas and, although I feel very confident with written articulation, I can be occasionally hesitant to explain my thoughts when put 'on the spot'. My doctoral study was focused on supporting children with English as an additional language, with one of the key focuses being on how we perceive the 'Other' - those different to ourselves - and how this can impact on the support provided to children. The message I particularly wanted to convey was that children with EAL often achieve at a very high level academically but that their abilities are often underestimated because their language levels are still developing. I was aware that high-achieving EAL learners often receive no specific language support because they are considered to be 'doing OK'. I was therefore surprised when one of my supervisors challenged me on my use of language which presented the children in a negative way. The language she had identified was my use of 'these children'; for example, 'The academic ability of these children might be overlooked when linguistic competence does not yet match cognition'. My supervisor felt that 'these children' could be perceived as derogatory and could place the learners in a category where the 'Other' is perceived as less able, needy, lacking potential etc. I was quite taken aback by this, as the meaning I had intended to convey was quite the opposite! This was a painful lesson, but one which raised my awareness of the need to be mindful of how the language we use - whether orally or written - can be misconstrued and interpreted.

Our vision

We would argue that it is essential to have a vision for our language-aware classrooms; a vision which enables us to confront and overcome challenges and which empowers us to adhere to our principles and push ourselves to be innovative and creative in our approaches. Pennycook (1998, p. 74) writes of the importance of maintaining 'a vision of possibility', and we hope that we have offered, throughout the book, ideas for developing these possibilities.

Virginia: It seems apt, Wendy, to finish the book with one of our conversations, as these have been so enjoyable throughout the process of writing this book! Coming full circle, and considering the title of our book – *Language Learning and Intercultural Understanding in the Primary School* – I wondered what your vision was for this as we move into an uncertain future?

Wendy: I have really enjoyed our many written and verbal exchanges writing this book during a year of unprecedented global challenge arising out of the COVID-19 pandemic. As I write today, it has been 12 months since I have seen you or any other of my work colleagues face-to-face in the same room, shaken a hand or hugged a friend. Perhaps that is why so many of our discussions have had such added poignancy for me.

Despite the dark days, I have also sensed a lot of hope as well as an eagerness for change. During the past year, I have had many personal cultural gains and have widened my connections across the world through virtual opportunities that would not have opened up to me previously (today, for instance, I was talking to teachers in Pakistan!). What I hope is that we will continue to develop new ways of communicating and connecting through both old and new technologies; but most of all I hope that we will retain our current 'pandemic' understanding of the importance of language, both verbal and non-verbal – including gesture, body language and touch – to engender a sense of belonging and relatedness for the children in our classrooms.

Virginia: My vision is education led by a recognition that each child arrives in school with useful and potentially transformative knowledge and experience and that flexible and innovative approaches are implemented which provide a space for children to demonstrate their existing understandings and to work collaboratively to share and develop their ideas. In this way, classrooms would be multilingual, dialogic spaces, where children and adults share funds of knowledge, leading to a transformation of learning. I would like to think that, by acknowledging that children living and learning in the 21st century require and use language practices which are 'multiple and ever adjusting to the multilingual multimodal terrain of the communicative act' (Garcia, 2009, p. 53), that education policy in England will begin to recognise the inappropriate nature of a monolingual, monocultural approach.

> Perhaps, the very best we can do as teachers who value and celebrate the diversity of language and culture within our classrooms is to follow Paulo Freire's words as he advises us to move beyond seeing groups as 'Others' and to 'become acquainted with their way of being in the world, if not become intimately acquainted then at least become less of a stranger to it' (Freire, 2001, p. 122).

References

Alexander, R. (2004) 'Still no pedagogy? Principle, pragmatism and compliance in primary education', *Cambridge Journal of Education*, 34, 1, pp. 7-33.

Barnes, J. (2020) 'Intimations of Utopia', in Bower, V. (ed.), *Debates in Primary Education*, Oxon: Routledge.

Biesta, G. J. J. & Tedder, M. (2007) 'Agency and learning in the lifecourse: Towards an ecological perspective', *Studies in the Education of Adults*, 39, 2.

Cordingley, P. Higgins, S. Greany, T. Buckler, N. Coles-Jordan, D. Crisp, B. Saunders, L. & Coe, R. (2015) *Developing Great Teaching: Lessons from the international reviews into effective professional development*, Teacher Development Trust, Available at www.teachertoolkit.co.uk/wp-content/uploads/2015/06/dgt-summary.pdf (Accessed 05.03.2021).

Dixon, M. (2016) 'Teacher beliefs in "testing" times: A lesson from Singapore', *Teaching Education*, 27, 3, pp. 327-339.

Freire, P. (2001) *Pedagogy of Freedom*, Oxford: Rowman and Littlefield.

Frost, D. (2006) 'The concept of "agency" in leadership for learning', *Leading and Managing*, 12, 2, pp. 19-28.

Fumoto, H. Hargreaves, D. & Maxwell, S. (2007) 'Teachers' perceptions of their relationships with children who speak English as an additional language in early childhood settings', *Journal of Early Childhood Research*, 5, 2, pp. 135-153.

Garcia, O. (2009) *Bilingual Education in the 21st Century: A Global Perspective*, London: Wiley-Blackwell.

Johnson, K. E. (2006) 'The sociocultural turn and its challenges for second language teacher education', *Tesol Quarterly*, 40, 1, pp. 235-257.Ofsted (2005) *Raising the Achievement of Bilingual Learners*, London: OfSTED ref.HMI 2513.

Pennycook, A. (1998) 'The right to language: Towards a situated ethics of language possibilities', *Language Sciences*, 20, 1, pp. 73-87.

Powney, J. & McPake, J. (2001) 'A fair deal for minority ethnic groups in Scotland?' *International Journal of Inclusive Education*, 5, 2-3, pp. 151-166.

Safford, K. & Drury, R. (2013) 'The "problem" of bilingual children in educational settings: Policy and research in England', *Language and Education*, 27, 1, pp. 70-81.

Zaidi, R. (2020) 'Dual-language books: Enhancing engagement and language awareness', *Journal of Literacy Research*, 52, 3, pp. 269-292.

INDEX

Note: Page numbers in *italics* indicates figures and page numbers in **bold** indicates tables.

accent 5, 25, 57, 153
accountability 72, 145-146, **177**
adjectival agreement 75-77, 86-87, 121, 135-136, 143
adjectives 19, 56, 76, 85, **121**, 123
agency 9, 22-24, 54, 68-70, 81, 102, 117, 169, 174, **177**, 180, 182
agreement 74-77, 85-87, 91-92, **121**, 135-136, 168
alphabet 16, 36, 74, 126, 130
alphabetical order 56
anxiety 7, 24-25, 53, 67-68, 79-81, 147, 151-152
art 47, 77, 79, 133-134, 138, 159
article(s) 85-86, **121**
artistry 173-174
assessment 8, 12, 52, 58, 94, 127, 129, 141-151, 154-155, 167-169, 181-182, **184**
assimilation 59
audio books 37
Australian 49, 93
autobiographical 67-69, 99, 185
autonomy 149, 182

barriers 17, 177
belonging 29, 52-53, 57, 67, 81, 174, **174**, 187
bias(es) 3, 84-85, 87-91, 95-97, 160, **163**, 176
big questions 8, 127, **127**, 129, 135-137, 145, 158-159, 161, **163**, 165, 172-173
bilingual 1, 6, 12-13, 28, 30-31, 33-41, 43, 55, 58, 100, 103-104, 110-111, 116, 125-126, 136, **164**, **174**, **178**
blocks 17, 48
body language 80, 187
brain 106

capital 289, 160-161
capitalise 11, 28, 57-58
capital letters 56, 115
character traits 77
circle time 77-78
citizenship 107, 159, 168-170, **177**
code-switching 26, 59, 70
cognate 111, 166
cognition 107, 116, 129, 139, 144, 146, 186
cognitive 17, 30, 32, 34, 41, 50, 58, 60, 69, 71, 100, **105**, 106-107, 110-111, 113, 117, 120, 130, 139, 143, 165, 173, **173**, 174, **178**
collaboration 33, 111, 137
collaborative 52, 60, 64, 69, 81, 106, 127, 139, 144-145, 153, **164**, 183, 187
communication 2, 10-11, 17, 35, 46-48, 59, 68, 70-71, 91, 104, 107, **107**, 109, 116, 122, 129, 139, 155, 167-168, 174, **178**, **184**
communicative competence 12, 16, 71, 81, 119-120, 122-123, 129, 139, 142, 144, 152
communicator 2, 30, 108
community(ies) 6, 10, 23, 26, 29, 31-32, 35, 37, 42-43, 46, 50, 52-54, 57-58, 67, 68, 78-79, 89, 106, 138, 144, 160, 165-172, 176, **177**, **178**, 183
complement 87-88
comprehension 12, 24, 33, 73, 124, 144, 166
conjugate(d) 74, 115
connectedness 7, 67-68, 74, 81
consonant(s) 56, 79, 112, 114, 126
Content and Language Integrated Learning (CLIL) 4, 7-8, 80, 100, 102-105, **105**, 106-108, 110, 113, 116, 120, 129, **184**

counting system 63
creative 2, 4, 7, 20, 24, 26, 31, 36, 40, 46, 72, 76, 78-80, 99-102, 108-109, 113, **127**, 135-136, 139, 142, 148, 150-151, 155, **163**, 166, 174-175, 183, 186
creative arts 8, **109**, 120, 126, **127**, 129-130, 135, 137
creativity 79-80, 100-101, **107**, 116, **127**, 129, 135-136, 160, 174, **177**, 183
criteria 147
cross-curricular 7, 75-76, 89, 100-102, **105**, 107, 133, 165-166
cross-linguistic transfer 111
curriculum 1-3, 6-8, 11-12, 14-18, 23, 28, 33, 36-38, 40-43, 52, 54, 60, 63, 77, 80, 89, 91, 99-102, 104, **105**, 106-107, **107**, 108, **109**, 113, 116, 119-120, 122, 126-127, **127**, 129, 134, 138-139, 141, 144, 146, 149, 158-163, **163**, 164, **164**, 165-168, 170, 172-174, **174**, 175-177, **177**, 178, **178**, 182-183, **184**, 185

deficit model 29, 33
dialect 5, 24-25, 43, 57
dialogic 32-33, 43, 181, 187
dialogue 6, 9, 19, 35, 144
dictionary(ies) 18, 86, 101, 114, 120, 123-126, 132, 136, 152, **174**
diminutives 85
directionality 55
disability(ies) 28, 138
discourse 33, 51, 58-59, 90, 122, 152
discrete 7, 100, **105**, 107
discrimination 7, 53, 84-85, 91
discriminatory 84, 93
display(s) 23-24, 38, 40, 105, 123, 171-172
divergent thinking 80
diversity 10, 12, 20, 23-24, 36-37, 42-43, 51, 54, 62, 64, 90, 96, 104, 138, 161, 171, **174**, 180-183, **184**, 188
drama 79-80, 95, 105, 144, **163**
draw(ing) **34**, 38, 126, 133-134
dual language 12-13, 20, 37, 41-42
Dutch 15, 166
dynamic assessment 144

early intervention 71
early years 5, 30, 32, 34, 36, 38, 67, 70-71, 79, 96, 161, 168
economic 50, 50, 52, 59, 62, 68, 160

embedded 1, 6-8, 28, 35, 57, 70, 100, 107, 116, 119, 141, 155, 171, 176, 181-183
emotion/emotional 7, 10, 18, 23, 57, 67-72, 75-81, 93-94, 96, 100-102, 106, 111-112, 129, 135, 138, 153, 161, 165, 174, 186
empathy 23, 34, 68, 145, 169
empower(ing) 6, 16, 23, 33, 42, 57, 111, 180-182, 187
engagement 20, 54, 104, 110, 129, 145, 160, 176, **177**
English 1, 3-4, 11-13, 15-16, **17**, 19-20, **21**, 22, 25, 28, 30-31, 33, 36-40, 42-43, 48, 53-54, **55**, 56-58, 61, 63, 71-72, 86-87, 102, 104, 109, 111-112, 115, 119, 123-126, 132, 134, 141, 150, 152, 159-160, 162-164, **164**, 165-167, **177**, **178**
English as an additional language (EAL) 3, 5, 11, 18, 24, 34-40, 42-43, 57-58, 73, 110, 112, 134, 141, 144, 146, 149, 154, 159, 162, 166, 168, 181, **184**, 186
environment/environmental 11-12, 29-30, 34, 36, 46-47, 56-58, 64, 68, 70-71, 79-81, 93, 100-101, 111, 134, 137, 139, 143, 145-146, 150-151, 154, 158, 164, **174**
error 14, 92, 119, 125, 151-155, 185
ethnic/ethnicity 47-48, 57, 59, 64
ethos 6, 22, 28, 31, 34-35, 42-43, 46, 49, 64, 76-77, 81, 93-95, 143, **174**, 176
e-Twinning 29, 171
etymology/etymological 14-15, 43
executive function(ing) 30, 100, 111-112, 116, 134, 139, 143
exemplar 113, 126-129

fairy tales 12-13, 22
family(ies) 3-4, 6, 10, 30-32, 37, 46-47, 49, 50, 53-55, **55**, 56-59, 63, 68-69, 94, 96, 106, **109**, 119, **127**, 142, 151, 160-161, 169, 176, 183, 186
feminine 85-86, **86**, 87, 89, 92, 96, 186
feminist 87, 89
formative 8, 23, 141-142, 145-146, 148
French 3-5, 12, 15-16, **21**, 56, 61-62, 71, 74-75, 78, **78**, 80-81, 85-86, 89, 104, **105**, 106, 109, **109**, 112, **113**, 114-115, 121, **121**, 122, **123**, 124, 126, 129, **132**, 136, 143, 150, 171
fronted adverbial 14, 19
funds of knowledge/language/culture/identity 29, 62, 187

games 12, 14, 17, 30, **34**, 35, 52, 60-62, 64, 73-74, 77, 106, 113-114, 133-134, 139, 144, **145**

gender 53, **55**, 57, 74, 76, 80, 84-93, 95-97, 121, 138, 158-159, 168, 176, 186
gender-binary 96
gendered 23, 85, 87, **88**, 89-90, 92-93, 95-96, 168
gender-inclusive 85, 89, 96-97
gender-neutral(ity) 85, **88**, 89, 92-93, 96-97
German 5, 15, **15**, **21**, 85, 110, 122, **132**, **136**, 138, **145**, 150, 171-172
gesture 25, 105, **109**, 112, **113**, 123-124, 143, 153, 174, 187
global 16, 29, 41, 53, 63, 84, 159-161, 165, 168, 170-171, **178**, **184**, 187
glossary(ies) 13, 18
grammar 4, 16, 19, 25, 59, 72-74, 91, 93, 101, 115-117, 120-122, 125, 134, 148, 152, 162, **164**, **174**, 186
grammatical form 14, **121**, 122
Greek 12, 16, 43, 126, 170
grouping(s) 33, 35, 64

happiness 68
health 7, 33, 52, 60, 67-68, 70-71, 73, 79, 81, 92-93, 99-100, 102, **109**, 111, **127**, **177**
holistic 1, 3, 33, 102, 120, 122, 129, 139, 144-145, 148, 162-163, 172
home language 28, 30, 56-57, 59, 127, 149, 167, 169, **178**
home-school 20
homework 14-15, 18, 29, **34**, 40
homophone(s) 73

identity(ies) 2, **2**, 3-6, 12, 20, 30, 46-47, 49, 50-54, 57-60, 62-64, 80, 85, 88, 91, 93, 97, 102, 107, **107**, 108, 142, 161, **163**, 165, 169, 180
immerse 5, 35, 39, 57, 60, 141, 165
immersion 35, 47, 110, 119
inclusion 6, 30-31, 46, 60, **177**, **184**
inclusive 24, 28-30, 33-34, 37, 41-43, 46, 64, 67-68, 75, 85, 88, 93, 96, 134, 158-159, 167, 169, **174**, 185
indigenous 28, 103
Indonesian 61
instruction 11, 23, 32, 47, 54, 103, 109, **109**, 113, 116, 122-123, 133, 144
integrated 3-4, 7-8, 47, 80, 100, 102, 106, 108, 110, 114, 116, 120, 137, **177**, 180
intercultural 47, **48**, 52

intercultural competence 20, 48-49, 52, 149
intercultural understanding 4, 32, 52, 60-62, 64, 68, 76, 120, 142-145, **145**, 146, 149-150, 155, 162, **174**, 180-181, 183, **184**, 187
interleave 100, 108
international 1, 4, 40, 62-63, 106, 147, 160, **164**, 165, 169, **184**, 185
intervention 18, 22, 71, 104, 106, 112, 154
intransitive 124-125
investigation 14-16, 23, 33, 55, 62, 64, 73, 90, 114, 116, 125, 135, 137, 146
ipsative 148
Italian 4, 12, 15-16, **21**, 53, 102, **132**, 136, 150, 165
iterative 69

Japanese 61
jokes 74, 124

knowledge about language 6, 10-11, 14, 18-19, 22, 26, 29, 105, 120, 181

labels 93
language awareness 2, *2*, 3, 6, 8, 10-15, 18, 22-25, 71, 103, 108, 132, 159, 162, 176, 180, *182*, **184**
language learning 1-2, 8, 10, 16, 24, 28-30, 37, 41-42, 52, 54, 57-58, 68, 75, 79-81, 100-102, 104-105, **105**, 106-110, 112, 119-126, 134, 137, 139, 141-142, 144-145, 147-152, 155, 159, **163**, 166, 174, **174**, 176, 181, **184**, 185, 187
language mat(s) 13, 37-41
language of the month 35, 38-39, 171
language system(s) 26, 72, 79, 85, 87, 111
Latin 4-5, 15-17, **17**, 126, 144, 148
lexical 13, 91, 119, 154, **154**, **155**
lexicon 57, 60
linear 107, 129, 144
literacy 1, 5, 20, 28, 30, 42, 52, 90, 96, 103-104, 107, 143, 162, 164-165, **174**, 184

Mantle of the Expert 134, 139
masculine 85-87, 89, 96
mastery 107
maths 16-18, 84, 88, 95, 100, 113-115, 117, 130, 164
meaning-making 59
memory 56, 69, 108-109, 111, 116, 131, 133, 147
mental health 7, 33, 67-68, 71, 92-93, 99
metalanguage 7, 119-120, 124, 139
Middle English 4, 16

migrant 51-52, 59
mindful 2, 23-24, 69, 75, 135, 151, 173
mindset(s) 52, 84, 160, 162, **163**
misgendering 7, 85, 91, 93
modelling 33, 54, 71, 113, 115
monolingual 22, 30, 33, 36, 38, *39*, 40, 42, 110-111, 181, 187
morphology 14, 122
mother tongue 103-104, 110, 165
motivated 71, 85, 106, **174**
motivation 8, 13, 54, **105**, 106, 120, 142, 150-153, 155, **174**
multicultural 16, 23, 37, 47, 54-55, 64, 85, 160, 171, **184**
multilingual(ism) 6, 17, 22-23, 28, 31, 36-38, 42, 103, 134, **164**, 187
multi-tasking 7, 100, 110, 116

NALDIC 34, 148, **184**
name 15, 18, 22, 25, 29, **34**, 35, 43, 52-55, **55**, 56, 56, 61, 63-64, 74, 92, 94, 112, **121**, **123**, 126, 132, 138, 143, 146, 169, 172, 186
narrative 3, 37, 183, 185
national 1, 47, 49-53, 57, 63, 68, 75, 84, 106, 108, 116, 138-139, 147, 149, 160, 162, **164**, 165, 169-170, **184**
native 1, 6, 11-12, 16, 28, 35, 38-39, 42-43, 50, 58-59, 80, 87, 124, 166, 172, **178**, 181
neuroscience 99
neuter 85
non-specialist 113, 128, 132, 142, 168
non-verbal 122, 187
norm 35, 84, 87, 122, 139, 147-148, 152
noun 43, 56, 72-74, 85-89, 91-92, 96, 99, 115-116, **121**, 124, 127, 135, 152, 154

objectives 32, 105, 121, 161-162
Old English 4, 15-16
oracy 52, 103, 162, **174**
oral 5, 12, 14, 24, 29-31, 33, 38, 57, 62, 124-125, 143-144, 166, 170, 181, 186
overload 105, 110-111, **178**

paradigmatic assumption 92-93
parents/parental 23, 29-32, 34-36, 41, 53-54, 57, 60, 63, 75, 78, 84-85, 96, 104-106, 134, 148, 159, 167-169, 171-172, **177**, **178**, **184**, 185

partner school(s) 53, 62, **164**, 168-169, 171-172, **177**, **178**
patterns 14, 20, 25, 34-36, 47, 72, 85-87, 92, 96, 125, 130-132, 136, 139, **164**
pedagogy 1, 3, 7, 20, 76, 100-101, 182, 185
phonics 73, 87, 120, 130
phonological awareness 11
phrase 13, 15, 19, 74, 88-89, 92, 94, 115, 119, 160
picture book 12, 41, 55, 90
planning 6-8, 18, 28, 32, 37, 51, 60, 62, 75-76, 80, 102, 104, **105**, 106, 109, 119-120, 126-127, 129, 138-139, 142, 146, 148, 158, 161, 172-173, 175-176, 180
play 7, 12, 15, 17, 60-62, 67, 71-74, 77-78, 80-81, 89, 95, 109, 113, 128-129, 134, 142-144, **145**
playful 17, 26, 73, 174
pluricultural 47-48, 64
plurilingual 11-13, 47, 149, **184**
poem 19, 29-30, 56, 72, **86**, 101, 135, 137, 175
poetry 56, 72-73, 101, 116, 124, 160, **163**, 175
policy 1, 3, 8, 100, 149, 159, 162, 164-168, 172, 176, 183, 187
Polish **15**, 38, 41-43, 49, 85
portfolio 147-150, 160, 169
Portuguese 5, 12-13, 15, **15**, 24, 102-103, 132, **132**, 155
positive pedagogy 7, 100-101
power 3-7, 11, 14-15, 19-20, 22-23, 26, 29, 33, 35, 37, 41-43, 46-47, 53-54, 57-59, 67, 72-73, 75, 78, 84, 88, 91, 95-96, 101, 111, 129, 142, 145-146, 151, 154, 160, 169-170, 175, 180-183, 186-187
practice 1, 3, 6, 17, 22-24, 29-32, 34-35, 37, 42, 49-53, 55, 57, 59-60, 63, 69, 75-76, 85, 90-92, 96, 100-101, 106-108, 110, 113-117, 120, 123, 130, 142-143, 145, 150, 155, 158, 160, 164, **173**, **174**, 176, 180-182, 185-187
pre-teach(ing) 18
prior learning 76, 105
problem solving 31, 39, 129, 144-145, **163**, **174**, **178**
prompts 7, 23, 72, 74, 76, 85, 89, 96, 102, 106, 109, 114, 123, 128, 137, 142, 145, **145**, 151-153, 159, 167, 173, **174**, 175-176, 185
pronouns 85, 87, 92, 96, **121**, 123, 186
pronunciation 24-25, 42, 72, 74-75, 115, 130, 143
pro-social 7, 68, 75, 85, 91, 97, 106
psychology 100, 116, 136
Punjabi 31, 43, 57

quality 28, 41, 67, 107, 129, 159, 162, 184-185
question 6, 8, 12-13, 15, 20, 24-25, 32, 35, 46-47, 50-51, 54, 56-57, 60, 69, 71-73, 79-80, 92, 97, 100, 107, 110, 114-115, 120-121, **121**, 122, **123**, 124-125, 127, **127**, 128, **128**, 129-130, 135-137, 139, 141, 143-147, 151-155, 158-162, **163**, 165, 168-169, 172-173, **174**, 175-177, 185-186

reading 4, 11, 13-14, 22-25, 33, 36-37, 41, 71-72, 80-81, 88, 90-91, 96, 110, 115, 137, 143-144, 145, 149, 159-160, 162, **163**, **164**, 166, 171, 176, **184**
recasting 154
Reception 34-35
reciprocity 32
reframing 95
refugee 23, 51-52, 55, 62-63, **184**
register **34**, 35-36, 77
registration 36
rehearsal 71
relational 7, 67, 81, 100, 106
relationship 2, 5, 10-13, 25, 32, 34, 46, **55**, 56-57, 63, 68, 70, 75, 91-94, 96-97, 108, 111, 161, 173-174, 186
religion 47, 53, 84
renaming 53
repetition 36, 76, 105, 107, 113, 115-116
resilience 8, 69, 75, 129, 141-142, 147, 155
resilient 93, 153
response 7, 11, 69, 71, 75, 78, 81, 85-86, 91, 95, 103-104, 106, 109, 122, 126, 128-129, 131, 136, 150-152, 154-155, 166, 174-176, **178**
rhyme 25, 29, 55, 61-62, 73-74, 105, 120, 143, **163**
rhythm 36-37, 55, 130-131
risk 72, 78, 81, 101-102, 117, 129, 139, 146
role model 34, 42-43, 71, 122, 137, **145**
role play 12, 80, 95, 142-144
routines 34-37, 42-43, 49, 60, 71, 79, 110, 164
rules 16, 49, 60, 72-73, 87, 94, 105, 114-115, 152, 170, **173**, 186

safe 34, 46, 62, 68, 78-81, 93, 97
scaffold 17, 33, 123
scheme of work 7, 80, 108, 119-121, 127, **174**
School in the Cloud 158
self-awareness 68, 177
self-concept(s) 54, 84
self-control 111, 116

self-esteem 5, 53, 58, 110, 152, 154
self-identify 93
Self-Organised Learning Environment (SOLE) 137, 158
self-regulate 93
sentence 11, 16, 19, 32, 41-42, 56, 73-74, 84, 87-89, 92, 96, 101, 106, 115, 122-125, 129, 133, 135, 144, 154
singular 57, 74, 92, 115, **121**
social advantage 30
social and emotional 7, 67-68, 70-71, 75, 77-79
social gender 7, 87-88, 90, 96-97
social justice 145, 170, 181
social shaping 90
socio-economic 68
song 29-30, 61, 74-75, 77, 105, 116, 120, 124, 126, 130, 135, 142-143, **163**, 171-172
Spanish 4, 12, 15-16, 20, **21**, 24-25, 40, 61, 64, 75, 77-78, **78**, 85, 86, **86**, 102, 122, 126, **132**, 136, 138, 150, 175
spirituality 136, 161
split infinitive 14, 16, 72
standard 25, 31, 58, 84, 147-148, 162-163
stereotyping 7, 76, 80, 85, 90, 182
story(ies) 12-13, 16, 18-19, 22, 30, 36-37, 42, 51, 62-63, 72, 77, 80, 91, 95, 96, 120, 124, 142-143, 171, **163**, 185
Stroop task 111-112
structures 17, 71, 75-76, 79-80, 105-106, 119-121, 123, 127, 129, 131, 133, 135-136, 166, 172, **173**, **174**, 175
subject/verb agreement 74, 91-92, 96
surveillance 146, 185
SWOT analysis 104, **105**, 176, **177**
symbolic annihilation 90
symbols 10, 17, 26, 53, 56, 58, 90, 125, **164**
syntactic 119
syntax 122

teaching assistant 18, 34, **34**, 35, 37, 43, 168, **178**
technology 15-16, 104, **105**, 109, **127**
test/testing 17, 52, 72, 92, 108, 112, 136, 143, 147-148, 150, 153, **173**
theme 6, 8, 10-11, 28, 38, 46, 62, 108, **109**, 110, 120, 124, 127, **127**, 128-130, 135, 143, 146, 158, 165-166, 171, **174**
third space 58-59
threads 48

tongue twisters 12, 73-74
topics 55, 100, 102, 107-108, **109**, 110, 127, **127**, 129, 131, 151
tradition 4-5, 8, 12, 14, 47, 51, 53-55, **55**, 59-62, 89, 107, 138, 141-142, 144, 161, **163**, 166
transgender 68, 91-92, 168
transition 2, 31, 58, 103, 109, 113, 126, 130, 137, 139, **178**
transitive 124-125
translanguaging 31, 35, 40
trauma/trauma-aware 68, 74
trust/trusting 32, 68, 70, 91, 93-94, 97, 102, **105**, 107, 117, **184**

values 8, 47, 59-60, 63, 84, 101-102, 107, **107**, 129, **145**, 158-161, 167, 180-183, 185
verb 72, 74-75, 77, 85, 88, 91-92, 115, **121**, 122-125, 134, 144, 187

verbal 88, 122, 144, 187
virtual 99, 147, 150-151, 187
vocabulary 13, 15, 17-19, 33, 38, 40, 59, 71, 79-81, 105, 120, 127, 130, 133, 135, 148, 162, **174**
voice 3, 5, 9, 22, 32-33, 36, 68, 75, 79, 91, 95, 106, 122, 159-160, 168-169, 172, **177**, **178**
vowel(s) 56, 79, 126
Vygotsky, L.S. 144

wellbeing 4, 7, 23, 33, 67-71, 75-79, 81, 99-100, 110-111, 116, 129, 151
word bank 123, 132, 136, **174**
word roots 17
writing 6, 11, 14, 22, 25, 39, 41, 60, 69-70, 73, 88, 92, 97, 99, 101-102, 105-106, 108, 113, 116, 123, 125-126, 137, 143, 149, 153, 160, 162, **164**, 166, 170, **174**, **184**, 186-187

For Product Safety Concerns and Information please contact our EU representative GPSR@taylorandfrancis.com
Taylor & Francis Verlag GmbH, Kaufingerstraße 24, 80331 München, Germany

www.ingramcontent.com/pod-product-compliance
Lightning Source LLC
Chambersburg PA
CBHW081946230426
43669CB00019B/2938